www.webopedia.com

Setting Up A Linux Internet Server

bestfume

bestfume

Visual Black Book

Hidenori Tsuji　　Acrobyte　　Takashi Watanabe

CORIOLIS™

The Coriolis Group:

President, CEO
Keith Weiskamp

Publisher
Steve Sayre

Acquisitions Editor
Charlotte Carpentier

Marketing Specialist
Tracy Schofield

Project Editor
Don Eamon

Technical Reviewer
Ivan McDonagh

Production Coordinator
Kim Eoff

Cover Designer
Jody Winkler

Translation By
DNA Media Inc:

President, CEO
Steven Forth

Project Manager/Editor
Tim Oftebro

Project Manager
Dave Paslawski

Layout Designers
Akie Higuchi
Junko Izumi

Production Coordinator
Marcel Cariou

Setting Up A Linux Internet Server Visual Black Book

Dekiru Linux Server Kochikuhen

The Coriolis Group, LLC
14455 N. Hayden Road
Suite 220
Scottsdale, Arizona 85260

480/483-0192
FAX 480/483-0193
http://www.coriolis.com

Library of Congress Cataloging-in-Publication Data
Tsuji, Hidenori, 1973-
    Setting up a Linux internet server visual black book/by Hidenori Tsuji and Takashi Watanabe.
        p. cm.
    ISBN 1-57610-569-5
    1. Linux. 2. Operating systems (Computers) 3. Internet (Computer network) I. Watanabe, Takashi, 1975- II. Title.
QA76.76.O63 T78 2000
005.7'13769--dc21
                                                            00-022693
                                                            CIP

Printed in the United States of America
10 9 8 7 6 5 4 3 2 1

14455 North Hayden Road • Suite 220 • Scottsdale, Arizona 85260

Dear Reader:

The CoriolisOpen™ Press was founded to create a very elite group of books: the ones you keep closest to your machine. Sure, everyone would like to have the Library of Congress at arm's reach, but in the real world, you have to choose the books you rely on every day *very* carefully.

To win a place for our books on that coveted shelf beside your PC, we guarantee several important qualities in every book we publish. These qualities are:

- *Technical accuracy*—It's no good if it doesn't work. Every CoriolisOpen™ Press book is reviewed by technical experts in the topic field, and is sent through several editing and proofreading passes in order to create the piece of work you now hold in your hands.

- *Innovative editorial design*—We've put years of research and refinement into the ways we present information in our books. Our books' editorial approach is uniquely designed to reflect the way people learn new technologies and search for solutions to technology problems.

- *Practical focus*—We put only pertinent information into our books and avoid any fluff. Every fact included between these two covers must serve the mission of the book as a whole.

- *Accessibility*—The information in a book is worthless unless you can find it quickly when you need it. We put a lot of effort into our indexes, and heavily cross-reference our chapters, to make it easy for you to move right to the information you need.

Here at The Coriolis Group we have been publishing and packaging books, technical journals, and training materials since 1989. We're programmers and authors ourselves, and we take an ongoing active role in defining what we publish and how we publish it. We have put a lot of thought into our books; please write to us at **ctp@coriolis.com** and let us know what you think. We hope that you're happy with the book in your hands, and that in the future, when you reach for software development and networking information, you'll turn to one of our books first.

Keith Weiskamp
President and CEO

Jeff Duntemann
VP and Editorial Director

About The Authors

Hidenori Tsuji
The Linux and Unix operating systems are Hidenori's life; not only in his everyday research, but also in his part-time jobs. Presently pursuing a Ph.D. at Tokyo University researching next-generation high-performance microprocessor architecture, he supports himself with various part-time work, including managing Unix workstations, configuring networks, programming, and writing books. He has written books including *Setting Up a Linux Intranet Server* (Impress Press) and *A Practical Guide to Dial-Up Routers* (Softbank Press).
Hidenori Tsuji E-mail: **hide@hide.net**

Takashi Watanabe
Takashi Watanabe started in the computer world by spending half of his time at elementary school writing frustratingly dysfunctional sample programs in FamilyBasic. After toying with N88BASIC and MS-DOS, in 1996 he made the move to Linux. At present, he is a graduate student at Waseda University and uses Linux at home and Solaris and FreeBSD at school. His favorite programming function is getopt_long. His main pastime is playing with the search engine Verno.
Verno: **http://verno.ueda.info.waseda.ac.jp/**
E-mail: **watanabe@hide.net**

Acrobyte
Acrobyte's focus is on PC-related books and magazines, but it is also involved in various projects, from software development and production of multimedia content right through to installing Unix OS systems and assembling servers for clients. Acrobyte is based in Akihabara in Tokyo. It supervised the translation of *Windows 98 Bible, Windows 98 Bible Professional, Windows 98 Secrets, Windows 98 Registry Blackbook*, and the *Can-do PC for Windows 98* (all by Impress Press).
URL: **www.acrobyte.co.jp/**

Acknowledgments

The Coriolis Group would like to thank the people who made things work at the Scottsdale part of this project: Stephanie Wall, acquisitions editor, who's drive and perseverance got this project off the ground; Don Eamon, project editor; Ivan McDonagh, technical reviewer, who—although in Western Australia— was instrumental in finessing the accuracy of the text and images; April Eddy, copyeditor; Kim Eoff, production coordinator; and Jody Winkler, cover designer. Coriolis would also like to thank Dan Fiverson (our in-house Linux connection) and Geoff Leach of Impress Group (for quick answers and much help with the fine points raised during all of the project's phases.

DNA Media Services Inc. would like to thank the following people who contributed to the translation, editing, localization, and production of this book. Tim B. Oftebro, Jon Babcock, Akie Higuchi, Junko Izumi, Marcel Cairou, Dave Paslawski, and all the rest of the DNA Media staff. DNA Media Services would like to make special mention to all the staff who went beyond the call of duty and made the extra effort to produce a quality book. This acknowledgment recognizes all those who were brave enough to give input to this book.

Contents At A Glance

Table Of Contents

Chapter 4
Installing Linux 45

Chapter 5
Mastering The Basic Operations Of Linux 77

Chapter 6

Chapter 7

Chapter 10
Operating A Secure Internet Server 177

Introduction

Recently, Linux has been in the spotlight. The reasons for Linux's popularity include dissatisfaction with personal computer environments such as Windows, a desire to explore the concept of open-source software, and the attraction of using a cost-free and easy-to-use operating system.

The Internet is where Linux can display its true worth. As a huge network connecting people all over the world, the Internet has grown using Unix operating systems, not Windows or Macintosh operating systems. Linux makes it easy to use Unix on a personal computer. At present, Unix is widely used at the core of the Internet, and with an unlimited number of small-scale servers using Linux, the percentage of personal computers running Unix will be substantial.

Although you may know that Linux can be used as an Internet server, it is difficult to build a full-fledged Internet server for the first time. Like the rest of the Unix family, you cannot use Linux without having some knowledge about it. This is why Unix has a reputation for being difficult to use. On the other hand, you do not need to be intimidated if you have a little knowledge about how to set up and use Linux. Linux is difficult only because there are not enough qualified people and sufficient materials to assist in training to make it easier to use. The goal of this book is to build an Internet server. To achieve this, this book provides a basic knowledge about the Internet and step-by-step instructions on how to build an Internet server. You may think that building an Internet server is a daunting task. If you read this book, however, you will be surprised to find that it is much easier than you expected. This book will not only show you how to set up an Internet server, but will also address the question of how the Internet works.

I am positive that reading this book will expand your knowledge about the Internet and Linux. I will be satisfied if you find new enjoyment in the Internet by building an Internet server.

In conclusion, I would like to thank my friends, who advised me in their capacity as Unix users, and Mr. Fukuura and other staff members in the Impress editorial department.

The Authors 1999

About This Book

This book describes how to build an Internet Server consisting of a DNS server, a mail server and other components. To build an Internet server using Linux, you must understand not only Linux but something of the Internet and your connection to it as well. Furthermore, the sequence of the steps in setting up a server is extremely important. Therefore, please read through the book in order, starting with the basics.

The procedures described in this book correspond to Red Hat Linux 6.0 and will not necessarily work with other versions of Linux, such as Red Hat Linus 5.2 or Turbo Linux. Please use the enclosed Red Hat Linux 6.0 in conjunction with the examples in the book.

The book is organized as follows:

A brief introduction to the basics of server construction

- **Chapter 1   Creating An Internet Server On Linux**
- **Chapter 2   Internet Basics**

In these chapters you will find a brief overview of an Internet server and a description of the Internet essentials needed to build one. TCP/IP, IP addresses, domains and other subjects you will need to know about to build an Internet server are introduced.

Preparing to connect your server to the Internet

- **Chapter 3   The Permanent Connection**

This is a description of different options for obtaining the permanent line needed to connect your Internet server to the Internet.

Building an Internet server

- **Chapter 4   Installing Linux**
- **Chapter 5   Mastering The Basic Operations Of Linux**
- **Chapter 6   Creating A DNS Server**
- **Chapter 7   Creating A Mail Server**
- **Chapter 8   Creating A Web Server**
- **Chapter 9   Using An Internet Server From A Client PC**
- **Chapter 10 Operating A Secure Internet Server**

This chapter gives details on connecting to a network. If you want to set up a network, read this chapter.

The remaining Appendixes are broken down into specific topics, such as connecting Windows and Macintosh and Web and mail settings. To avoid making incorrect settings when you are setting up the Linux intranet server, read all the chapters, in order, from Chapter 1.

How To Use The Command Notation In This Book

Command Notation

Command line operations are described here.

A history of your previous choices is indicated in gray. Use this history to confirm the operation just prior to executing it.	Commands that you must enter are indicated by bold characters. If ⏎ is displayed next to a command, press the Enter key after typing the command.

```
[root@server /root]# cd /usr/local
[root@server local]# cd / ⏎_
[root@server /]# _
```

Shows a description of the location from the command prompt. Use this to confirm the current directory and user.

About Red Hat Linux 6

Red Hat Linux 6.0 from Red Hat Software is available in two ways: either on CD-ROM or by download from the Internet. For all exercises in this book, we used the CD version of Red Hat Linux 6. If you purchase the CD-ROM, you will also receive additional open source and commercial software packages for Red Hat Linux. The Linux configuration files are also included on the disk. These files will be necessary as you read through the book. If you want to download the Red Hat Linux distribution from the Internet, you should go to the Red Hat Software home page at **www.redhat.com.** This web page also contains a large amount of documentation and many links to other Linux related web pages. Even if you don't intend to download the distribution, it is recommended that you visit this page on a regular basis.

An alternative download site is MetaLab (which used to be called Sunsite and is still frequently referred to by that name). The MetaLab home page is **http://metalab.unc.edu.** The Red Hat distribution is available from the MetaLab ftp server at **ftp://metalab.unc.edu/pub/Linux/distributions/redhat/redhat-6.0.** In this directory (folder), you will find additional directories specific to the different platforms for which Red Hat Linux is available. Choose your platform (i386 for the most common Intel 386-, 486-, and Pentium-based computers), and then the welcome message will be displayed, which tells you how to download the distribution. The MetaLab Web site is a huge repository of Linux software and is the home of the Linux Documentation Project. Start from the home page (**http://metalab.unc.edu**) and browse the site.

Before deciding to download the distribution from the Internet, it is worth considering that, depending on the speed of your Internet connection, you may require 12 or more hours of actual downloading time. If you are subject to long-distance, time, and/or download charges or limits, you may find it substantially cheaper to purchase the CD-ROM. Another point to consider is that if you make a mistake during the installation, you may have to start again... from scratch. Do this two or three times, and you'll soon be wishing you had purchased the CD-ROM.

Some of the different Linux distributions are discussed briefly in Appendix. The Red Hat Linux distribution has become popular because of its ease of use and the availability of high-quality commercial support (included when you purchase the CD-ROM package). Because of this and its high availability, this is the distribution we have chosen to use in this book.

About The Included CD-ROM

The CD-ROM that is included with this book contains Red Hat Linux 6.0 from Red Hat Software. There are no restrictions on its use, so you may use it freely at will. The CD-ROM also contains several free software programs related to Linux and some configuration files. Use them as needed while you work through the book.

See Chapter 4 for how to install Red Hat Linux.

"Red Hat" is a registered trademark of Red Hat Software, Inc. Used with permission.

Chapter 1
Creating An Internet Server
On Linux

The true charm of the Internet is in creating servers.
If you create your own Internet server, you can handle email,
Web services and other Internet related services as you like.
This type of Internet server can be created easily using Linux.
This chapter explains why Linux is suitable for use as an
Internet server and just what an Internet server is.

Contents Of This Chapter

6.2

Creating An Internet Server

The Linux Advantage

Linux is an operating system (OS) like Windows and MacOS that provides the environment necessary to start up and use a computer. Linux is provided with a full suite of functions for local area network (LAN) and Internet use and is very stable and reliable. Moreover, Linux is highly flexible for use on the Internet and, because of this, is an OS suited for use as an Internet server. The low cost of Linux is also extremely attractive to many. Using Linux will allow you to create a stable and reliable Internet server easily and cheaply.

What Type Of OS Is Linux?

An OS provides the environment necessary to start up and use a personal computer (PC). Linux is an OS much like the Windows and Mac operating systems you may find installed on the computers around you. The Windows and Mac operating systems are designed for ordinary users. Linux is a suitable OS for ordinary users or for users who also want to run servers that connect to the Internet. Linux has the stability that an Internet server requires. Moreover, the programs Linux supports have a long history of actual practical use on the Internet. Finally, because the OS and software applications can be obtained at a low cost and installed on a PC, the cost of introducing a new system can be kept down.

Strong Points Of Linux

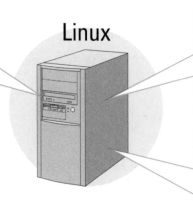

Stability

Linux enables the user to restart or quit a specific application that is experiencing problems without the need to restart the computer itself.

Reliability

Today, Linux is used extensively throughout the world as an Internet server. The many programs and servers that run on Linux have excellent track records.

Low Cost

Instead of using expensive specialized servers, Linux and its associated software are available at low cost and can be installed on PCs.

Linux Is Intimately Connected With The Internet

The Internet was originally developed together with the Unix OS. Server functions within the Internet are provided by a variety of Unix systems. Even now, the majority of Internet servers run on a Unix OS of one kind or another. Linux was created so that this flavor of Unix could be used on PCs. Consequently, Linux also is intimately connected with the Internet and is eminently suitable for use as an Internet server. Another appealing point is that many programs with excellent Unix track records are readily available for Linux.

Varieties Of The Unix OS

- **Solaris** (Sun Microsystems)
- **SCO UNIX** (SCO)
- **BSD/OS** (BSDI)
- **AIX** (IBM)
- **HP-UX** (HEWLETT PACKARD)

The above versions of Unix are sold as commercial products.

Unix Operating Systems

- **Linux**
- FreeBSD
- NetBSD
- OpenBSD

The above versions of Unix are freely available either by downloading from the Internet or by purchasing inexpensive software packages.

Red Hat Linux 6.0

Strictly speaking, Linux is the name of a program called a kernel. A kernel is the core of an OS and acts as an intermediary between the computer hardware and all of the processes and programs being run by the OS. The OS that surrounds the Linux kernel was developed and contributed by GNU (**www.gnu.org**), so what is usually called *Linux* should more properly be called *GNU/Linux*. The kernel, the OS, basic tools, and applications are installed as a compiled set known as a *distribution*. There are many varieties of distributions. The Red Hat Linux 6.0 that is provided on the CD-ROM included with this book is one of the most widely used distributions today. This book describes how to install and to use Red Hat Linux.

What Is An Internet Server?

Types Of Internet Servers

When you use the Internet to view your favorite Web page or to exchange email with friends and colleagues, a server located somewhere on the Internet is inevitably employed. On the Internet, different types of servers provide functions such as publicly opening Web pages and exchanging email.

The general name for these is *Internet servers*. The Domain Name System or Service (DNS) server, Mail server, and Web server are the specific types of Internet servers that should first command your attention.

Internet Use Means Server Use

Many people use telephone lines to dial-up and connect to their *Internet Service Provider (ISP)* and access the Internet. When viewing Web pages and reading email there is invariably a server located somewhere on the Internet that has been accessed and is providing the Web page and email functions. Additionally, the very act of accessing the Internet is the process of employing a server located somewhere on the Internet.

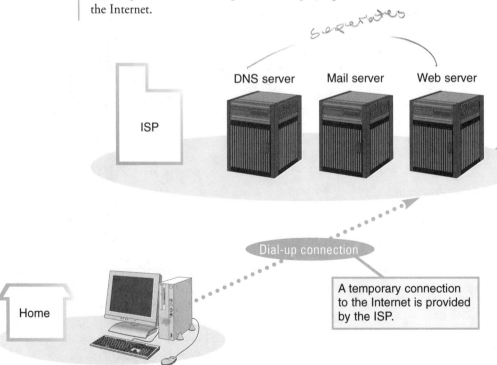

DNS server   Mail server   Web server

ISP

Dial-up connection

Home

A temporary connection to the Internet is provided by the ISP.

Types And Roles Of Internet Servers

An Internet server provides many different functions that can use the Internet to exchange email, display Web pages, and so on. Basically, a server operates 24 hours a day to allow access to and from the Internet at any time.

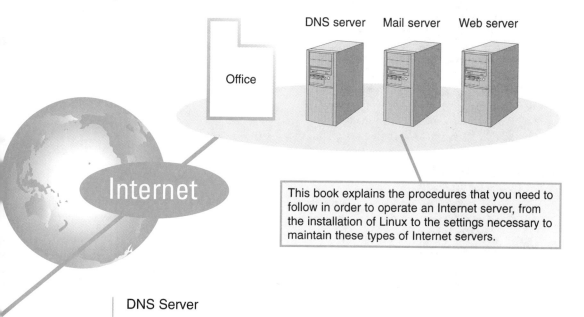

This book explains the procedures that you need to follow in order to operate an Internet server, from the installation of Linux to the settings necessary to maintain these types of Internet servers.

DNS Server

A DNS server maintains a database of information about each machine or device (host) that exists within its own segment of the worldwide DNS database and makes that information available to other name servers throughout the entire Internet. The most important information is the address of each host within its own jurisdiction. The DNS server manages these addresses for the purpose of distinguishing devices that are being used on the Internet. A DNS server must be used when exchanging email and viewing Web pages.

Mail Server

This server carries out the operations of email exchange. When you send email to a specific address, the email goes to the Mail server (located somewhere on the Internet) that is in charge of delivering email to the address you specified.

Web Server

This server publicly serves up Web pages. When you specify a URL to view a Web page, your request goes to the Web server located somewhere on the Internet that is in charge of serving up the Web page that you specified by URL address.

Using An Internet Server

The Use Of A Dedicated Connection To The Net

For Internet users to view Web pages and exchange email when they please, Internet servers must be connected to the Internet at all times. To achieve this, a 24-hour-a-day dedicated connection to the Internet is required.
A dedicated connection is a necessity for an Internet server, but there is also the appeal of being able to allow local network users of the Internet server simultaneous access to the Internet at any time as well.

A Dedicated Connection Is A Necessity For An Internet Server

The Internet is a huge network used by people all over the world. Vast numbers of people from all over the world have discretionary access to Internet servers. Internet servers must be connected to the Internet at all times to allow all of these people immediate access. Consequently, a 24-hour-a-day connection to the Internet is required, not just a dial-up connection that connects to the Internet temporarily.

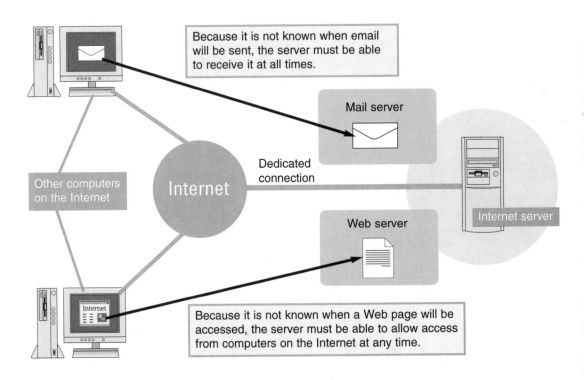

Because it is not known when email will be sent, the server must be able to receive it at all times.

Mail server

Dedicated connection

Other computers on the Internet

Internet

Internet server

Web server

Because it is not known when a Web page will be accessed, the server must be able to allow access from computers on the Internet at any time.

Making It Possible To Own An Internet Server

If you own an Internet server, the settings of the server depend on you. You can use a domain name, an email address, and a Web home page URL that you create. Furthermore, you can add or subtract email addresses as you see fit, and the capacity of your Web site is limited only by the capacity of your computer or computers.

Internet server

Original domain name
yourcoolcompany.com

Creating a Mail server using an original domain name

you@yourcoolcompany.com

You can use an easy to remember email address that combines your company name and personal name.

Owning a home page with a URL that uses an original domain name

www.yourcoolcompany.com

You can use an easy to remember URL—for example, your company name.

Creating only the required addresses

 ...

Because there is no limit to the number of email addresses that can be used, you can issue precisely the number of email addresses that you need.

Configuring the server capacity and its programs

You can freely configure each of the different parameters: disk capacity as a Web server; the usage of programs, including computer graphics interface (CGI): and the capacity of the hard disk connected to the server.

Advantages Of A Dedicated Connection

Although a dedicated connection is a necessity for an Internet server, it is also very convenient for local users who can simultaneously access the Internet at any time. This is much more appealing than for each user to dial up the Internet individually, because each user can gain access at any time while maintaining costs at a fixed rate.

● 24-Hour Internet Access At A Fixed Cost

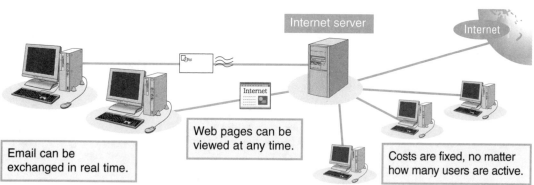

Internet server

Internet

Email can be exchanged in real time.

Web pages can be viewed at any time.

Costs are fixed, no matter how many users are active.

Let's Identify The Main Stages Of Construction

Steps In Creating An Internet Server

Using this book you will create an Internet server using Linux. To accomplish this, you must not only install Linux, but also obtain a dedicated connection to the Internet then connect your Linux Internet server to it. You must follow a set of procedures to set up the Internet server itself.

It isn't necessary at this point to concern yourself with the different types of Internet servers that can be built and the processes needed to create them. This will become clear as you proceed through the book.

Obtaining An Original Domain Name

Apply for and obtain a domain name to use with the Internet server. You can request a domain name when you apply for your dedicated access line or you can obtain one by yourself directly. For many, the simplest way to obtain a domain name is to request one when you apply for a dedicated line.

yourcoolcompany.com

Original domain name
Obtain your own original domain name using your company name or group name.

Placing A Dedicated Access Line Into Service

To operate an Internet server, you need a dedicated connection to the Internet. Because there are many services that provide dedicated access lines, select the service that is best suited for your purposes.

Building The Internet Server

Installing Linux
Using the CD-ROM included with this book, install Red Hat Linux 6.0. During the installation, you must set up the network in accordance with the specific information that is included in your agreement with your ISP.

Setting Up The Internet Server
Select the type of server you want to install (DNS server, Mail server, or Web server). Install the server's components, and then configure it. If you follow the procedures for installation and configuration outlined in this book, you should have no difficulty setting up your server. It will be necessary, however, for you to change certain settings to conform to the specifics of your own network .

Install Red Hat Linux 6.0.

Set up as your Internet server.

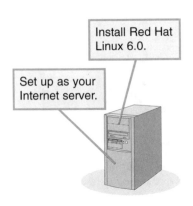

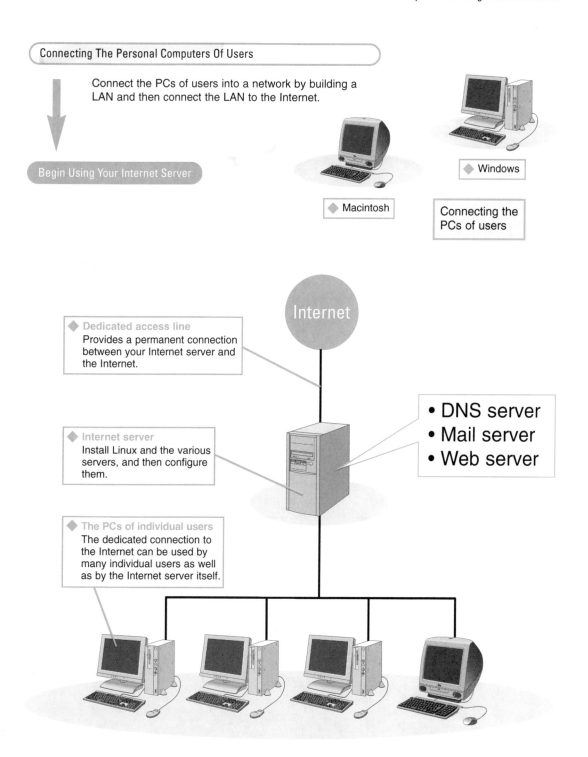

Connecting The Personal Computers Of Users

Connect the PCs of users into a network by building a
LAN and then connect the LAN to the Internet.

Begin Using Your Internet Server

◆ Windows

◆ Macintosh

Connecting the
PCs of users

Internet

◆ Dedicated access line
Provides a permanent connection
between your Internet server and
the Internet.

• DNS server
• Mail server
• Web server

◆ Internet server
Install Linux and the various
servers, and then configure
them.

◆ The PCs of individual users
The dedicated connection to
the Internet can be used by
many individual users as well
as by the Internet server itself.

STEP UP

What Kind Of OS Is Linux

Linux refers to a Unix-like, GNU-based OS (built around the Linux kernel) for PCs. The kernel was created through the global cooperative efforts of people working through the Internet, led by Linus B. Torvalds of Finland. The first version of Linux was released on October 5, 1991, and its daily evolution has continued ever since. The term Linux originally referred to just the kernel of the OS. In reality, however, when you install Linux you are also installing a set of basic utilities and applications that, when combined, allow Linux to be used as a Unix-style OS. This is called a *Linux distribution,* and there are many different distributions available throughout the world. Generally, when you say Linux you are not referring to the kernel alone but to the kernel plus the GNU OS as packaged in one or the other of these distributions. There are many basic distributions available, and each has made improvements to the installation base and enhanced ease of use. Derivatives of these distributions also exist in languages of various countries. The most widely used distributions in the United States are Red Hat, Slackware, and Debian and their derivatives such as Caldera, Mandrake, SuSe, TurboLinux, and Storm Linux.

Free Software And Open Source

Some Unix applications are open-source software (OSS)—the source code is publicly available)—but most are proprietary. Most Linux applications, on the other hand, are OSS. There are a number of criteria for the distribution of OSS, as explained in the Open Source Definition (OSD).

Open source software programs are publicly available, and permission is granted to anyone to modify these programs. The software itself is usually available at no cost. The acquired programs can be improved and distributed in accordance with the licensing provisions, making it possible for people anywhere to join in the continued development of these programs, thereby constantly improving their quality. Nearly all of the many tools required to use Linux and the applications that run on Linux are OSS and are licensed in accordance with the conditions stipulated in the first and most popular of the licenses for free software, the General Public License (GPL) of the Free Software Foundation (FSF), written by Richard M. Stallman.

OSD	**www.opensource.org**
GNU (FSF)	**www.gnu.org**

Chapter 2
Internet Basics

When creating an Internet server, you must specify many different types of information. To do this correctly, you must understand the meaning of this information. This chapter summarizes the basic Internet knowledge required to set up an Internet server.

Contents Of This Chapter

Understanding The Internet

Overall Structure Of The Internet

The Internet ties many different networks from all over the world together creating one huge worldwide network. The many different networks include individuals, homes, businesses, universities, and Internet Service Providers (ISPs), as well as many others.

Usually, one portion of the network of an ISP is devoted to handling dial-up connections for users who, in general, do not realize that they are actually connecting to the Internet as a part of their ISP's local network.

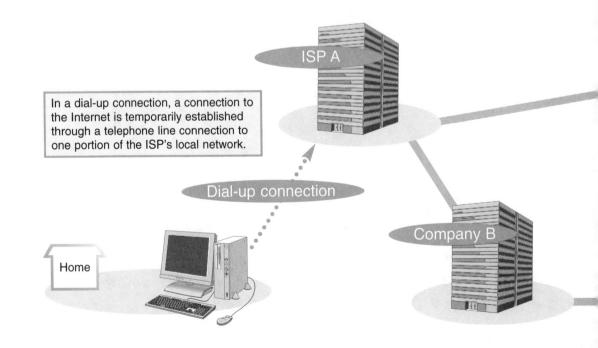

In a dial-up connection, a connection to the Internet is temporarily established through a telephone line connection to one portion of the ISP's local network.

ISP A

Dial-up connection

Company B

Home

An ISP Has One Network Within The Internet

A network connected to the Internet is one portion of the Internet. When someone says they are connecting to the Internet through an ISP using a dial-up connection, a part of the local network of the ISP is being used temporarily. Because the local network of the ISP providing the dial-up access is connected to the Internet, it's possible to connect to the Internet through dial-up access to that ISP.

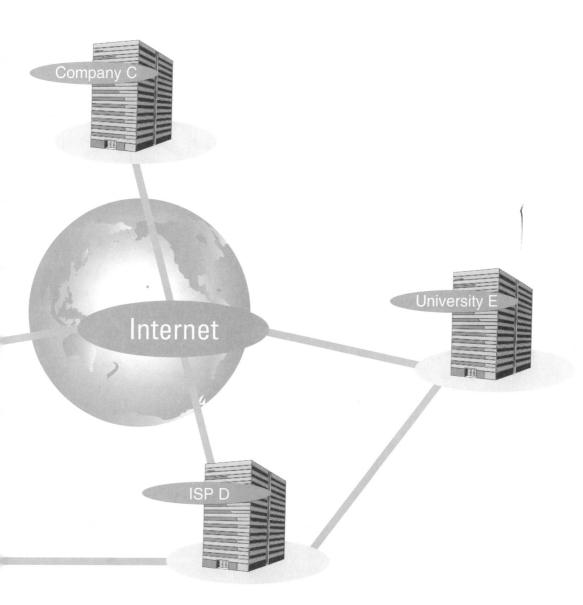

How The Internet Is Connected

The Internet ties together millions of different networks, large and small; but how are these networks connected? If each different network throughout the world used a "one-to-many" form of network connection, the total number of connections would be nearly infinite, and the Internet itself would be an impossibility.

In reality, although each separate network isn't directly connected to *every* other network, a network can connect to any other network by sending its packets of data through indirect, interconnected routes. Consequently, it becomes possible to access any location desired by connecting to the Internet at any particular point.

Individual Networks Are Connected By Routers

The Internet is a connection of many different networks, but this doesn't mean that each network is connected to every other network, directly, one-to-one. The beauty of the Internet is that it's possible for two networks that are not directly connected to connect to each other via other networks. For example, access from ISP A to University E is possible via other networks, even though ISP A and University E are not connected directly. Access to a network anywhere in the world is possible by going through multiple networks.

• Route To Access The University E Server

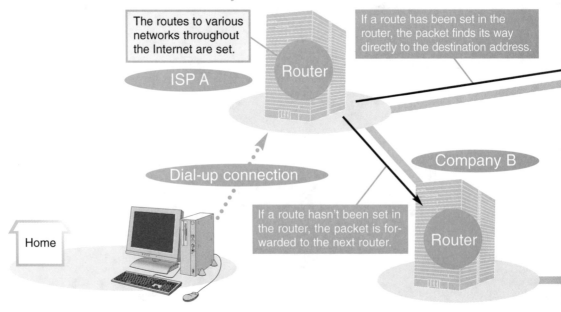

The routes to various networks throughout the Internet are set.

If a route has been set in the router, the packet finds its way directly to the destination address.

ISP A

Router

Dial-up connection

Company B

Home

If a route hasn't been set in the router, the packet is forwarded to the next router.

Router

Many Types Of Routers

When multiple networks are connected to a specific network, which of these many networks provides the best means of access to that particular network? Routing answers this question by selecting which network to pass through and by determining the optimal path for forwarding the packets to that destination. On the Internet, the router carries out this routing procedure.

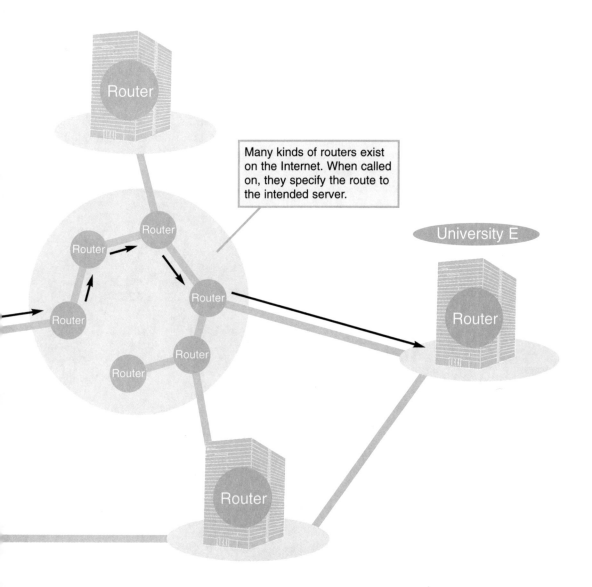

Many kinds of routers exist on the Internet. When called on, they specify the route to the intended server.

172.16.102.2

Understanding TCP/IP

TCP/IP

On the Internet, information flows throughout the networks following communication protocols called *TCP/IP*. TCP/IP is an acronym for a set of protocols used on the Internet to define how computers talk to each other. TCP/IP refers to the two most important of those protocols - Transmission Control Protocol and Internet Protocol.

In a TCP/IP network, devices are distinguished by numbers called *IP addresses*. Consequently, it's necessary to assign a unique IP address to each device on the Internet. On the Internet, IP addresses are grouped sequentially and managed logically. This section explains what is meant by a network address and how network masks are required to manage them.

What Is TCP/IP?

A set of protocols (TCP/IP) is used throughout the Internet. In a TCP/IP network, numbers (IP addresses) are used to distinguish devices located on the network. Each device connected to the network has its own unique IP address. Throughout the Internet not even one device has the same IP address as another device. The work of determining where access originates and where it is directed completely depends on the use of IP addresses.

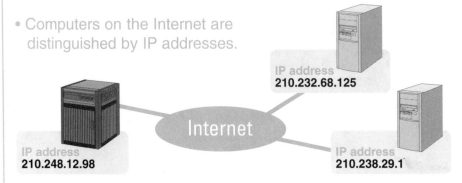

• Computers on the Internet are distinguished by IP addresses.

IP address
210.232.68.125

Internet

IP address
210.248.12.98

IP address
210.238.29.1

An IP address is composed of four decimal numbers, each ranging from 0 to 255, all separated by dots (.). Each of the four numbers represents a combination of eight bits (one byte). Because IP addresses are used to identify each computer on the Internet uniquely, you cannot assign them freely as you please. When connecting to the Internet, you must use the IP addresses that have been assigned to you by your ISP.

◆ IP address

210 . 248 . 12 . 98

A combination of four numbers, each ranging from 0 to 255, separated by dots (.).

Use Of IP Addresses

When placing a dedicated access line into use, a group of successive IP addresses are assigned. A network address and a net mask are used to identify these successive IP addresses. Moreover, an IP address called a *broadcast address* has special meaning within a network.

Network Address

This is the initial IP address of the group of successive IP addresses that were assigned to the network. This IP address is not normally assigned to a device connected to the network.

Net Mask

In conjunction with the network address, a *net mask* is used to identify the range of successive IP addresses that have been assigned to a network. A net mask is also called a *subnet mask*.

Broadcast Address

This is the last IP address of the group of successive IP addresses assigned to the network. When this IP address is accessed, all devices within the network are accessed. This IP address is not normally assigned to a device connected to the network.

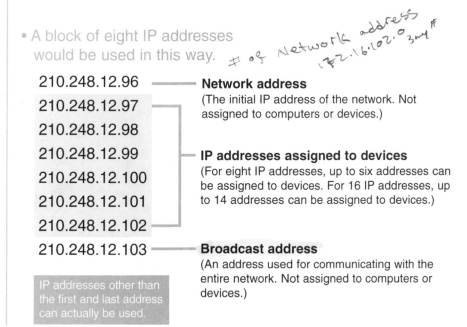

• A block of eight IP addresses would be used in this way.

# of Network address 172.16.102.0 3my #

210.248.12.96 —— **Network address**
(The initial IP address of the network. Not assigned to computers or devices.)

210.248.12.97
210.248.12.98
210.248.12.99 —— **IP addresses assigned to devices**
(For eight IP addresses, up to six addresses can be assigned to devices. For 16 IP addresses, up to 14 addresses can be assigned to devices.)
210.248.12.100
210.248.12.101
210.248.12.102

210.248.12.103 —— **Broadcast address**
(An address used for communicating with the entire network. Not assigned to computers or devices.)

IP addresses other than the first and last address can actually be used.

Understanding The Meaning Of A Net Mask

To better understand the meaning of the value of a net mask, you must first understand the close relationship IP addresses have to the binary number system. Additionally, you should also understand something about the structure of net masks.

Representing An IP Address As A Binary Number

An IP address is a 32-digit (32-bit) binary number. In the realm of computers, binary numbers are often separated into 8-bit (1 byte) units. An IP address is also separated into 8-bit units. Each 8 bit value is represented as a Base 10 (decimal) number in the range of 0 to 255. Consequently, the 32-bit value of an IP address is written with four numbers, each with a value ranging from 0 to 255. (The STEP UP section of this chapter explains binary numbers.)

When represented as a decimal number: 210 . 248 . 12 . 98

When represented as a binary number: 11010010 | 11111000 | 00001100 | 01100010

Structure Of A Net Mask

A net mask is represented as a binary number in the same way. When a net mask is represented by a binary number, you can see that there are two portions, one consisting of a continuous stream of ones (1) and the other consisting of a continuous stream of zeros (0). Direct your attention to the portion consisting of a continuous stream of ones (1). This portion is called a *mask*.

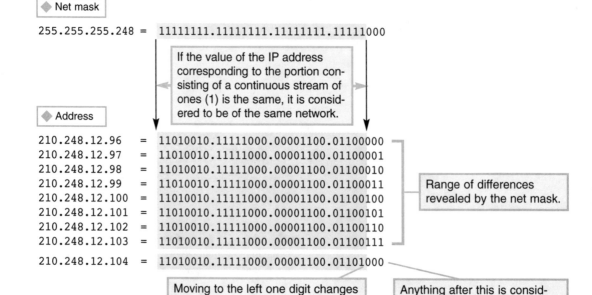

◆ Net mask

255.255.255.248 = 11111111.11111111.11111111.11111000

If the value of the IP address corresponding to the portion consisting of a continuous stream of ones (1) is the same, it is considered to be of the same network.

◆ Address

210.248.12.96	=	11010010.11111000.00001100.01100000
210.248.12.97	=	11010010.11111000.00001100.01100001
210.248.12.98	=	11010010.11111000.00001100.01100010
210.248.12.99	=	11010010.11111000.00001100.01100011
210.248.12.100	=	11010010.11111000.00001100.01100100
210.248.12.101	=	11010010.11111000.00001100.01100101
210.248.12.102	=	11010010.11111000.00001100.01100110
210.248.12.103	=	11010010.11111000.00001100.01100111
210.248.12.104	=	11010010.11111000.00001100.01101000

Range of differences revealed by the net mask.

Moving to the left one digit changes the value of the masked portion.

Anything after this is considered to be a separate network.

When the values of the masked portions of a group of IP addresses are the same, they are considered to belong to the same network. For example, because the value of the masked portions for both IP addresses 210.248.12.96 and 210.248.12.103 are the same, they belong to the same network. However, because the value of the masked portions for IP addresses 210.248.12.103 and 210.248.12.104 are different, they do not belong to the same network.

Using A Net Mask To Determine The Number Of IP Addresses That Can Be Used On A Network

When a net mask is represented by a binary number, it is possible to know the number of IP addresses that belong to the network if you focus on the portion consisting of a continuous stream of zeros (0). For example, for the IP address 255.255.255.248, the zero (0) portion occupies three bits thereby allowing eight IP addresses. If you understand binary numbers, you can use the net mask to determine the number of IP addresses that are available for use on a particular network.

```
255.255.255.  0 = 11111111.11111111.11111111.00000000
                                        8 bits = 256 addresses
255.255.255.192 = 11111111.11111111.11111111.11000000
                                        6 bits =  64 addresses
255.255.255.240 = 11111111.11111111.11111111.11110000
                                        4 bits =  16 addresses
255.255.255.248 = 11111111.11111111.11111111.11111000
                                        3 bits =   8 addresses
```

Precautions When Specifying A Net Mask

When representing a net mask as a binary number, at a specific place, all of the digits to the right must be zeros (0) and all the digits to the left must be ones (1). Consequently, the only net mask values that can be specified are those where the delimiting digits shifted. For example, the value 255.255.255.15 cannot be specified.

◆ Values that can be specified as a net mask   Ones (1) ← → Zeros (0)

```
255.255.255.192 =  11111111.11111111.11111111.11000000
```

                                           Ones (1) ← → Zeros (0)

```
255.255.255.  0 =  11111111.11111111.11111111.00000000*
```

◆ A value that cannot be specified as a net mask

```
255.255.255. 15 =    11111111.11111111.11111111.00001111
```

This cannot be divided into two portions, i.e., a zero's only portion and a one's only portion.

19

Understanding Domain Names

Domain Name Rules

The domain names used to identify network affiliation are constructed on the basis of certain rules. A domain name is made up of several parts, which are separated by dots (.), and each of the separate parts means something. Just like an IP address, a unique domain name must exist on the Internet.

In this book, because an original domain name is obtained to build an Internet server, you should recognize the basic parts of a domain name and understand how it is constructed.

Domain Name Notation

A full domain name consists of several labels, separated by dots (.). Each separate label indicates a certain level in the hierarchy of the Internet. The first label on the right is called the *top-level domain name*. Immediately to its left is the second label, and subsequently the left-most label which can be a selectable name. In the United States, the top-level domain name identifies the type of organization, such as .com (for commercial firms), .edu (for educational institutions), and so forth. Elsewhere, the top-level domain name identifies the country, such as .jp (for Japan), .ca (for Canada), and so on. In the .jp domain and in other similar similar domains, the second level indicates the type of organization. In the U.S., the management of domain names is controlled by InterNIC (**www.internic.net**). The assignment of domain names is handled by a number of registrars that are listed on the InterNIC Web site.

◆ Domain name

dekiru.gr.jp

◆ **Third level.**
You can apply for any name you like for this level, as long as it hasn't already been assigned.

◆ **Second level.**
Countries outside the U.S. use a two-letter code to indicate the type of organization. Here are examples from the .jp domain.

co	Company, bank, credit union, credit cooperative
gr	Volunteer group (club, hobby group)
or	Medical organization, religious organization, cooperative group
ne	Network service (such as an ISP)
ac	Academic institution, national university, private university, educational organization
go	Government, national organizations
ad	JPNIC member network
ed	Elementary, junior, and high schools

◆ **Top level.**
This is usually omitted in the U.S.; elsewhere, it represents the name of the country by means of a two-letter country code.

jp	Japan
uk	England
fr	France
it	Italy
de	Germany
ca	Canada

Attribute Type Domain Names And Location Type Domain Names

A domain name that uses two letters to represent the type of organization in the second level of the domain name (as in the .jp domain) is called an *attribute type domain name*. A domain name can also have the name of a geographic location as its second level label which is known as a *location type domain name*. A location type domain name represents the name of prefectures (as in Japan), or of the names of cities or towns, using the actual geographic names as the label in the domain name. These appear to the left of the two-letter country code, such as .jp.

A location type domain name can be obtained by those who are not classified as organizations, such as private individuals. For example, when a person who resides in the Chiyoda ward of Tokyo wants to obtain a domain name, he or she would belong to chiyoda.tokyo.jp.

◆ Location type domain name

--- .chiyoda.tokyo.jp

◆ **Organization label**
This part identifies a group or an individual and can be freely used for private individual or company names.

◆ **City, town, ward label**
This part identifies the city, town, or ward following the prefecture where the applicant of the domain name resides.

◆ **Prefecture, district label**
This part identifies the location of the applicant of the domain name.

Domain Names Not Differentiated By Country

Although the top level of a domain name was described as identifying a country by means of a two-letter code, domain names also exist that omit the name of the country and assign an organizational classification to the top level. This type of domain name is often used in the U.S., which is where the Internet originated. For example, using "yourcoolnetwork.net", "net" doesn't represent the name of a country but rather is a domain that indicates a network service. These types of domains that do not belong to any country in particular are managed by an organization named InterNIC (**www.internic.net**). InterNIC lists accredited registrars such as (**www.networksolutions.com**) and many others throughout the world.

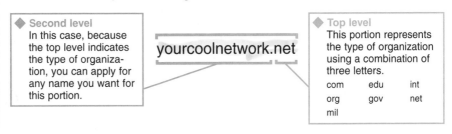

◆ **Second level**
In this case, because the top level indicates the type of organization, you can apply for any name you want for this portion.

yourcoolnetwork.net

◆ **Top level**
This portion represents the type of organization using a combination of three letters.

com	edu	int
org	gov	net
mil		

Understanding The Relationship Between IP Addresses And Domain Names

Domain Name System/Service (DNS)

Host names are given to computers and devices on the Internet and are different from IP addresses. An easily remembered host name can be used in place of the series of numbers that is the IP address, which is difficult to remember. Just like an IP address, a host name specifies computers and devices on the Internet.

You may specify either a host name or an IP address, and it is possible to convert one to the other. A server on the Internet with a database to handle this conversion is called a Domain Name Server/Service (DNS) server, or *name server*.

Host Names And Domain Names

The domain name identifies the network to which a computer or device belongs. When a particular name is given to that computer or device, this, together with the domain name, makes up the host name, also called the *fully qualified domain name* (FQDN). A host name or FQDN has two portions: the domain portion that shows network affiliation and the host portion that shows the name of the computer or device. For example, in **www.yourcoolcompany.com**, the domain name (domain portion) is yourcoolcompany.com and the computer name (host portion) is www.

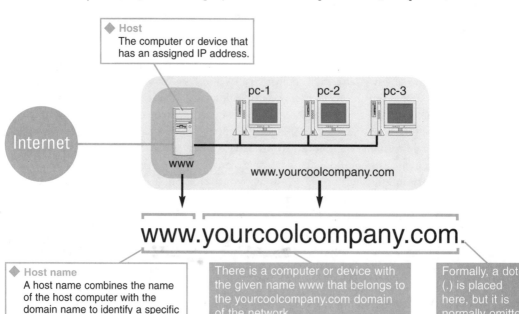

◆ **Host**
The computer or device that has an assigned IP address.

pc-1   pc-2   pc-3

Internet

www   www.yourcoolcompany.com

www.yourcoolcompany.com.

◆ **Host name**
A host name combines the name of the host computer with the domain name to identify a specific computer or device on the Internet.

There is a computer or device with the given name www that belongs to the yourcoolcompany.com domain of the network.

Formally, a dot (.) is placed here, but it is normally omitted.

Host Names And IP Addresses

Unique IP addresses are assigned to all computers and devices connected to the Internet and are used during Internet access. It is not easy, however, to remember IP addresses represented by numbers. Usually, the Internet is accessed by humans using a host name. A host name corresponds to an IP address and, wherever a host name is specified, an IP address is also implicitly specified. In the opposite case — where you know only the IP address — you can also determine the host name is as well.

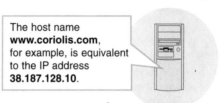

The host name **www.coriolis.com**, for example, is equivalent to the IP address **38.187.128.10**.

IP and domain name (FQDN)

Role Of The DNS Server

All network connections are made by using IP addresses. When specifying an address using a host name, the host name needs to be converted to an IP address before the connection can be made. This conversion is called *name resolution*. The database in the Internet that carries out this name resolution is the domain name service (DNS). When a DNS server is given a host name, it returns the corresponding IP address and given an IP address, it returns the corresponding host name.

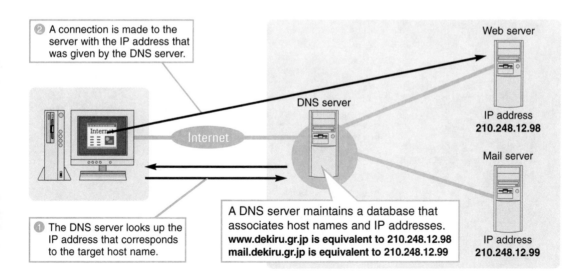

② A connection is made to the server with the IP address that was given by the DNS server.

Web server

DNS server

IP address
210.248.12.98

Mail server

① The DNS server looks up the IP address that corresponds to the target host name.

A DNS server maintains a database that associates host names and IP addresses.
www.dekiru.gr.jp is equivalent to 210.248.12.98
mail.dekiru.gr.jp is equivalent to 210.248.12.99

IP address
210.248.12.99

What Services Will The Server Provide?

Choosing Services

When you convert a host name to an IP address, view a Web page, or exchange email, you use services that respond to these requests. A server is not just a personal computer with Linux installed; it also refers to the programs that provide these services. For example, a Web server refers to a program that serves up Web pages.

Servers that provide different services operate independently of each other. Consequently, more than one server can run on a single Linux machine.

One Computer Can Run Several Servers

Server refers to a program that provides certain services as well as to the machine which the program runs on. A Web server is a program that serves up Web pages. In Linux, server programs operate independently of each other. It is possible to run each program on its own separate computer with Linux installed; it is also possible to run all the server programs on one Linux machine. Therefore, if you set up one Linux machine, you can run it as a server that offers various services at the same time.

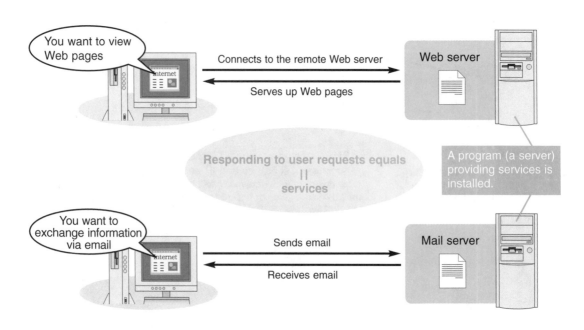

Services And Protocols

Each service, whether it allows you to resolve a host name and IP address, serves up a Web page, or exchanges email, follows different communication protocols within a TCP/IP network. For example, a specific protocol, hypertext transfer protocol (HTTP), is used to serve Web pages. Another protocol, simple mail transfer protocol (SMTP), is used to send email. A third protocol, post office protocol (POP), is used to receive and distribute email to clients. Using one Linux machine, you can allow various servers to operate even though their protocols are different. Consequently, Linux allows you to run a single machine, an Internet server, that provides multiple services.

• Exchanging Information Using
  The Different Protocols Of Each Server

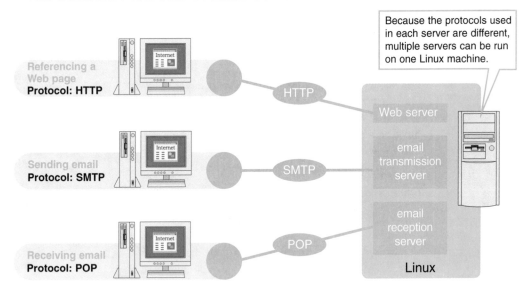

Because the protocols used in each server are different, multiple servers can be run on one Linux machine.

Referencing a Web page
Protocol: HTTP

HTTP

Web server

Sending email
Protocol: SMTP

SMTP

email transmission server

Receiving email
Protocol: POP

POP

email reception server

Linux

Servers And Programs Used In This Book

DNS servers, Web servers, and mail servers are programs that provide various types of services and they all run on Linux. For any given service, several programs are available for Linux. In the Internet server built using this book, Berkeley Internet name domain (BIND) is used as the DNS server, Apache is used as the Web server, Sendmail is used as the mail transfer server, and qpopper is used to receive and distribute email. These server programs are widely used by many people throughout the world and have solid track records of reliability.

STEP UP

Understanding The Difference Between Base 2 And Base 10 Numbers

People use decimal (Base 10) numbers when counting things. Computers, however, are based on the binary number system (Base 2). A computer operates on electricity. Inside a computer, the only decision that can be made is whether or not electricity is flowing. A state in which electricity is not flowing is 0, a state in which electricity is flowing is 1. This state in which only a 0 or a 1 can exist is the digital world of binary numbers. Computers express all numeric values as 0 or 1.

In the Base 10 number system, there are 10 numbers (0 to 9). When counting beyond 9, a digit is carried over. In the binary number system, there are only two numbers (0 and 1), so the digit carries over quickly. If this is understood, the binary number system is not difficult. Furthermore, because only 0 and 1 exist in the binary number system, the number of digits increases rapidly. One digit in the binary number system is called a *bit*. When you hear someone say, "32 bits" or "64 bits," 32 bits represents a numeric value of 32 digits in the binary number system.

Base 10		Base 2
0	=	0
1	=	1
2	=	10
3	=	11
4	=	100
5	=	101
6	=	110
7	=	111
8	=	1000
9	=	1001
10	=	1010

Converting From Base 2 To Base 10

Let's examine the correspondence of each digit in a binary number system to the value of a digit in a Base 10 number system. You can see from the table that each time a digit carries over, the decimal value doubles itself (increases by two), i.e., if the nth digit is 1, then 2^{n-1}. When converting binary numbers to Base 10 numbers, the corresponding Base 10 number can be found by adding the decimal value (see table) of all of the non-zero binary digits, as in the following example.

Number of digits		Value
1	-	1
10	-	2
100	-	4
1000	-	8
10000	-	16
100000	-	32
1000000	-	64
10000000	-	128

$$11000000$$
$$\|$$

1	1	0	0	0	0	0	0
128	64	32	16	8	4	2	1

$$\|$$

128 + 64 + 0 + 0 + 0 + 0 + 0 + 0 = 192

Chapter 3
The Permanent Connection

Before you can use Linux to create an Internet server,
you must obtain a permanent connection to the Internet and
set up your private network. This chapter gives you
information about choosing the kind of permanent
connection that best suits your needs and where to get your
own domain name. A leased T1 line is used here as an
example of a dedicated line.

Contents Of This Chapter

Why Do You Need A Dedicated Line?

The Internet

To run an Internet server, you must have a permanent connection to the Internet. To connect user machines at your site to the Internet, you must set up a *local area network* (LAN). The Internet server is in the middle, between the permanent line to the Internet and your LAN. As such, it must be set up to deal with the Internet on the outside and your private network on the inside.

You need to understand some points about the relationship between the two networks and what activities this relationship involves.

3.1

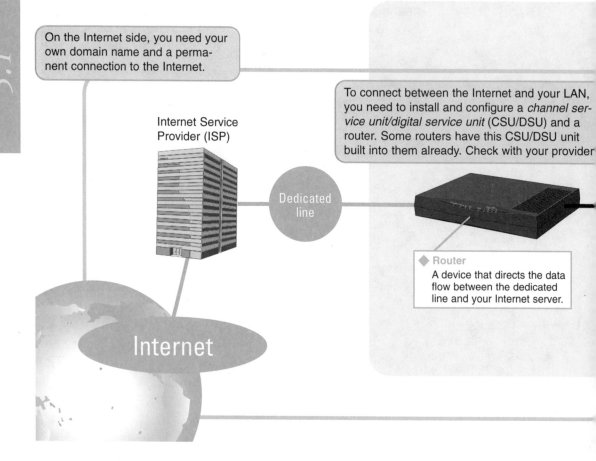

On the Internet side, you need your own domain name and a permanent connection to the Internet.

Internet Service Provider (ISP)

To connect between the Internet and your LAN, you need to install and configure a *channel service unit/digital service unit* (CSU/DSU) and a router. Some routers have this CSU/DSU unit built into them already. Check with your provider

Dedicated line

◆ Router
A device that directs the data flow between the dedicated line and your Internet server.

Internet

Ethernet Is Used To Construct A LAN

Your permanent or dedicated line is accessed through the router. Ethernet is used on the LAN that ties the router and all of the users on your private network to the Internet server. Ethernet protocol is the most popular method used to construct a LAN and is available in two speeds: Base 10, which provides a transfer rate of 10Mbps (10,000,000 bits per second), and Base 100 (Fast Ethernet), which provides a transfer rate of 100Mbps. Cable and connectors similar to common telephone cable and its modular jacks are the most commonly used standard for wiring together both 10Base-T and 100Base-TX networks.

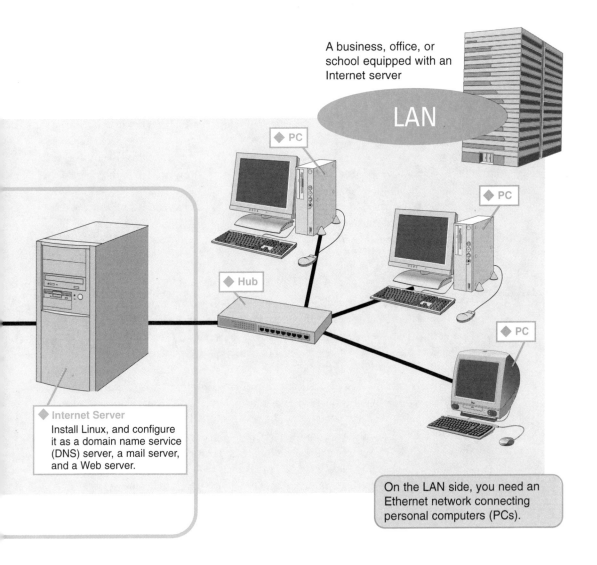

A business, office, or school equipped with an Internet server

LAN

PC

PC

Hub

PC

Internet Server
Install Linux, and configure it as a domain name service (DNS) server, a mail server, and a Web server.

On the LAN side, you need an Ethernet network connecting personal computers (PCs).

Getting Permanently Connected

How To Choose A Line

To use an Internet server, it must be permanently connected to the Internet. Permanent connections vary from one location to another and differ widely in price and quality of service. In the end, it is up to you to decide which type of connection best fits your specific situation. In this book, we will use a T1 or fractional T1 (FT1) leased line as an example of one approach.

The Higher The Speed, The Higher The Price

A number of different types of permanent connections are available, but in any particular location, the choice may be limited. At any given location, the higher the speed, the more you will pay for that connection. Generally, the better the quality you receive, the higher the price you pay. The speed and quality of service you will receive at a given price, however, varies widely from location to location. Better quality usually means higher speed, but it doesn't necessarily refer to the rated speed. For example, a cable connection may not deliver its full rated speed when it is shared by many others. A good quality connection provides its rated speed, or very close to it, any time of day or night.

What Is A Dedicated Line?

A *dedicated line* is a permanent line that is set up for the exclusive use of connecting a particular user to the ISP. Unlike a cable modem connection and a dial-up line, it is not a shared line. The speed is guaranteed between the user and the ISP. A dedicated line usually refers to a leased line with speeds ranging from 56Kbps to 1.54Mbps (T1) or even 45Mbps (T3). Fractional T1 lines (at 128, 256, 384, 512Kbps, and so forth) are also available. If cost is the controlling factor, investigate a digital subscriber line (DSL). DSLs are available in several varieties, but the most common is asymmetrical DSL, where the upload speed is slower than the download speed. For an Internet server, make sure that your agreement with your DSL provider allows for the connection of name servers, Web servers, mail servers, FTP servers, and so on to your DSL line and that you can obtain the necessary minimum number of static IP addresses. Agreements for leased T1 or FT1 lines, usually assume that the user will be connecting various Internet servers to the line.

The critical difference between a dedicated line and the other types of permanent connections is the guaranteed bandwidth. Both lines allow you to be connected all the time, but only the dedicated line guarantees the constant availability of a certain amount of bandwidth. For this, you pay more.

Conceptual Differences Between Dedicated Lines And Permanent Connections

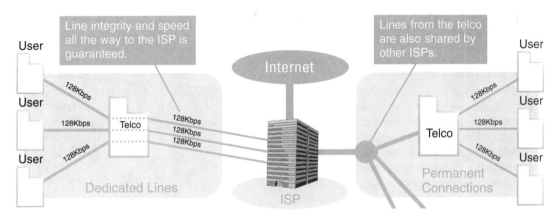

A Permanent Connection At Low Cost

If cost is the decisive factor, instead of a leased T1 or FT1, consider an integrated services digital network (ISDN) line or DSL. One of these does not necessarily provide a better connection than a dedicated leased line, but the price is likely to be cheaper.

Types Of Permanent Connections Available

Available Service

Check with the ISPs as well as the telephone companies that service your area. If you are lucky enough to have several options determine the difference in price between a leased T1 or FT1 and the various flavors of DSLs that are offered. If the leased line is too expensive and a DSL not yet available, investigate an ISDN line.

Web Sources

For general information about DSL visit **http://dslreports.com**.
For an example of one telco DSL and ADSL provider, see
www.pacbell.com/Products_Services/Business/.
One example of an ISP with these services can be viewed at **www.prismnet.com**.

Your Own Domain Name

How To Get A Domain

If you want your Internet server to be able to use a name that you like, you must obtain your own domain name. You have a choice of belonging to one of six top-level domains. The likely candidates are .com or .org. Besides choosing the category of top-level domain to which you want to belong, you must choose the specific name of your own domain. Your name must be different from any other name belonging to that top-level domain. To save time, check whether or not the name you want to use is unique before you apply for your domain name.

Domain Name Search

1 Accessing the InterNIC database of domains.

InterNIC home page.

http://www.internic.net

① Click list of Registrars.

Part of the List of Registrars on Internic.net.

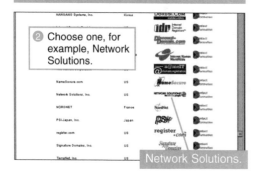

② Choose one, for example, Network Solutions.

Network Solutions.

2 Searching for the domain name you want to use.

http://www.networksolutions.com.

For example, type cjk.com.

Type the desired domain name.

TIP!

Allowable domain name characters

Restrict the characters to U.S. ASCII letters, digits, and the hyphen. A domain name cannot begin or end with a hyphen. Spaces are not allowed. The maximum number of characters is 67, including the three-letter top-level domain name.

Note that all three-letter domain names and most common four-letter English words have been already assigned.

3 Results of the search.

Name Is Not Available

Your desired domain name has already been assigned to someone else.

Name Is Available

Your desired domain name has not been assigned. You may apply for it.

Applying For A Domain Name

You may apply for a domain name at the same time that you set up an account with your ISP or your dedicated connection provider. In effect, you are asking them to apply for you. You may also apply for a domain name directly. For many, the first method may be more convenient, but applying yourself is not difficult.

Allowing your ISP to apply for you may be slower because the name you want to use may have already been taken by the time your application is submitted. For the fastest service, if you have all of the required information on hand, you may apply for a domain name directly through one of the companies, called *registrars*, which handle domain name registration. The place to start is **www.internic.com** where you will find a list of registrars. Explore their Web sites and choose the one that most appeals to you. In our examples, we use Network Solutions.

The Router

To actually use the dedicated line that you have had installed, you must have a router. There are many routers on the market, but we will talk about a router used to connect to a dedicated T1 or FT1 line. In other words, we are not discussing units for use with an xDSL line. Although we use the specific example of a Compatible Systems 1200i router, the same functionality is available in any of the other routers shown on the next page.

Role Of The Router

A *router* is the gatekeeper of a network. The router determines whether any given data packet is allowed to pass in or out of the network for which it works. Both you and your ISP have a router on your respective ends of the dedicated line that connects both of you. All traffic into and out of your private Ethernet network must first check with your router for permission to come in or go out. It could be said that effective communication between networks is only possible through the good graces of their respective routers.

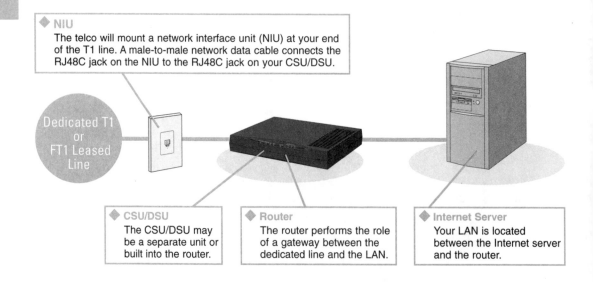

◆ **NIU**
The telco will mount a network interface unit (NIU) at your end of the T1 line. A male-to-male network data cable connects the RJ48C jack on the NIU to the RJ48C jack on your CSU/DSU.

Dedicated T1 or FT1 Leased Line

◆ **CSU/DSU**
The CSU/DSU may be a separate unit or built into the router.

◆ **Router**
The router performs the role of a gateway between the dedicated line and the LAN.

◆ **Internet Server**
Your LAN is located between the Internet server and the router.

Points To Consider In Selecting A Router

There are plenty of router choices on the market. The ones mentioned are for use with a dedicated leased T1 or FT1 line. Many routers also have a secondary port that allows them to connect to a modem, 56Kbps CSU/DSU, or ISDN terminal adapter. All of the routers listed below may be configured by connecting a VT 100 terminal or terminal emulator directly to the console port. An alternate method is to use a crossover cable connected to the router's LAN port. If the networking on a workstation has been temporarily reconfigured to use the router's default IP addresses, or the router has been minimally configured by means of one of the methods just mentioned, the router can be configured by telnetting to it over the network.

- Is the DSU/CSU included or is it purchased as a separate unit?
- Besides a T1 DSU/CSU, what else can the router connect with?
- Does the router include a LAN interface (hub)?
- How do you configure it? Web browser, terminal, Windows program?

Examples Of Routers

Compatible Systems
1200i Office Router

Compatible Systems 1250i Office
Router (includes CSU/DSU)

Cisco 1601R
(includes CSU/DSU)

Lucent Pipeline 130
Router

The 1200i

The Compatible Systems 1200i router meets our requirements. It has a good track record of trouble-free use. A similar Compatible Systems model that belongs to one of our technical editors has performed flawlessly for five years. Technical support for initial set-up was quick and accurate; subsequent technical support hasn't been needed. This model has a secondary wide area network (WAN) port that will connect with a modem, 56K CSU/DSU, or ISDN terminal adapter, if needed. It includes a standard RJ-45 10Base-T Ethernet port and is configurable through a VT100 terminal emulator or a Windows graphical user interface (GUI) program.

The Big Picture

Putting It All In Perspective

Now it's time to step back and take an overall look at your plan for an Internet server. Permanently connecting an Internet server to the Internet isn't something to take lightly. You will be responsible for protecting users and their computers on your private network from technical problems that come in through your Internet connection. While you provide content to the world at large, you are also assuming an obligation to do your best to ensure its availability and accessibility. If your Internet server is an integral part of a business plan, you have additional reasons to do it right.

Key Points In Establishing Your Permanent Presence On The Internet

We have covered many of these topics already and some will be discussed in greater detail in following pages, but now is a good time to look at the big picture. This should help you to understand what you really want to do with an Internet server, as well as how to do it.

Server Location

You will need a cool, clean, convenient, and secure location for the machine that runs your server and related equipment.

Uptime

If you intend to maintain a 24/7 (24 hours a day, 7 days a week, all year) DNS, Mail, Web, or File Transfer Protocol (FTP) presence on the Internet, you must be able to ride out power outages, maintain contingency plans for equipment failures, and perform unassisted reboots. If the telco (telephone company) line or the ISP's name server goes down, you need to know who to call and what to do at your end.

How Much Bandwidth

Most would say, the more available bandwidth, the better. It's a practical world, however; adding more bandwidth must be weighed against the additional cost. A stable, well maintained Web site that offers only static content and has a relatively small number of hits per day can operate smoothly on a 56Kbps link. Dynamic content or a high volume of hits demands more bandwidth. Because your need for bandwidth may change quickly, it's important to know how easy it is to scale your bandwidth up or down.

Your Domain Name

You will want to summon all your ingenuity to find an appealing but as yet unassigned name. To request a domain name, you need to provide the registrar company with the name of your administrative, technical, and billing contacts, and the IP addresses of your primary and secondary DNS name servers, although it is possible to reserve a name for a certain amount of time without knowing those IP addresses.

Selecting The Hardware

Like bandwidth, how much CPU speed, RAM, and storage capacity you need depends on how much content you intend to serve up over a given interval. It also depends on the bandwidth of your dedicated line. For example, there is little point in outfitting a server with powerful CPUs, for example, if you publish mostly static pages, and the most data you can push out through your line is 64Kbps. Besides the computer that you will use to run your Internet server, the router, a DSU/CSU, hubs, network interface cards, network cables, and a power backup unit must also be selected and acquired.

Ordering The Line

You will need to give the leased line provider and your ISP (they may be the same company) certain information. Schedule the installation of your line at a time that is convenient for you and the telco. An agreement with the line provider will have to be signed, and initial payments may have to be made.

You And Your ISP

You will probably not have much ongoing contact with your leased line provider unless the line goes down. Ideally, this will be true of your ISP, too. They provide you with a port into the Internet through a single router. There is no filtering, no content monitoring, and no interference of any kind. They may run your secondary name and mail servers, but you take care of everything else. Keep in mind, however, that, even in this scenario, your continued presence on the Internet is completely dependent on your ISP. A good relationship is a necessity.

The Key Points In Detail

You will become familiar with these key issues as you proceed to build your Internet server and make it available on the Internet. Your specific response to these issues and how they can be handled best will change over time. The answers may vary, depending on the set of conditions at a specific time and place. The questions, on the other hand, will generally remain the same. Our approach, using a dedicated leased T1 or FT1 line, is only one among several options. You may chose to use an XDSL or ISDN line.

Location

The best place for your server might be a closet or small room. The location must be convenient for your access as well as that of the T1 line. You should have enough room either to work on your server or to easily move the server out of the closet for upgrades and maintenance. Restrict casual access by locking the door. You don't want someone accidentally resetting the server or unplugging the T1. Finally, have a telephone next to the server and a telephone log or bound telephone notebook to record communications with your ISP and the telephone company. Install wall vents near the ceiling so that warm air can escape, and make sure that cooler air has a way to enter somewhere near the floor. (Cutting off 1/2 to 3/4 inch from the bottom of the door may work.) If heat is a big problem, you may need an air conditioner or forced venting. Clean the floor and walls regularly, and install screens over your inlet vents if the outside air entering the space gets especially dusty. The cooler and cleaner the ambient air around your server is, the better the server will run.

Uptime

The first line of defense is to guard against electrical power outages by means of an *uninterruptible power supply* (UPS) backup power unit. How long the UPS can keep your server and associated equipment running will depend on its own rating and the total power demanded by your equipment. You can extend your uptime by shutting down all nonessential equipment, such as the server's monitor. Most power outages last less than a few seconds, so a unit that will run your server for 10 to 20 minutes is usually adequate for all but the worst cases. If you must prepare for outages longer than 90 minutes, consider using a generator. Most UPS's do not work properly with off-the-shelf portable generators, however, so be sure to review carefully before you buy.

The UPS will clean up the power to your computer, helping to extend its life, but power supplies, fans, and hard drives will fail sooner or later. How much redundancy you have will depend on how concerned you are about keeping the server on line continuously and on your budget. Hot swappable power supplies hard drives, and redundant array of independent disk (RAID) systems, and even completely redundant computers can be used.

Bandwidth

The bandwidth of an FT1 leased line can be scaled up or down, depending on your needs. If you use the same T1 line with DSU/CSU, the router will run just as well at the low end as it does at the high end of the bandwidth spectrum. You can start with 128Kbps and bump it up in steps to full T1 speed, as needed. Technically, changing the bandwidth of the line (resetting the DSU/CSU units on both ends of the line to the new speed), is simple, but the change in the billing and in your agreement with your ISP or telco might be more difficult. When you make your initial agreement, ask your leased line provider for an estimate of the time that would be required to change your bandwidth.

Domain Name

You need to find an appealing but unassigned domain name. To apply for it, you must determine your administrative contact, technical contact, billing address, and IP addresses of your primary and secondary DNS name servers. If you are planning to set up your own DNS name server, you need to have someone else—probably your ISP—perform this service until you are ready to take over. It's also possible to reserve a domain name without knowing beforehand what DNS name servers you will eventually use. There may be an extra charge for this.

Hardware

In addition to the NIU provided by the telco, you need a DSU/CSU (or an ISDN terminal unit, if you're hooking up ISDN), a router, and the proper cables. Some router models (e.g., compatible systems 1250i) have the DSU/CSU built in. The minimum computer hardware configuration for Red Hat Linux is an Intel 486 or higher CPU, 16MB RAM, approximately 500MB disk space, and a 3.5-inch floppy drive. This set-up certainly would have to be the absolute minimum for an Internet server. Besides increasing bandwidth, the next most obvious measure to increase the performance of your Internet presence is to increase your RAM. If you're not sure, start with 64MB or more. If you will be serving up dynamic Web content, you want something faster than a 486 MHz CPU. Again, if you're not sure, start with a Pentium 120 or higher CPU.

The Line

If you obtain your leased T1 or FT1 directly from the telephone company or through your ISP, they need to know how much bandwidth you want to pay for and when it will be convenient to schedule the installation. Confirm with them that the line will terminate in an NIU supplied by the telephone company and the type of jack that will be available to connect to your DSU/CSU, probably an RJ48C. Make sure that they understand that they will be bringing the wire all the way to your desired point of termination inside your house or office. Also, make sure that you know who to call and how to refer to your line (by circuit ID number), in case a problem arises. After you are permanently wired, billing will begin, so be ready to bring your other equipment, your new domain name, and your Internet server online quickly.

Your ISP

Who is responsible for what? If you run your own primary mail server, will the ISP handle the secondary? If you run the primary DNS name server, will your ISP handle the secondary? Do you need a few dial-up accounts to access the Internet when you're away from your private network? Will there be any filtering on packets directed to your domain, or will they pass straight through so that you can deal with any filtering you want to use? How fast is the ISP's own connection to the Internet? If you decide later to turn over the DNS name server completely to them later, what will you have to do and about how long will it take? Who is the technical contact (get a name) with whom you should deal? No other Internet relationship is more important to the well-being of your presence in cyberspace than the one you have with your ISP. Cultivate it, be diplomatic, and ask questions politely. Also, keep your eye open for alternatives, in case you need to move.

What You Need For Your Local Network

Getting The Hardware To Set Up Your Private Network

From the router on your dedicated line on in, Ethernet is used to build your private network. You must install a network interface card (NIC) in each computer that is attached to your network. To connect each one of your computers to the network, you will need a hub and a cable of the correct length.

This section provides information about selecting a NIC and other necessary components, and some key points about Ethernet.

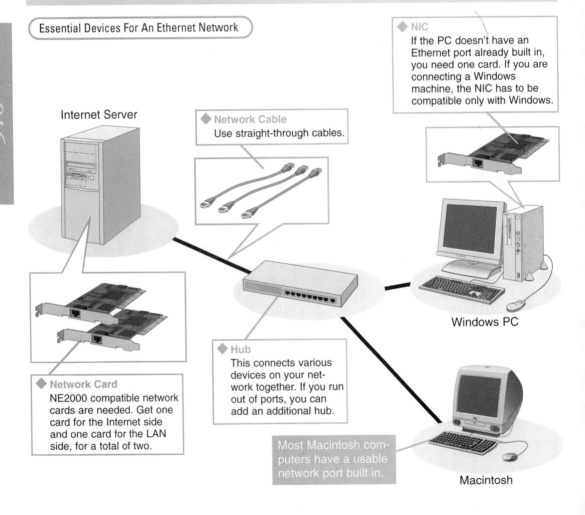

Essential Devices For An Ethernet Network

◆ NIC
If the PC doesn't have an Ethernet port already built in, you need one card. If you are connecting a Windows machine, the NIC has to be compatible only with Windows.

Internet Server

◆ Network Cable
Use straight-through cables.

Windows PC

◆ Network Card
NE2000 compatible network cards are needed. Get one card for the Internet side and one card for the LAN side, for a total of two.

◆ Hub
This connects various devices on your network together. If you run out of ports, you can add an additional hub.

Most Macintosh computers have a usable network port built in.

Macintosh

Network Interface Cards

A great number of NICs made by many different manufacturers are available. They come with a wide variety of feature sets and prices. For Linux, the easiest choice is one of the NE2000 compatible cards or a card that has been certified to work with Linux. Ask the store or online hardware retailer that sells the cards about compatibility or consult a Linux hardware compatibility list. (Red Hat maintains a good one on their Web site, **www.redhat.com/support/hardware/**.)

You usually have a choice between a card that is compatible with an industry standard architecture (ISA) slot or a peripheral connection interface (PCI) slot. We recommend you select the PCI cards. Because an NE2000 compatible card is not absolutely guaranteed to work on Linux, it may be best to purchase several different kinds of cards that are known to work on the Windows machines, and then swap these between Linux and Windows, if necessary.

- Choose an NE2000 compatible NIC or a card known to work on Linux.
- Get a card designed for a PCI slot.

Two Cards Are Needed In The Server

When you have many client PCs on your private network and you haven't been assigned enough IP addresses to connect each one directly to your dedicated line, a network address translator (NAT) is often used. To use a NAT, you need to install two NICs in your Internet server. These two cards can be NE2000 compatible cards or any other NIC that you know will work with Linux.

Network Cables

A number of cable types can be used with Ethernet, but the easiest to find and most compatible cable for use with both 10Base-T and 100Base-TX is called a *category 5 unshielded, twisted-pair (UTP) cable*, often shortened to *cat 5*. It is readily available for purchase both in stores and over the Internet. Do not inadvertently buy crossover cables, which are used to connect two computers directly together and cannot be used to connect computers to a hub. You want straight-through cables, not the crossover type.

- Choose category 5 cable.
- Only straight-through cables will work.
- Cable lengths should be appropriate for the distances between each machine and its hub.

Hubs *repeater*

A hub is a hardware device used to connect various networked computers or devices together. Hubs come in all sizes, from four-port models to models with dozens of ports. Because it's easy to run out of ports, the most economical place to start is with an eight-port hub. If you need more than eight ports, you can buy a hub with more ports, or you can combine several eight-port hubs. Generally, 10Base-T hubs can connect only to other 10Base-T hubs, and 100Base-TX hubs can connect only to other 100Base-TX hubs. If you want to mix the two together on the same network, you must use dual-speed hubs.

• Choose a hub that has the right number of ports for your setup.

When You Want To Connect More Devices To Your Network

Just because you want to connect more computers or devices to your hub than the number of available ports on your hub doesn't necessarily mean that you must buy a hub with more ports. You can add ports by connecting one of the regular ports on one hub to the cascade port on another hub. Connecting hubs in this way is called *cascading*. If you use a stackable hub, because you can connect to the stack port, you can increase the number of available ports without cascading.

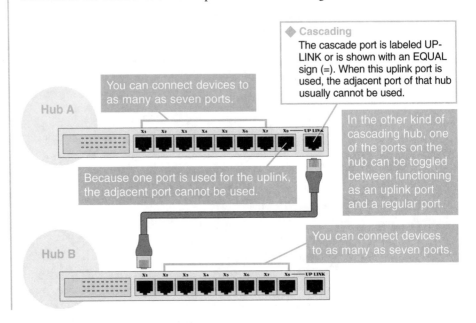

◆ Cascading
The cascade port is labeled UP-LINK or is shown with an EQUAL sign (=). When this uplink port is used, the adjacent port of that hub usually cannot be used.

You can connect devices to as many as seven ports.

Hub A

In the other kind of cascading hub, one of the ports on the hub can be toggled between functioning as an uplink port and a regular port.

Because one port is used for the uplink, the adjacent port cannot be used.

You can connect devices to as many as seven ports.

Hub B

• Hints On Cascading

Usable Ports

When cascading, the uplink port of one hub is connected to one of the regular ports of another hub. You cannot connect the uplink port of one hub to the uplink port of the next hub or a regular port of one hub to a regular port of the next hub. Depending on the hub, you have a choice of two types of uplink ports. In one of these types, the two adjacent ports at either the left or the right end of the bank have the same number. One of these is an uplink port, and the other is an ordinary port. Only one of these two ports can be used at any one time. In the other type of hub, a switch near the port determines whether it will function as an uplink port or a regular port.

• The Number Of Hubs Required

In cascading, you must pay attention to how many hubs the data packets pass through. In a situation such as the one illustrated in the following figure, the packets pass through one hub to go from client A to client B, but must go through two hubs to get to client C. In an Ethernet LAN, the maximum number of hubs that data packets can pass through is four. This is further restricted to two hubs in the case of 100Base-TX.

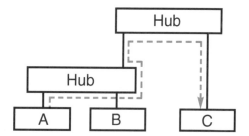

A Few Thoughts On Efficient Use Of Hubs

Because the speed of your dedicated line will be so much slower than the speed of a LAN, a 10Base-T is quite sufficient to connect your router to your Internet server. It's nice, however, to have the faster speed provided by a 100Base-TX when transferring data between users on the LAN. To acquire this speed, you can use a dual-speed hub, tying together the 100Base-TX LAN and the 10Base-T Internet server.

When additional users are added to the LAN or when certain users require more speed, consider using a switching hub. A switching hub helps to reduce network confusion by managing the traffic on each port so that you achieve better flow throughout the network. Moreover, most 100Base-T switching hubs are *dual speed* (they can handle either speed equally well). Finally, in the case of a cascade connection, at the moment when the data packets pass through a switching hub, the hub count is reset to zero.

STEP UP

The Router Is The Gateway

The router is used to isolate a particular network. It stands between your private network and all of the other networks, and it mediates the exchange of information between these two realms.

The router looks for addresses in the data flow on your private network. When the router finds data with an address outside your local network, it routes the data out to an external network. On the other hand, when the router sees data that has a local address, it does nothing. This is its most basic function, to determine whether or not data should leave your private network. Because it is like a gate standing between the local network and all other networks, it's sometimes called a *gateway*.

A large-scale network may have more than one gateway. In this case, information must be available so that the right router can be chosen to move the data outside the local network. When the information isn't specific about which gateway should be used, the data is directed to the *default gateway.* path to the Wan

When the connection to the Internet is via a single dedicated line (as has been the case in our examples in this book), it's best if a single router is used. It will then function as the default gateway.

Chapter 4
Installing Linux

To create an Internet server using Linux, you must perform several tasks. This chapter explains the procedure for configuring the router and installing Linux in preparation for creating an Internet server.

Contents Of This Chapter

Things To Know Before Installing Linux

IP Address And Domain Name Verification

Before installing Linux, verify the configuration of the network that you will be building. The network settings include the domain name to be used, network address, netmask, server's host name and assigned Internet Protocol (IP) address, router's IP address and domain name service (DNS) server's IP address. These network settings are not only required during

installation, but are also required later during the configuration of various types of servers. Make sure to record them so that you don't forget them.

Internet Environment To Be Used In This Book

In this book, various Internet servers are built using eight IP addresses assigned by a hypothetical Internet Service Provider (ISP).

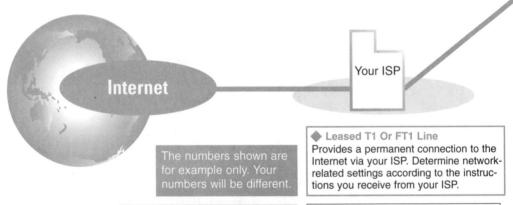

Your ISP

The numbers shown are for example only. Your numbers will be different.

Check with your ISP to verify that the items shown at the right have correct IP addresses.

◆ **Leased T1 Or FT1 Line**
Provides a permanent connection to the Internet via your ISP. Determine network-related settings according to the instructions you receive from your ISP.

Allocated Range Of IP Addresses
  210.248.12.96
  to 210.248.12.103
DNS Server Specifications
Primary DNS Server
  ns.dekiru.gr.jp
  210.248.12.98
Secondary DNS Server
  ns-tk02ocn.ad.jp
  203.139.160.104
Router's IP Address Specification
  210.248.12.97

TIP!
Verify Your IP Address Assignments With Your ISP

The IP address of the router is the second address in the block assigned to you by your ISP. Usually, your DNS server's IP address is the third address. Make sure that your ISP concurs with your IP address assignments.

◆ Server PC
Personal computer on which Linux is to be installed for servers. Servers such as the DNS server, Web server, and mail server will run on this machine.

◆ Router
The router and the DSU/CSU are connected to the T1 or FT1 leased line.

Router's Host Name And IP Address
router.dekiru.gr.jp
210.248.12.97

Domain Name
dekiru.gr.jp
Allocation Range Of IP Addresses
210.248.12.96 to 210.248.12.103

Host Name And IP Address Of Server PC
server.dekiru.gr.jp
210.248.12.98
Net Mask
255.255.255.248

List Of Network Settings For dekiru.gr.jp, The Example Used In This Chapter

Network settings differ for each network. In the following table, enter the actual information for your network in the fields that correspond to the settings used in this book, then substitute your settings while reading the remainder of this book.

Item	Setting Used In This Book	Setting You Will Use
Domain name	dekiru.gr.jp	[ ]
Range of IP address to be used	210.248.12.96 to 210.248.12.103	[ ]
Netmask	255.255.255.248 (29 bits)	[ ]
Network address	210.248.12.96	[ ]
Broadcast address	210.248.12.103	[ ]
Router's IP address (default gateway)	210.248.12.97	[ ]
Server PC's IP address	210.248.12.98	[ ]
Server PC's host name	server.dekiru.gr.jp	[ ]
Primary DNS server's IP address	(Same as server)	[ ]
Secondary DNS server's IP address	203.139.160.104	[ ]
DHCP allocation range	210.248.12.99 to 210.248.12.102	[ ]

Connecting Your LAN To The Internet

Router Configuration

To use your permanent connection, you must connect your local area network (LAN) to the dedicated line through the router and digital service unit (DSU) and configure the router. Connect the network interface unit (NIU) to the DSU and the DSU to the router and the router to a hub on your LAN. Then configure the router with the correct IP addresses and test your connection to the Internet.

The router can be configured by directly connecting a PC running a terminal emulation program to the console port. Once minimally configured, subsequent configuration can be done over the network. This section explains the procedure using the Compatible Systems Micro Router 1200i as an example.

1 Connect your LAN to the T1/FT1 line.

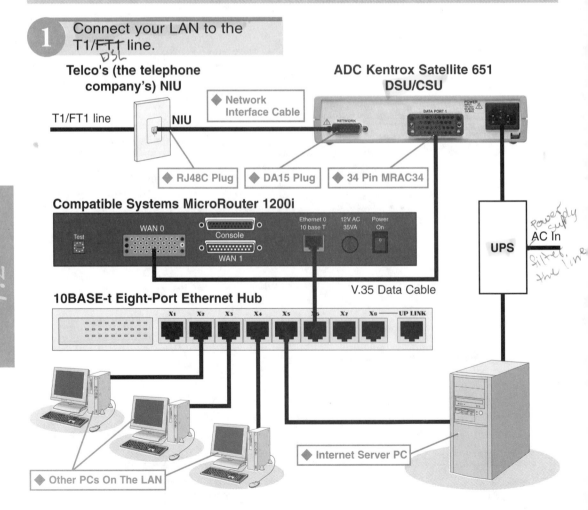

Telco's (the telephone company's) NIU

ADC Kentrox Satellite 651 DSU/CSU

T1/FT1 line — NIU

◆ Network Interface Cable

◆ RJ48C Plug ◆ DA15 Plug ◆ 34 Pin MRAC34

Compatible Systems MicroRouter 1200i

V.35 Data Cable

10BASE-t Eight-Port Ethernet Hub

UPS — AC In

◆ Internet Server PC

◆ Other PCs On The LAN

2 Connect an out-of-band management console to the router.

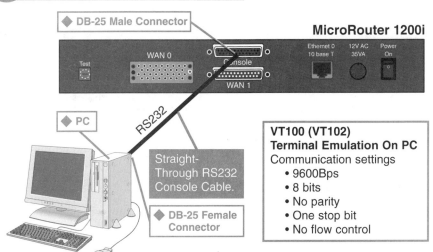

◆ DB-25 Male Connector

MicroRouter 1200i

◆ PC

RS232

Straight-Through RS232 Console Cable.

◆ DB-25 Female Connector

VT100 (VT102)
Terminal Emulation On PC
Communication settings
• 9600Bps
• 8 bits
• No parity
• One stop bit
• No flow control

3 Log in to the router.

Use the default password that is printed in the router's documentation.

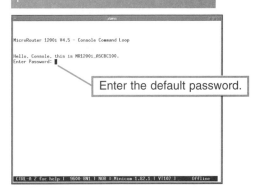

Enter the default password.

TIP! Commands and section name
keyword-value pairs

There are two types of commands: configuration and managment commands. For example, when you type the "**configure**" command, you will enter the configuration editor and then choose a section, like "**general**", "**ip**", or "**ip ether 0**". Within a section, you add or modify settings using keyword-value pairs. For example, **mode=routed**. Other examples of management commands are "**help**", "**exit**", "**save**", and "**show config**".

4 Change the default password and the device name.

Note: Change the insecure, default password to a new one to use until you have finished configuring the router. You can give this password to technical support, if necessary. After the router is configured and working properly, change the password again.

❶ Enter the "**config general**" command.

❷ Enter the default "**password**".

❸ Enter "**yes**".

❹ Enter the "**password=** *yournewpasswordhere*" keyword-value pair.

❻ Enter the "**exit**" command.

❼ Enter the "**save**" command.

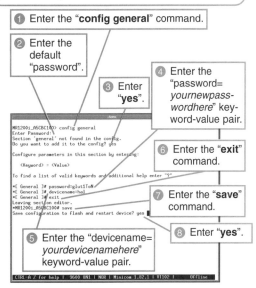

❺ Enter the "**devicename=** *yourdevicenamehere*" keyword-value pair.

❽ Enter "**yes**".

⑤ Set the basic Ethernet interface.

❶ Enter "**configure ip ether 0**" command.

❷ Enter your router password.

❸ Enter "yes".

❹ Enter your IP address for the router.

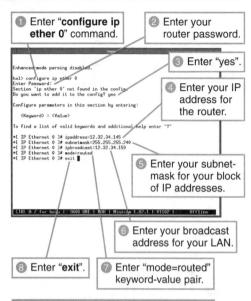

❺ Enter your subnet-mask for your block of IP addresses.

❻ Enter your broadcast address for your LAN.

❽ Enter "**exit**".

❼ Enter "mode=routed" keyword-value pair.

When these settings are set properly, a Telnet client can find the router and all further configuration can be done over your LAN or over the Internet.

Note: Correct command line syntax must be followed for command line management. The commands are not case-sensitive and they can be abbreviated.

TIP! **Don't forget to save the new configuration to Flash ROM.**

If you don't save it, the router will continue to ignore all your new settings.

⑥ Set the basic WAN interface.

❶ Enter "**ip wan 0**" command.

❷ Enter your router password.

❸ Enter your IP address for the router.

❹ Enter your sub-netmask for your block of IP addresses.

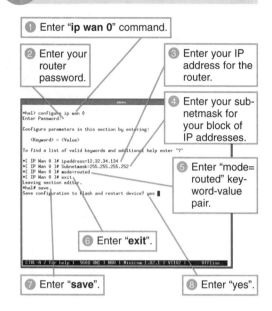

❺ Enter "mode=routed" keyword-value pair.

❻ Enter "**exit**".

❼ Enter "**save**".

❽ Enter "yes".

⑦ Set the static route interface for actual routing.

❶ Enter "**edit config ip static**" command.

❷ Enter your password.

❸ Enter "yes".

❹ Enter "append 1".

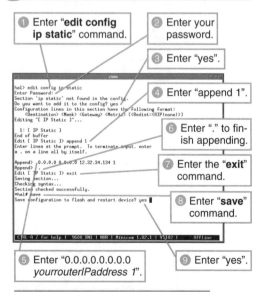

❻ Enter "." to finish appending.

❼ Enter the "**exit**" command.

❽ Enter "**save**" command.

❺ Enter "0.0.0.0 0.0.0.0 *yourrouterIPaddress* 1".

❾ Enter "yes".

When these parameters are set properly, actual routing can begin.

8 Check the router's configuration.

❶ Enter "**show config**".

❷ Enter your password.

```
hal> show config
Enter Password:

[ General ]
EthernetAddress        : 00:00:a5:cb:c1:00
SoftwareVersion        : MicroRouter 1200i V4.5
DeviceType             : MicroRouter 1200i
ConfiguredOn           : Timeserver not configured
ConfiguredFrom         : Command Line, from Console
DeviceName             : "hal"
Password               : "glut1ToN"

[ IP Ethernet 0 ]
Mode                   : Routed
IPBroadcast            : 12.32.34.159
SubnetMask             : 255.255.255.240
IPAddress              : 12.32.34.145

[ IP Wan 0 ]
Mode                   : Routed
SubnetMask             : 255.255.255.252
IPAddress              : 12.32.34.134

[ IP Static ]
0.0.0.0 0.0.0.0 12.32.34.134 1

Configuration size is 685 out of 65500 bytes.
hal#
```

Note: If any settings are not correct, you will have to go back to "configure" and reset them.

10 Verify that your network can be reached from outside.

❶ Ask your ISP or someone else outside your LAN to ping (or trace-route) to your router.

❷ Substitute the IP address of your router.

```
michael@cog:~$ ping 12.32.34.145
PING 12.32.34.145 (12.32.34.145): 56 data bytes
64 bytes from 12.32.34.145: icmp_seq=0 ttl=37 time=202.3 ms
64 bytes from 12.32.34.145: icmp_seq=1 ttl=38 time=227.8 ms
64 bytes from 12.32.34.145: icmp_seq=2 ttl=37 time=273.9 ms

--- 12.32.34.145 ping statistics ---
3 packets transmitted, 3 packets received, 0% packet loss
round-trip min/avg/max = 202.3/234.6/273.9 ms
michael@cog:~$ /usr/sbin/traceroute 12.32.34.145
traceroute to 12.32.34.145 (12.32.34.145), 30 hops max, 38 byte packets
 1  la.creatureshop.henson.com (38.243.102.1)  14.293 ms  0.760 ms  0.785 ms
 2  38.24.14.1 (38.24.14.1)  16.375 ms  17.367 ms  17.648 ms
 3  rc2.sw.us.psi.net (38.1.44.2)  21.299 ms  19.994 ms  22.100 ms
 4  rc1.sw.us.psi.net (38.1.24.193)  22.416 ms  22.017 ms  20.538 ms
 5  38.1.10.173 (38.1.10.173)  37.741 ms  51.032 ms  33.672 ms
 6  psi-gw.affca.ip.att.net (192.205.31.66)  37.650 ms * *
 7  gbr2-p40.affca.ip.att.net (12.123.12.230)  37.095 ms  42.478 ms  40.159 ms
 8  gbr4-p70.affca.ip.att.net (12.122.1.109)  40.069 ms  37.695 ms  35.911 ms
 9  12.122.2.62 (12.122.2.62)  82.951 ms  83.217 ms  87.392 ms
10  ar1-a300a1.st6wa.ip.att.net (12.127.6.133)  87.393 ms  87.468 ms  89.868 ms
11  12.127.65.86 (12.127.65.86)  289.747 ms  179.708 ms 12.127.65.82 (12.127.65.
82)  213.637 ms
12  12.32.34.145 (12.32.34.145)  172.907 ms  180.074 ms  195.191 ms
michael@cog:~$
```

9 Verify the router's presence on the LAN.

Enter "**ping router**" command.

```
~/z4.2$ /usr/sbin/traceroute 12.32.34.145
traceroute to 12.32.34.145 (12.32.34.145), 30 hops max, 38 byte packets
 1  12.32.34.145 (12.32.34.145)  3.182 ms  3.067 ms  3.010 ms
~/z4.2$
~/z4.2$ ping router
PING router.kanji.com (12.32.34.145): 56 data bytes
64 bytes from 12.32.34.145: icmp_seq=0 ttl=48 time=2.8 ms
64 bytes from 12.32.34.145: icmp_seq=1 ttl=48 time=2.8 ms
64 bytes from 12.32.34.145: icmp_seq=2 ttl=48 time=2.8 ms
64 bytes from 12.32.34.145: icmp_seq=3 ttl=48 time=2.8 ms
64 bytes from 12.32.34.145: icmp_seq=4 ttl=48 time=2.0 ms
64 bytes from 12.32.34.145: icmp_seq=5 ttl=48 time=2.8 ms
64 bytes from 12.32.34.145: icmp_seq=6 ttl=48 time=2.8 ms
64 bytes from 12.32.34.145: icmp_seq=7 ttl=48 time=2.8 ms

--- router.kanji.com ping statistics ---
8 packets transmitted, 8 packets received, 0% packet loss
round-trip min/avg/max = 2.8/2.8/2.8 ms
~/z4.2$ date
Fri Mar 24 11:47:00 MST 2000
~/z4.2$
```

TIP!

Change Your Password

After you verify that your router is working properly, it's a good idea to change your password again.

Preparing The PC For The Installation

Hardware Preparations

To build an Internet server with Linux, you must have a PC on which you can install Linux. The copy of Red Hat Linux on the CD-ROM included with this book is for an Intel 386 compatible (or higher) PC. This designation refers to the entire line of PCs running Intel 386, 486, Pentiums, PII, PIII, and compatible central processing units (CPUs).

Before installing Linux, install one network interface card (NIC) and a small computer system interface (SCSI) card, if one is to be used. This allows the installation program to recognize the hardware automatically.

Preparations For Installing Linux

To install Linux, you must prepare the following two items:
- **The computer**
- **A boot disk**

Use a Windows PC to prepare the boot disk to be used for the Linux installation. Also, before installing Linux, determine whether your computer is equipped properly.

i386 Based PC

The Red Hat Linux included with this book can be installed only on an i386 (486 or later preferred) compatible computer.

> **Caution:** Always make sure that the PC is turned off or unplugged before removing the case cover from the computer.

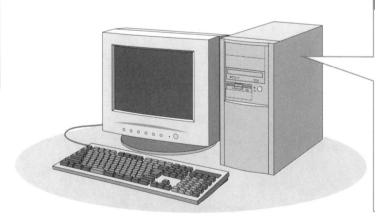

Recommended Specifications

Hard Disk Size, At Least 2GB
Linux itself is approximately 300MB in size, and a large amount of free space is required for storing Web data and mail. A PC with a 2GB or larger hard disk must be available.

At Least Two Empty PCI Slots
At least one PCI slot will be used by the NIC for the Internet connection. Because an additional slot is required to create a setup in which multiple computers can access the Internet, you should select a PC that has several open PCI slots.

4.3

Preparing The PC For Linux Installation

Installing The Network Interface Card

Because Ethernet is used for the connection to the router, install an NIC in the PC to be used for the Linux installation. To use a network address translation (NAT), install only one of the two NICs. Install a PCI-type NIC in the PC before installing Linux.

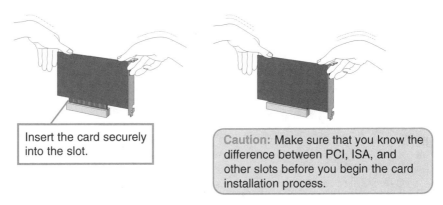

Insert the card securely into the slot.

Caution: Make sure that you know the difference between PCI, ISA, and other slots before you begin the card installation process.

Connecting The Router To The Internet Server Machine

Use a straight-through cable to connect the server machine to the Ethernet port of the router. Be careful not to connect the cable to the Up-Link port, and be sure not to use a crossover cable.

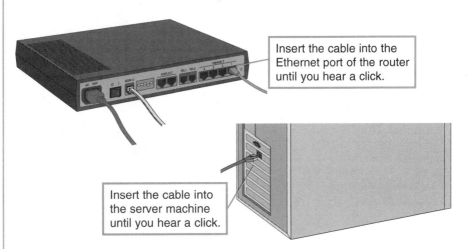

Insert the cable into the Ethernet port of the router until you hear a click.

Insert the cable into the server machine until you hear a click.

No Mouse Is Required

Because the explanations in this book do not use a mouse, you do not need to configure the server machine for use with a mouse. Unplug the mouse before installing Linux.

Creating An Installation Disk

Creating A Boot Disk

Because Red Hat's installation program is used for installing Linux, first create a floppy disk for installation (boot disk), and then start the PC from that floppy disk.
The file named boot.img located in the images folder of the included CD-ROM is required to create an installation disk.

Use the Windows special-purpose tool named rawrite.exe to write boot.img to the floppy disk.

1   Insert the included CD-ROM.

Create a boot disk on a Windows PC.

Insert the CD-ROM.

2   Start up the disk creation tool.

❶ Open items in the following order.

🖳 My Computer
  💿 CD-ROM drive
    📁 dosutils

❷ Double-click rawrite.

3   Specify the image file.

Specify the boot disk image file.

Caution: Be sure to enter the file name correctly.

Type "..\images\boot.img".

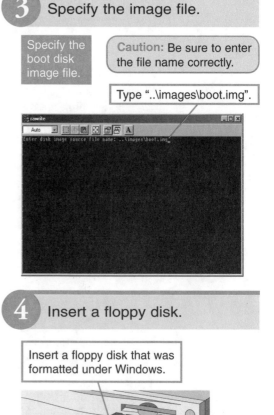

4   Insert a floppy disk.

Insert a floppy disk that was formatted under Windows.

5 Specify the location of the floppy disk.

Type "a".

6 Create the boot disk.

Press [Enter].

Creation will take a few minutes.

TIP!

Booting Directly From The CD-ROM

The CD-ROM included with this book enables you to boot Linux directly from the CD-ROM. If your PC supports a CD-ROM boot, you can install Linux from the CD-ROM without creating a boot disk. You need to set the PC basic input/output system (BIOS) or the SCSI BIOS if you have an SCSI CD-ROM to enable support for a CD-ROM boot. If you can't determine your current setting, create a boot disk to install Linux.

---

7 End the MS-DOS session.

The Linux installation disk is ready.

Click Close.

The Linux installation boot disk is ready.

TIP!

Using Pre-Compiled Image Files

The included CD-ROM provides three other image files in addition to the boot disk image file.

• Network Installation (bootnet.img)

This image file enables you to install Linux over a network, (either the Internet or a company's internal LAN,) by using the File Transfer Protocol (FTP) or Hypertext Transfer Protocol (HTTP) and specifying a Red Hat Linux mirror site.

• PCMCIA (pcmcia.img)

Use this image file to install Linux in a PC equipped with a Personal Computer Memory Card International Association (PCMCIA) interface.

• Rescue Disk (rescue.img)

Use this emergency image file for recovery if your Linux system has been fatally damaged. You'll be asked for this rescue disk shortly after you type "rescue [Enter]" at the first boot disk prompt. If the rescue disk is used to boot the computer, a version of Linux containing the minimum management commands will start; however, only individuals with a fair degree of Linux technical knowledge will actually be able to use this minimum Linux operating environment effectively.

Installing Linux, Part 1

Starting The Installation Program

Install Red Hat Linux by using the boot disk that you created. The general installation procedure consists of starting up the installation program, configuring the installer, initializing the hard disk, copying files, recognizing and configuring hardware, and defining Linux operation settings.

This section covers the installation procedure from starting the installation program to partitioning your hard disk with fdisk.

1 Insert the boot disk.

Insert the boot disk that you created (as described previously) into the floppy disk drive of the PC where Linux is to be installed.

Insert the boot disk.

2 Turn on the PC.

Turn on the power.

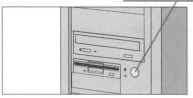

TIP!

CD-ROM Boot Drive

If your PC supports a CD-ROM boot, no floppy disk is needed. In this case, boot up by inserting the CD-ROM included with this book and turning on the PC.

3 Start the installer.

A message for confirming the Red Hat Linux installation method appears.

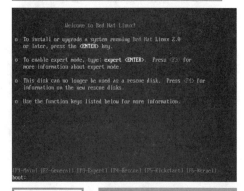

Press [Enter]. Program loading begins.

4 A message is displayed.

An installation message
is displayed.

Press Enter.

5 Select the language used during installation.

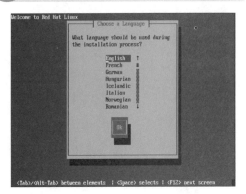

Confirm that English is selected
and press Enter.

TIP!

Changing A Setting Using The Back Button

If you realize that you made a mistake during the
installation procedure, you can sometimes use the
Back button to return to the preceding operation.
Carefully check each operation, because some setting changes cannot be undone.

6 Select the type of keyboard.

❶ Use the ↑ and ↓
keys to select us.

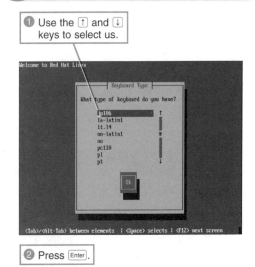

❷ Press Enter.

7 Select the installation source.

Because you are using the CD-ROM
included with this book for installation,
select Local CDROM.

Confirm that Local CDROM
is selected and press Enter.

8 Insert the included CD-ROM.

❶ Insert the CD-ROM.

❷ Press [Enter].

9 The CD-ROM is initialized.

The CD-ROM drive is initialized so that the CD-ROM can be used from Linux.

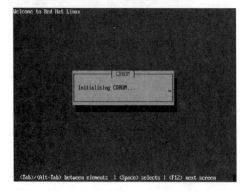

10 Select the installation method.

Because you are performing a new installation of Linux, select Install.

❶ Confirm that Install is selected and press [Enter].

Because you are installing Linux with settings suited for an Internet server, select Custom.

❷ Confirm that Custom is selected and press [Enter].

TIP!

If The CD-ROM Drive Is Not Recognized

Linux cannot automatically recognize some ATAPI-type CD-ROM drives. If you configure such a CD-ROM drive manually, Linux will be able to recognize it. For details, see page 86.

11. Select whether you have any SCSI adapters installed.

A message asking you whether you have any SCSI adapters appears.

If any SCSI adapters are installed, select Yes; otherwise, select No. Press [Enter].

12. Select the tool for initializing the hard disk.

Because the entire hard disk is to be used as an Internet server, initialize the entire hard disk.

Use fdisk for initialization here.

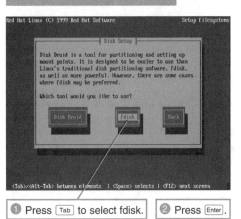

❶ Press [Tab] to select fdisk.   ❷ Press [Enter].

TIP!

When An SCSI Adapter Is Used

To use an SCSI-type hard disk or CD-ROM drive, you must install an SCSI adapter. Often the installation program will probe your system and discover the existence of SCSI adapters automatically. Sometimes, it will ask you if any SCSI adapters are installed. If the answer is yes, you will be given a list of SCSI drivers. Select the one that best matches your SCSI adapter. You will be able to specify options for the SCSI at this point.

13. Execute fdisk.   *jump to pg 66*

Make sure that the hard disk to be initialized is listed.

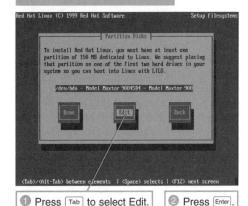

❶ Press [Tab] to select Edit.   ❷ Press [Enter].

Caution: If more than one hard disk is installed on your PC, all of their names are displayed here. Select the hard disk for which /dev/hda is displayed.

The fdisk screen appears.

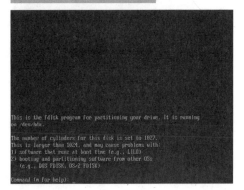

Installing Linux, Part 2

Using fdisk

The fdisk tool divides the storage space on the hard disk into separate partitions for different purposes. Because a PC that is set up as an Internet server will run continuously after it has been booted, it need not be able to boot another operating system (OS). Let's configure the hard disk so that the entire disk will be used by Linux.

A hard disk that is used by Linux is usually divided into two main divisions: a swap partition and a filesystem partition. In this book, the filesystem area is divided into three partitions: one for a minimal OS, one for temporary storage of mail and the like, and one for data.

Creating Partitions Suitable For An Internet Server

For this part of the installation, allocate 64MB for the swap partition, 256MB for the root (/) partition, 512MB for the /var partition, and the remaining area for the /usr partition. The minimum Linux system will be placed in the / partition. Data used by various types of server software (such as the system log, mail spool, or proxy cache) will be placed in the /var partition. Programs or documents will be installed in the /usr partition.

Hard Disk Used By Linux (Example: For An 8GB Hard Disk)

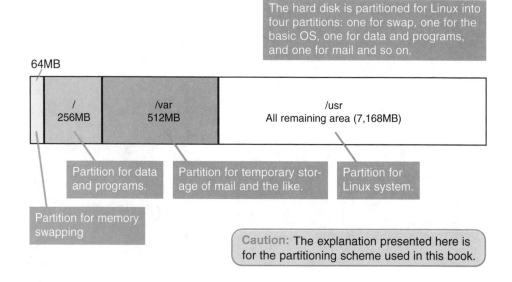

The hard disk is partitioned for Linux into four partitions: one for swap, one for the basic OS, one for data and programs, and one for mail and so on.

64MB

| / 256MB | /var 512MB | /usr All remaining area (7,168MB) |

Partition for data and programs.

Partition for temporary storage of mail and the like.

Partition for Linux system.

Partition for memory swapping

Caution: The explanation presented here is for the partitioning scheme used in this book.

4.6

1 Check to see what the fdisk commands do.

Note: Enter "commands" to perform fdisk operations. You can display a list of available commands by entering the letter "m" in lowercase.

When this prompt string appears, a command can be executed.

① Enter **m** in lowercase.

```
Command (m for help): m
```

② Press Enter.

```
Command (m for help): m↵
Command action
   a   toggle a bootable flag
   b   edit bsd disklabel
   c   toggle the dos compatibility flag
   d   delete a partition
   l   list known partition types
   m   print this menu
   n   add a new partition
   o   create a new empty DOS partition table
   p   print the partition table
   q   quit without saving changes
   t   change a partition's system id
   u   change display/entry units
   v   verify the partition table
   w   write table to disk and exit
   x   extra functionality (experts only)

Command (m for help): _
```

A list of commands is displayed. If you are unsure of what each command does, display this list for help.

As soon as one command is completed, another command can be entered.

2 Check the contents of the hard disk.

Note: The **p** command displays the partitions that exist on the hard disk.

TIP!

fdisk Commands Used In This Book

a	Flags a partition as bootable
d	Deletes a partition
m	Displays available fdisk commands
n	Creates a new partition
p	Displays partitions
q	Quits without saving changes
t	Changes the type of partition
w	Writes the changes and quits

Enter "**p**".

Information about the hard disk partitions is displayed.

```
Command (m for help): p↵
Disk /tmp/hda: 255 heads, 63 sectors, 1027 cylinders
Units = cylinders of 16065 * 512 bytes

   Device Boot    Start     End   Blocks   Id  System
/tmp/hda1   *         1    1027  8249364    c  Win95 FAT32 (LBA)

Command (m for help): _
```

The partition number is displayed as "hda1".

All data contained on the hard disk is deleted, and a Linux partition is created.

Caution: The numbers and partition configuration will differ for each PC.

61

3 Delete the existing partition.

❶ Enter "d".

Note: The **d** command deletes a partition.

```
Command (m for help): d↵
Partition number (1-4): 1↵

Command (m for help): _
```

Because hda1 is to be deleted, enter 1.

❷ Enter "1".

4 Check the contents of the hard disk.

Note: The **p** command displays the partitions on the hard disk.

Enter "p".

```
Command (m for help): p↵

Disk /tmp/hda: 255 heads, 63 sectors, 1027 cylinders
Units = cylinders of 16065 * 512 bytes

   Device Boot    Start       End    Blocks   Id  System

Command (m for help): _
```

The partition that had been used by Windows was deleted.

Use the **d** command to delete all remaining partitions.

5 Create a new partition.

❶ Enter "n".

Note: The **n** command creates a new partition.

Swap partition (64MB)

```
Command (m for help): n↵
Command action
   e   extended
   p   primary partition (1-4)
p
Partition number (1-4): 1↵
First cylinder (1-1027): _
```

Create a new partition as your primary partition.

❷ Enter "p".

❸ Enter "1".

❹ Enter "1".

Because you are creating the first partition, select 1.

```
Command (m for help): n
Command action
   e   extended
   p   primary partition (1-4)
p
Partition number (1-4): 1
First cylinder (1-1027): 1↵
Last cylinder or +size or +sizeM or +sizeK ([1]-1027): +64M↵

Command (m for help): _
```

Because this partition will be created starting from the first cylinder of the hard disk, enter 1.

64MB is allocated to the first partition.

❺ Type "+64M".

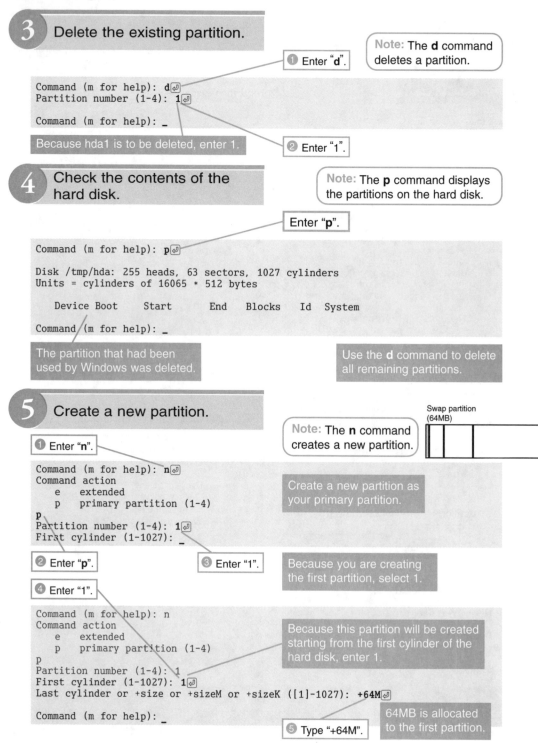

6 Confirm that the partition was created.

Enter "**p**".

Note: The **p** command displays the partitions on the hard disk.

```
Command (m for help): p⏎

Disk /tmp/hda: 255 heads, 63 sectors, 1027 cylinders
Units = cylinders of 16065 * 512 bytes

   Device Boot    Start      End    Blocks    Id  System
/tmp/hda1              1        9    72261    83  Linux native

Command (m for help): _
```

Starting and ending numbers of hard disk cylinders in the partition.

Size of the partition.

Type of partition.

7 Change the partition type.

Change the partition type from "Linux native" to "Linux swap".

TIP!

What Is A Linux Swap Partition?

A Linux swap partition uses hard disk memory in place of RAM memory when RAM memory is insufficient.

Note: The **t** command displays partition information.

❶ Enter "**t**".   ❷ Enter "**1**".   ❸ Enter "**L**".

A list of partition types is displayed.

```
Command (m for help): t⏎
Partition number (1-4): 1⏎
Hex code (Type L to list codes): L⏎

 0  Empty           a  OS/2 Boot Manag  65  Novell Netware   a6  OpenBSD
 1  DOS 12-bit FAT  b  Win95 FAT32      75  PC/IX            a7  NEXTSTEP
 2  XENIX root      c  Win95 FAT32 (LB  80  Old MINIX        b7  BSDI fs
 3  XENIX usr       e  Win95 FAT16 (LB  81  Linux/MINIX      b8  BSDI swap
 4  DOS 16-bit <32M f  Win95 Extended   82  Linux swap       c7  Syrinx
 5  Extended        48 Venix 80286      83  Linux native     db  CP/M
 6  DOS 16-bit >=32 51 Novell?          85  Linux extended   e1  DOS access
 7  OS/2 HPFS       52 Microport        93  Amoeba           e3  DOS R/O
 8  AIX             63 GNU HURD         94  Amoeba BBT       f2  DOS secondary
 9  AIX bootable    64 Novell Netware   a5  BSD/386          ff  BBT
Hex code (Type L to list codes): _
```

The Hex code for Linux swap is 82.

❹ Type "**82**".

```
Hex code (Type L to list codes): 82⏎
Changed system type of partition 1 to 82 (Linux swap)

Command (m for help): _
```

The partition type was changed to Linux swap.

8 Continue to create partitions.

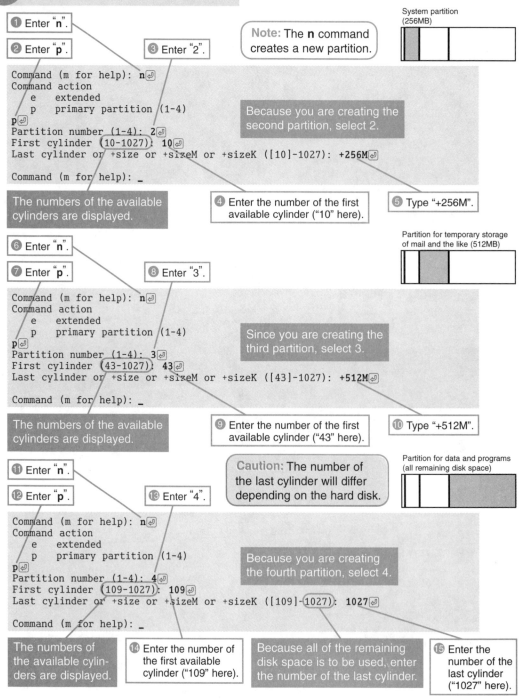

① Enter "**n**".

② Enter "**p**".

③ Enter "2".

Note: The **n** command creates a new partition.

System partition (256MB)

```
Command (m for help): n⏎
Command action
   e   extended
   p   primary partition (1-4)
p⏎
Partition number (1-4): 2⏎
First cylinder (10-1027): 10⏎
Last cylinder or +size or +sizeM or +sizeK ([10]-1027): +256M⏎

Command (m for help): _
```

Because you are creating the second partition, select 2.

The numbers of the available cylinders are displayed.

④ Enter the number of the first available cylinder ("10" here).

⑤ Type "+256M".

⑥ Enter "**n**".

⑦ Enter "**p**".

⑧ Enter "3".

Partition for temporary storage of mail and the like (512MB)

```
Command (m for help): n⏎
Command action
   e   extended
   p   primary partition (1-4)
p⏎
Partition number (1-4): 3⏎
First cylinder (43-1027): 43⏎
Last cylinder or +size or +sizeM or +sizeK ([43]-1027): +512M⏎

Command (m for help): _
```

Since you are creating the third partition, select 3.

The numbers of the available cylinders are displayed.

⑨ Enter the number of the first available cylinder ("43" here).

⑩ Type "+512M".

⑪ Enter "**n**".

⑫ Enter "**p**".

⑬ Enter "4".

Caution: The number of the last cylinder will differ depending on the hard disk.

Partition for data and programs (all remaining disk space)

```
Command (m for help): n⏎
Command action
   e   extended
   p   primary partition (1-4)
p⏎
Partition number (1-4): 4⏎
First cylinder (109-1027): 109⏎
Last cylinder or +size or +sizeM or +sizeK ([109]-1027): 1027⏎

Command (m for help): _
```

Because you are creating the fourth partition, select 4.

The numbers of the available cylinders are displayed.

⑭ Enter the number of the first available cylinder ("109" here).

Because all of the remaining disk space is to be used, enter the number of the last cylinder.

⑮ Enter the number of the last cylinder ("1027" here).

Check the details of the partitions.

Enter "p".

Note: The **p** command displays the partitions that exist on the hard disk.

```
Command (m for help): p↵

Disk /tmp/hda: 255 heads, 63 sectors, 1027 cylinders
Units = cylinders of 16065 * 512 bytes

    Device Boot    Start      End   Blocks   Id  System
/tmp/hda1              1        9    72261   82  Linux swap
/tmp/hda2             10       42   265072+  83  Linux native
/tmp/hda3             43      108   530145   83  Linux native
/tmp/hda4            109     1027  7381867+  83  Linux native

Command (m for help): _
```

Four partitions were created on the hard disk.

Because you cannot boot Linux if there is no boot partition, set one.

10 Create a boot partition.

Because the second partition is used for the Linux system, set this partition as the boot partition.

❶ Enter "a".

Note: The **a** command sets a bootable partition.

```
Command (m for help): a↵
Partition number (1-4): 2↵

Command (m for help): p↵
```

❷ Enter "2".

❸ Enter "p".

```
Disk /tmp/hda: 255 heads, 63 sectors, 1027 cylinders
Units = cylinders of 16065 * 512 bytes

    Device Boot    Start      End   Blocks   Id  System
/tmp/hda1              1        9    72261   82  Linux swap
/tmp/hda2    *        10       42   265072+  83  Linux native
/tmp/hda3             43      108   530145   83  Linux native
/tmp/hda4            109     1027  7381867+  83  Linux native

Command (m for help): _
```

An asterisk (*) is displayed for the boot partition.

11 Save the changes and quit fdisk.

Note: The **w** command writes the changes to the partition table to disk and quits fdisk.

Enter "w".

TIP! **The System Cannot Be Returned To Its Original State After The w Command Is Entered**

After you save the partition changes, programs and data that were stored in deleted partitions will no longer be available. Therefore, use the **p** command to display partition information and carefully examine the details. Save the changes only after you make sure that there are no mistakes.

```
Command (m for help): w↵
The partition table has been altered!

Calling ioctl() to re-read partition table.
Syncing disks.
```

Installing Linux, Part 3

Installing Red Hat Linux

When partitioning is complete, assign the partitions so that they can be used by different parts of your Linux filesystem, and then install components. Many peripheral devices will be recognized automatically. Even if a device is not recognized automatically, you can select it from a displayed list.

This book is concerned only with the components needed to build an Internet server. If you select other components, you may have to reconfigure your video card and other settings. Also, server settings that appear later may be affected by these additional components.

---

1 Complete the allocation of partitions.

① Use Tab to select Done.

② Press Enter.

2 Set the root mount point.

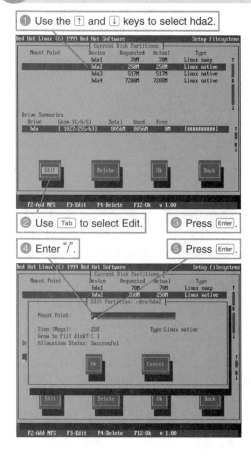

① Use the ↑ and ↓ keys to select hda2.

② Use Tab to select Edit.

③ Press Enter.

④ Enter "/".

⑤ Press Enter.

TIP!

What Is Mounting?

To use a hard disk or CD-ROM, Linux must first make it part of the directory hierarchy under the root directory (/). This operation is called *mounting*.

Directory ? pg 67 or 81
go to pg 81

What Are /, /var, And /usr?

/ (root) is the mount point (name) of the region assigned to the Linux OS. /var is the name of the region assigned to system logs and server data. /usr is the name of the region where non-system data or programs are stored.

If Mount Point Names Are Invalid, Linux Cannot Be Installed Properly

If you set the name of a mount point such as /, /var, or /usr incorrectly, an error may occur during installation due to insufficient free disk space or some other reason. Note that the names are case sensitive. That is, a distinction is made between uppercase and lowercase letters.

3 Set the /var mount point.

① Use the ↑ and ↓ keys to select hda3.

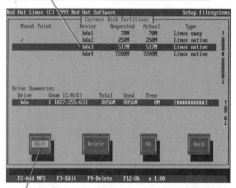

② Use Tab to select Edit.

③ Press Enter.

④ Type "/var".

⑤ Press Enter.

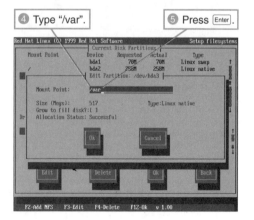

4 Set the /usr mount point.

① Use the ↑ and ↓ keys to select hda4.

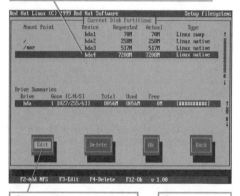

② Use Tab to select Edit.

③ Press Enter.

④ Type "/usr".

⑤ Press Enter.

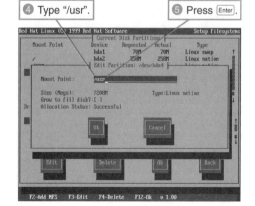

5 Save the settings.

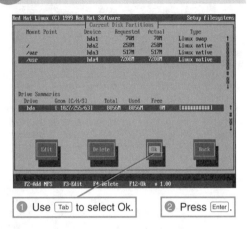

1 Use `Tab` to select Ok.   2 Press `Enter`.

7 Format other partitions.

1 Use the spacebar to prepend an asterisk (*) to all entries.   2 Use `Tab` to select Ok.   3 Press `Enter`.

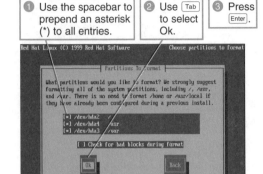

6 Format the swap partition.

Confirm that an asterisk (*) appears here.

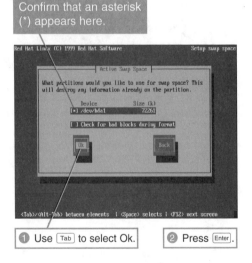

1 Use `Tab` to select Ok.   2 Press `Enter`.

8 Select the components to install.

1 Use the space-bar to prepend an asterisk (*) to the components you want to install.

Note: Components group packages of programs according to the functionality they provide.

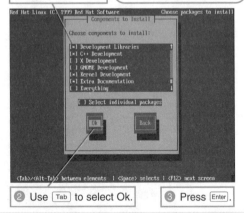

2 Use `Tab` to select Ok.   3 Press `Enter`.

The components used in this book are shown in the following list. Use the spacebar to remove the asterisk (*) from any other component.

Networked Workstation
DNS Name Server
Network Management Workstation
C Development
Development Libraries
C++ Development
Kernel Development
Extra Documentation

9 Verify the location for saving log files.

A message indicating the location for saving log files is displayed. | Press Enter.

A filesystem is created in each partition.

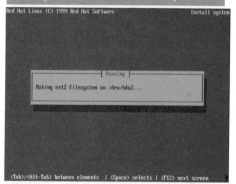

10 Installation of components begins.

The installation status is displayed. | The installation of components may take a long time to complete.

11 A confirmation message is displayed.

When no mouse is connected, a message indicating that the mouse type could not be found is displayed.

Press Enter.

12 Set the option indicating that no mouse is used.

Because no mouse is required, do not set a mouse.

1 Use the ↑ and ↓ keys to select No Mouse.

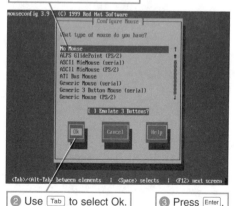

2 Use Tab to select Ok. | 3 Press Enter.

13 Begin to configure networking.

Note: When Linux is used as an Internet server, the network-related settings are important. Be sure to configure the following settings correctly.

A message confirming whether you want to configure networking is displayed.

Press [Enter].

14 The network card is recognized automatically.

The network card was recognized automatically.

Press [Enter].

15 Select the method of acquiring an IP address.

Because Linux will be used as an Internet server, select Static IP address to directly specify the IP address.

① Use the [↑] and [↓] keys to select Static IP address.

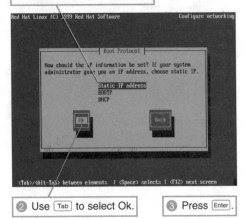

② Use [Tab] to select Ok.   ③ Press [Enter].

16 Specify IP addresses.

① Enter the IP address.   ② Enter the netmask.   ③ Enter the IP address of the router.

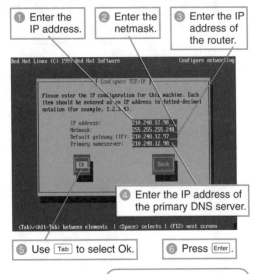

④ Enter the IP address of the primary DNS server.

⑤ Use [Tab] to select Ok.   ⑥ Press [Enter].

Note: See Section 4.1 for the network settings.

17 Set the domain name.

❶ Enter the domain name ("dekiru.gr.jp" here).

❷ Enter the host name ("server.dekiru.gr.jp" here).

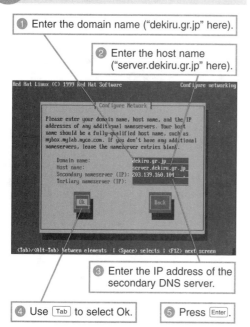

❸ Enter the IP address of the secondary DNS server.

❹ Use Tab to select Ok.

❺ Press Enter.

18 Set the time zone.

❶ Use Tab to move to the list of time zones and then use the ↑ and ↓ keys to select your local time zone.

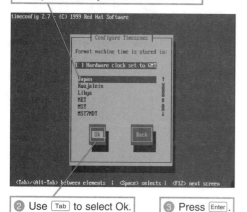

❷ Use Tab to select Ok.

❸ Press Enter.

19 Select the services to start automatically on reboot.

Select the services that will start automatically when you reboot Linux.

❶ Use the spacebar to prepend an asterisk (*) to the services that are to be started.

ntsysV - command

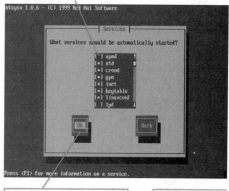

❷ Use Tab to select Ok.

❸ Press Enter.

The services that will start automatically in the example used in this book are listed below. Use the spacebar to remove an asterisk (*) from any other service.

atd
crond
gpm
inet
keytable
linuxconf
named
network
portmap
random
sendmail
syslog

20 A confirmation message is displayed.

A message asking if you want to configure a printer is displayed.

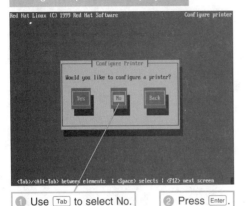

1 Use Tab to select No.   2 Press Enter.

21 Set a password for the Linux administrator.

Note: Enter at least six alphanumeric characters for the password.

Set a password for the Linux administrator (called root).

1 Enter the password and press Enter.

2 Enter the password again and press Enter.   3 Press Enter.

Note: The entered password is not displayed on screen.

Caution: The password entered here is required to use Linux. Do not forget it.

22 Set the password management method.

Because the standard settings can be used, proceed without changing any settings.

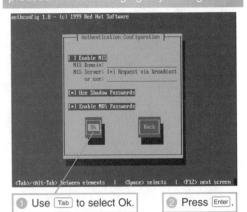

1 Use Tab to select Ok.   2 Press Enter.

23 Create a boot disk.

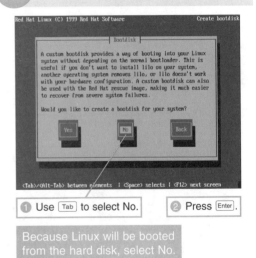

1 Use Tab to select No.   2 Press Enter.

Because Linux will be booted from the hard disk, select No.

TIP!

Choose A Password Carefully

A password can consist of alphanumeric characters and symbols, and uppercase letters are distinguished from lowercase ones. Do not set a password that can be easily guessed, such as a part of a word or an abbreviation. Create a password by combining uppercase letters, lowercase letters, symbols, and numbers.

24 Select the installation location for Linux Loader (LILO).

Install the boot manager (the startup program) in the system partition.

1 Use the ↑ and ↓ keys to select /dev/hda2.

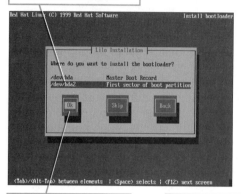

2 Use Tab to select Ok.

3 Press Enter.

Note: LILO is the standard boot manager for Linux.

25 Set boot options.

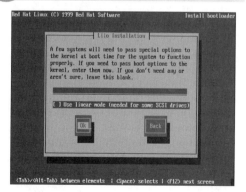

Press Enter.

Since no special option need be set, proceed to the next step.

26 Finish the install.

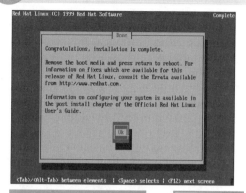

Remove the floppy disk.

Press Enter.

Caution: When a CD-ROM boot is used, remove the CD-ROM after rebooting.

Caution: When you press Enter, the PC is rebooted.

27 Linux starts.

The Linux installation succeeded, and the login prompt appears.

Troubleshooting Problems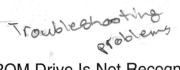

When An ATAPI CD-ROM Drive Is Not Recognized

Some ATAPI CD-ROM drives (for example, PIONEER DR-A24X) aren't recognized automatically by Linux. You can enable such a CD-ROM drive by specifying that it is a CD-ROM drive at the boot prompt that is displayed when the installer is started.

Example: When the CD-ROM drive is connected to a primary slave (hdb)

```
boot: hdb=cdrom hdb=noprobe↵
```

Example: When the CD-ROM drive is connected to a secondary master (hdc)

```
boot: hdc=cdrom hdc=noprobe↵
```

After you have completed the installation, if you want to use a CD-ROM drive that must be specified in this way, enter a similar specification as a boot option parameter during the LILO installation in step 25 shown on page 73.

Booting Problems After Installation

LILO is used to boot Linux. If LILO is operating properly, the word "LILO" is displayed before Linux is booted. If you type "linux↵" at this prompt, Linux starts. Alternatively, Linux boots after five seconds if nothing is entered. If Linux doesn't boot after installation, LILO is usually the culprit.

The Install Program Starts (No LILO Prompt)

This happens when Linux is booted from the floppy disk or CD-ROM. Remove the floppy disk or CD-ROM and then press ⎡Ctrl⎤+⎡ Alt ⎤+⎡Delete⎤ to reboot.

No LILO Prompt And "No Boot Device" Is Displayed (Message Differs Depending On Computer Model)

This happens if no boot flag was assigned when the hard disk partitions were created. Start the install program again and use the **a** command to assign a boot flag to the partition (/dev/hda2 in the example in this book) that was allocated to the system root directory(/) in step 10 of the fdisk procedure shown on page 65. Then use the **w** command to write the change, exit fdisk, and press ⎡Ctrl⎤+⎡ Alt ⎤+⎡Delete⎤ to reboot.

The LILO Prompt Is Only Partially Displayed And Digits Are Displayed And Stopped

In almost all cases, this happens when LILO cannot recognize the boot disk information correctly. Although there is no definite way to resolve this problem, selecting the Us Linear Mode global option in step 25 of the LILO installation procedure shown on page 73 may enable Linux to boot successfully.

Linux Still Will Not Boot

Linux may boot properly if you use the Install program to create the boot disk that was not created in step 23 shown on page 72. In this case, if you insert the created boot disk in the floppy drive and turn on the power, the LILO prompt appears. If you type "linux⏎" at this prompt or wait 10 seconds, Linux starts to boot. After the login screen is displayed, you can remove the floppy disk. If this method does not work, try to install Linux again from the beginning. If this doesn't work, determine whether Linux can be used on your PC.

STEP UP

The Procedures In This Book Are Based On Red Hat Linux 6.0

This book assumes that you will use Red Hat Linux 6 as the OS for your Internet server. From the next chapter on, the procedures for building an Internet server are based on Red Hat Linux 6. Therefore, to create a server according to the procedures described in this book, you must install Red Hat Linux 6, which can be found on the CD-ROM that is included with this book.

Although the various types of server programs that are used in this book are generally used in Unix-like OSes and are not limited to Linux, the procedures described in this book cannot necessarily be used directly on all of them. And because Linux itself differs by distribution, you will not necessarily be able to use the same procedures. This may be true even if the version of Red Hat Linux differs. Unless you have enough experience to be able to read the procedures described in this book for the servers that are installed and configured and to convert them accordingly for use with another Unix-like OS, you should use the included Red Hat Linux 6.

If Red Hat Linux 6.0 Is Not Used...

To use a different distribution of Linux or another Unix-like OS to install and configure the servers described in this book, you must have sufficient experience. Although the basic procedures and configuration files are the same, details will differ. You must be able to convert and apply the book's descriptions to the specifics of the other OS. This requires familiarity with the procedures and documentation for installing and configuring new programs, especially server programs, on the other system. To use an OS other than Red Hat Linux 6, be prepared to work out the changes in these procedures yourself.

Chapter 5
Mastering The Basic
Operations Of Linux

To use Linux to create an Internet server, you must know
how to perform basic Linux operations. You perform
operations by typing commands. This chapter explains
the basic knowledge you must acquire concerning
file systems in order to use Linux. How to enter
commands and other information required for
building an Internet server is also discussed.

Contents Of This Chapter

Working In Linux

Login And Logout

su -1

Work in Linux begins with login and ends with logout. Only people who have been given a user account can use Linux. Login is the operation that confirms whether a person has already been given a user account.
The login command not only allows you to begin your work, it also lets Linux know which users are using the system. You cannot use Linux without first logging in. Also, when you have finished your work session with Linux, you should log out.

How To Start Working With Linux

After the system boots, Linux displays a login prompt, inviting you to log in.

```
Red Hat Linux release 6.0 Publisher's Edition (Hedwig)
Kernel 2.2.5-15 on an i686

server login: _
```

The cursor is displayed at the location where you can enter characters.

❶ Type "root", which is the username for the Linux administrator, using lowercase letters and press Enter.

```
Red Hat Linux release 6.0 Publisher's Edition (Hedwig)
Kernel 2.2.5-15 on an i686

server login: root⏎
Password: _
```

Enter the root password at the prompt.

❷ Enter the administrator password that was set during installation, and press Enter.

```
Red Hat Linux release 6.0 Publisher's Edition (Hedwig)
Kernel 2.2.5-15 on an i686

server login: root
Password:
[root@server /root]# _
```

The password is not displayed on the screen.

A prompt is displayed indicating that Linux is ready to go to work.

Working With Linux Begins With Login

To work with Linux, you must begin by logging in. Login verifies whether or not you have a user account on the system and allows Linux to identify which users are currently logged on. Each user has a username and password. During login, you enter both of these so that Linux can verify that your account exists. After you finish logging in, you can start to work. When you finish working, you should log out. Otherwise, another person could use your account to access the system. You log out by typing "exit" at the command prompt.

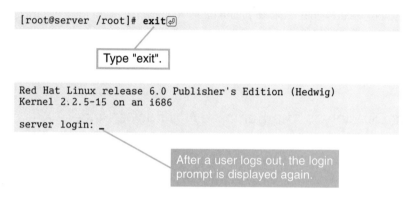

The Meaning Of Prompts

A *prompt* is a character string displayed on the screen, that prompts the user for input. The meaning of the character string indicates what kind of input is requested at the cursor position.

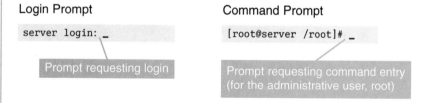

Linux Users

Not just anyone can access Linux directly. More than one person can use Linux simultaneously via a network, but only if each person has a user account that was created in advance. Such people are called *users*. When Linux is first installed, only the user named root is provided with a user account. The root user account has been set up for Linux system administration, and that user is called a superuser to distinguish it from ordinary users. Normally, anyone who will have access to a specific Linux system will have been given a user account. The method used to create new users is explained in Section 5.6.

Understanding Directories

Linux Directory Structure

All Linux files are placed in locations called *directories*, which correspond to Windows or Macintosh folders. Because other directories can also be placed within a directory, the directory structure is nested.

In Linux, the root portion of this nested structure is called the "root directory," and the representation of the positional relationship between files and directories is called a "path." Paths are required when performing operations from the command line. Make sure that you understand how they work.

A Linux Directory Is The Same As A Windows Folder

A Linux directory corresponds to a Windows or Macintosh folder. Like a Windows or Macintosh folder, a directory can contain other directories.

If directory B is contained in directory A, A is called the "parent directory" of B, and B is called "subdirectory" of A. In Linux, if you continue to follow a path back along parent directories, you will end up at the root directory. All directories and files in Linux are contained in the root directory.

Linux Directory Hierarchy

Viewed from the root directory, directories form a hierarchy. Names for commonly used directories are fixed. The same directory name is often used to classify different content by positioning it at a different level in the hierarchy.

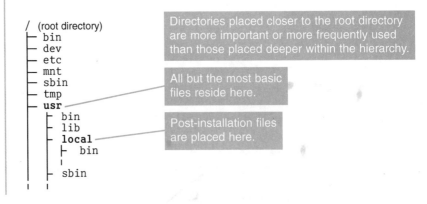

/ (root directory)
- bin
- dev
- etc
- mnt
- sbin
- tmp
- usr
  - bin
  - lib
  - local
    - bin
  - sbin

Directories placed closer to the root directory are more important or more frequently used than those placed deeper within the hierarchy.

All but the most basic files reside here.

Post-installation files are placed here.

Standard Directory Names

Name	Contains
bin	Essential command binaries
sbin	Essential system administration command binaries
dev	Peripheral device representation files
etc	System-wide configuration files
lib	Shared libraries (code snippets and data)
mnt	Mount point of temporary partitions
tmp	Temporary files

In Linux, the system root directory is represented by a / (pronounced "slash" or "root"). If directory A is contained in the root directory, it is represented by /A. If directory B is contained in /A, a / is used to separate the two directories, therefore /A/B. This second /, and all subsequent use of a / in the path, is for separation only; these slashes do not mean root. This method of representing a file or directory location by using directory names and slashes (/) is known as path. In Linux, all directories and files can be specified by using paths from the root directory (/). The specification of a path from the root directory (/) such as /A/B is referred to as an *absolute path*.

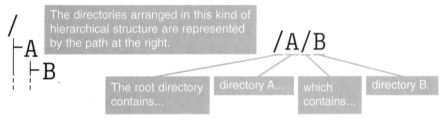

The directories arranged in this kind of hierarchical structure are represented by the path at the right.

/A/B

The root directory contains...   directory A...   which contains...   directory B.

Current Working Directory

Rather than use an absolute path each time you specify a file location, you can use ".." to refer to the parent directory of your present working directory.

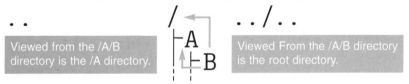

Viewed from the /A/B directory is the /A directory.

Viewed From the /A/B directory is the root directory.

Again, the directory in which you are currently working is called the *current directory* or *present working directory*. Not preceding the pathname with a slash (/) means that the file location is represented relative to the current directory and is known as a *relative path*.

Linux Is Case-Sensitive

File and directory names in Linux are case-sensitive. Uppercase letters are distinguished from lowercase ones in Linux file or directory names. For example, /usr and /USR are treated as totally different directories. Therefore, pay careful attention to case when entering file or directory names and commands.

Using Commands

Commands

The command-line interface is basic to all Linux operations. A command is entered; the system responds. At the command prompt, you type in a specific character string that runs a script or program. You can change the way a command operates or specify the target of a command through the use of arguments, separated by spaces, immediately following the command.

Commands And Their Arguments

You perform all Linux operations by entering commands. A *command* is a character string that represents an operation. At the command prompt, type a command, press "enter", and the command is accepted. After processing the accepted command, a response appears on screen, and Linux prompts for the next command.

Some commands may be followed by one or more arguments, separated by spaces, that can be used to specify the target of the command or to control the way in which a command operates. To specify an argument that includes a space, enclose the argument in single quotes (').

Enter one or more spaces between the command and its arguments.

```
[root@server /root]# command argument argument
```

If the argument contains a space, enclose the argument in single quotes (').

How To Use Options

An *option* is a type of command argument. You specify an option when you want to execute a variation on the standard function of the command. The syntax of the option may differ somewhat, depending on the command, but most options begin with a hyphen (-).

Example: Using an option with the **ls** command

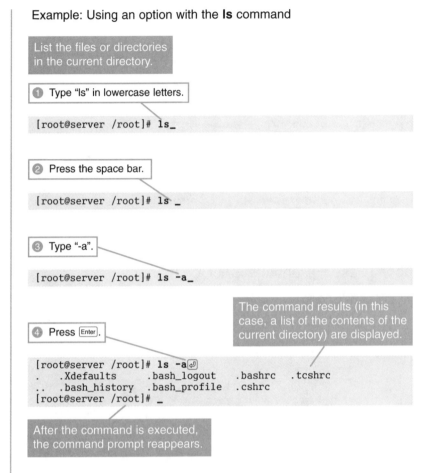

List the files or directories in the current directory.

① Type "ls" in lowercase letters.

```
[root@server /root]# ls_
```

② Press the space bar.

```
[root@server /root]# ls _
```

③ Type "-a".

```
[root@server /root]# ls -a_
```

④ Press Enter.

The command results (in this case, a list of the contents of the current directory) are displayed.

```
[root@server /root]# ls -a⏎
.    .Xdefaults     .bash_logout   .bashrc   .tcshrc
..   .bash_history  .bash_profile  .cshrc
[root@server /root]# _
```

After the command is executed, the command prompt reappears.

Some Commands Do Not Display Their Results

Part of a command's job is to respond. No screen output also can be a response, and whether or not it occurs depends on the specific command. For some commands, nothing is displayed on screen, even if the command has been accepted and processing was correctly performed.

In Linux, an error message is always given if the command is invalid or if an incorrect operation occurred. No response can mean that the operation succeeded.

Mastering Basic Commands

cd, ls, cp, mv, rm, And mkdir

Nothing is more basic to Linux than performing operations on files. This section describes commands that are required for manipulating files. **cp**, **mv**, **rm**, and **mkdir** are commands for manipulating files or directories; **cd** and **ls** are commands that are needed to use these commands:

cd	Changes current directory.
ls	Lists directory contents.
cp	Copies files or directories.
rm	Removes (deletes) files or directories.
mv	Moves (renames) files.
mkdir	Creates a directory.

Remember These Essential Linux Commands

cd Changes Current Directory

The **cd** (change directory) command changes the current directory to a different directory.

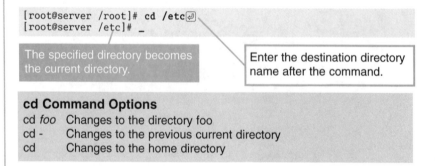

The specified directory becomes the current directory.

Enter the destination directory name after the command.

cd Command Options
cd *foo*   Changes to the directory foo
cd -   Changes to the previous current directory
cd   Changes to the home directory

ls Lists Directory Contents

The **ls** (list directory) command lists the contents of a directory. When a specific directory is given, it lists the contents of that directory. When no directory is given, it lists the contents of the current directory.

Enter a directory name after the command.

A list of the contents of the specified directory appears.

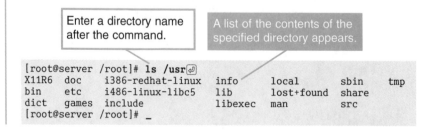

ls Command Options

ls -a   Lists all file names, including hidden files that begin with a dot (.).
ls -d   Lists directory entries instead of contents.
ls -l   Lists file names in long format, with details.
ls -F   Appends indicator (one of * / = @ or |) to entries.

cp   Copies Files Or Directories

mv   Moves Files Or Directories

Use the **cp** (copy) or **mv** (move) command to copy or move a file or directory. You can also use the **mv** command to rename a file.

cp [**mv**] *source_file_name destination_directory_name*

When a directory is specified for the destination, the source file is copied (moved for **mv**) to the destination directory.

cp [**mv**] *source_file_name destination_file_name*

When file names are specified for both the source and destination, the file at the source is copied (**cp**) or moved (**mv**) to the file name specified by the destination.

rm   Deletes File Or Directory

The **rm** (remove) command deletes the path specified by the argument. Be aware that a deleted file or directory cannot be recovered.

cp, mv, Or rm Command Options

cp[mv, rm] -i   Copies (moves or deletes) with confirmation.
cp[mv, rm] -f   Forcibly copies (moves or deletes) without confirmation.
cp[rm] -r   Recursively copies (deletes) everything within the directory.

mkdir   Creates A Directory

The **mkdir** (make directory) command creates the directory specified by the argument.

TIP!

Entering A File Name - A Shortcut

When entering a command, it can be difficult to specify a file name using an absolute path or to specify a long file name. In these cases, simplify your entry by typing the first few characters of the path or name followed by Tab to complete the entry automatically.

Press Tab midway through the entry of the directory name.

```
[root@server /root]# cd /u Tab
```

```
[root@server /root]# cd /usr/
```

The directory name is completed and entered automatically.

Understanding Permissions

Permissions

Besides the owner and affiliated group that are set for all files and directories in Linux, permissions are also assigned. Permissions indicate whether a particular user in Linux can access a file. This information is listed with the -l option of the **ls** command.

You can manage files and directories precisely in Linux through the use of permissions.

Permissions Represent File Or Directory Access Rights

An owner, an affiliated group, and permissions settings are assigned to every file and directory. Permissions determine whether or not a user will be given access to a particular file or directory. When the -l option is appended to the **ls** command, the nine-character sequence consisting of the characters r, w, x, and -, which appears on the left side, is the permission information. This is the mode of the file or directory. This sequence consists of three sets of rwx arranged from left to right. An r, w, or x indicates that the corresponding type of access is permitted. A hyphen (-) indicates that the corresponding type of access is not permitted. The three sets from left to right indicate the access rights of the owner, the affiliated group, and others on the system.

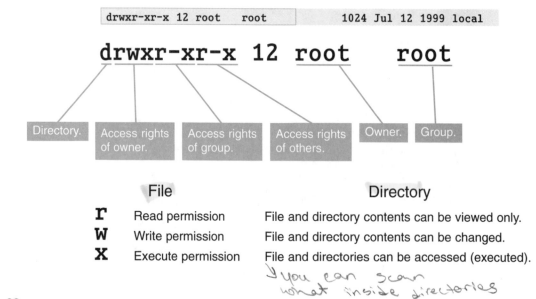

```
drwxr-xr-x 12 root    root            1024 Jul 12 1999 local
```

drwxr-xr-x 12 root   root

Directory.

Access rights of owner.

Access rights of group.

Access rights of others.

Owner.

Group.

	File	Directory
r	Read permission	File and directory contents can be viewed only.
w	Write permission	File and directory contents can be changed.
x	Execute permission	File and directories can be accessed (executed).

↓ you can scan
what inside directories

rwxr-xr-x For A Directory (Owner root, Group root)

drwxr-xr-x   12 root   root

The initial d means that this is a directory.
- If the user is root, the user can list (r) the files and directories, change (w) those files and directories, and access or execute (x) those files and directories.
- If the user belongs to the root group, the user can list (r) the files and directories, and access or execute (x) those files and directories.
- If the user is not root and does not belong to the root directory, the user can list (r) the files and directories, and access or execute (x) those files and directories.

rwxr-xr-x For A File (Owner root, Group root)

-rwxr-xr-x   1   root   root

The initial hyphen means that this is a regular file.
- If the user is root, the user can read the contents of the file, write to the file, and execute the file.
- If the user belongs to the root group, the user can read the contents of the file and execute the file.
- If the user is not root and does not belong to the root directory, the user can read the contents of the file and execute the file.

How To Set Permissions

Each rwx character string is represented by a single digit, and the entire set of nine permissions is expressed using three digits. The value taken by each rwx character string is the sum of the numbers corresponding to the access rights that are permitted (r=4, w=2, and x=1). For example, rwx is represented by the number 7.

```
4 2 1
r w x    4 + 2 + 1 = 7
r - x    4 + 0 + 1 = 5
r w -    4 + 2 + 0 = 6
r - -    4 + 0 + 0 = 4
```

Because rwx takes the value 7 and r-x takes the value 5, the permissions rwxr-xr-x are expressed by the number 755.

```
r  w  x      r  -  x      r  -  x
4 + 2 + 1    4 + 0 + 1    4 + 0 + 1
   7            5            5
```

This number is used when changing or setting the permissions of a file or directory.

Creating Users

Users are created in Linux so they can not only log in, but also identify who is using the system. All operations are managed in terms of an individual user. A user is the basic unit for dealing with work areas, file access rights, and other aspects of Linux.

Even the system administrator should not log in directly as root. Instead, the system administra-tor should log in as a user and then switch to root with the **su** command.

Use the **useradd** command to create a new user in Linux.

1 Log in as root.

```
Red Hat Linux release 6.0 Publisher's Edition (Hedwig)
Kernel 2.2.5-15 on an i686

server login: root
Password:
Last login: Sun Jul 11 22:51:36 on tty1
[root@server /root]: _
```

Type "root", and enter the root password.

The system is ready to use.

2 Create a new user.

Create a user named "bob" who belongs to the group "users".

Enter the command.

```
Red Hat Linux release 6.0 Publisher's Edition (Hedwig)
Kernel 2.2.5-15 on an i686

server login: root
Password:
Last login: Sun Jul 11 22:51:36 on tty1
[root@server /root]: useradd -g users -p '' bob
[root@server /root]: _
```

Since you are specifying an empty password, enter two single quotes with no space between them.

useradd Command
useradd foo   Adds the user foo.

useradd Command Options
-g *group*   Includes the new user into one or more groups.
-p *password*   Sets the new user's password.

Role Of A User

Because Linux can be used simultaneously by more than one person on a network, users are identified by their usernames. For example, users may be distinguished in the following ways (to distinguish users on the basis of services applies mostly to an Internet server);

- Distinguishing users on the basis of services.
  (These will be mail addresses, URLs, and so on.)
- Allocating work areas by home directories.
  (Personal Web pages are also placed in home directories.)
- Distinguishing users on the basis of file and directory access rights.

Verifying New Users

Use the **id** command to verify whether a user was registered correctly. Specify the username you want to verify, and execute the **id** command. If the specified user is registered, their username and group memberships will be displayed.

```
[root@server /root]: id bob⏎
uid=500(bob) gid=100(users)
[root@server /root]: _
```

Username.

Affiliated group names.

Deleting A User

Use the **userdel** command to delete a registered user. A user's home directory and its contents are not deleted and remain unchanged when you delete a user.

```
[root@server /root]: userdel bob⏎
[root@server /root]: _
```

Basic Linux Rule: Do Not Log In Directly As root

After you create a user account for yourself, do not log in directly as root again. If you log in directly as root, it will not be clear in the logs who was operating as root. Therefore, always log in as a user, and then use the **su** command to switch to root. The **su** command is not an abbreviation for super user. It represents substitute user or switch user.
The **su** command changes users. If you execute it without specifying an argument, it switches you to root.

Changing Passwords

Passwords are set so that only the registered user of an account can use it. A password is required at login with a username. A password is a combination of single-byte alphanumeric characters and symbols. It can be set and changed using the **passwd** command.

A password is the only key to each user's information. Do not choose an obvious password and keep your password secret.

1 Log out.

To change the password of a user, log in as that user.

Enter the **exit** command.

```
[root@server /root]# exit⏎
```

```
Red Hat Linux release 6.0 Publisher's Edition (Hedwig)
Kernel 2.2.5-15 on an i686

server login: _
```

The login screen appears.

2 To change the password of a user, log in as that user.

Enter the username.

```
Red Hat Linux release 6.0 Publisher's Edition (Hedwig)
Kernel 2.2.5-15 on an i686

server login: bob⏎
[bob@server bob]$ _
```

Because a password hasn't yet been set, you can log in with the username alone.

TIP!

Characters For Passwords

Do not choose an obvious password, such as a single word or common abbreviation that can be easily guessed by others. Ideally, a password should be a combination of uppercase and lowercase letters, symbols, and numbers. Only the first eight characters of a password are actually used. Strings of less than six characters or those that consist of only one type of character, such as lowercase letters, will not be accepted by the system.

3 Change the password.

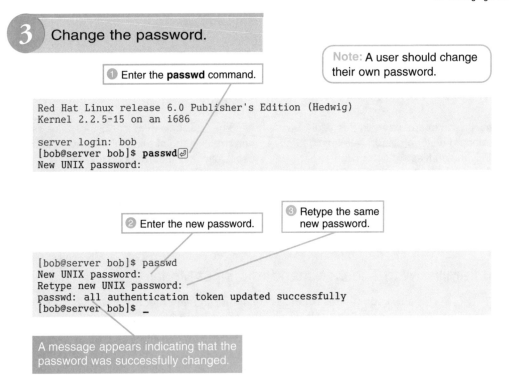

Note: A user should change their own password.

1 Enter the **passwd** command.

```
Red Hat Linux release 6.0 Publisher's Edition (Hedwig)
Kernel 2.2.5-15 on an i686

server login: bob
[bob@server bob]$ passwd⏎
New UNIX password:
```

2 Enter the new password.

3 Retype the same new password.

```
[bob@server bob]$ passwd
New UNIX password:
Retype new UNIX password:
passwd: all authentication token updated successfully
[bob@server bob]$ _
```

A message appears indicating that the password was successfully changed.

A Password Is An Important Key

A password is the only key safeguarding each user's information. Whoever knows your password can log in to Linux with your username. Even if you are both on the same network, you will not know exactly what the impostor is doing. Manage your password carefully, especially with the Internet, because people can access your Linux machine from anywhere in the world. Also, if your password is stolen, it is a mistake to think that only you will be adversely affected. You must consider the possibility that the impostor may cause trouble for others.

Forgetting Passwords

If a user forgets their password, switch to root to overwrite that user's password with a new one. If you execute the **passwd** command and specify the username as an argument, you can set the user's password. Set a simple password so that the user can log in, and then have the user set a new password.

```
[root@server /root]# passwd bob⏎
Changing password for user bob
New UNIX password:
Retype new UNIX password:
passwd: all authentication tokens updated successfully
[root@server /root]# _
```

Editing Configuration Files

The vi Text Editor

To configure an Internet server, this book uses **vi**, a standard editor provided with Linux, to edit the configuration files.

The **vi** text editor has a command mode and an input mode. In the input mode, you enter characters; in the command mode, you enter commands. At first, the **vi** text editor may seem hard to use but after repeated use, you will become familiar with its operations. This section explains the **vi** text editor basics and lists especially useful editing commands. You can also use one of two special versions of **vi** to edit password files (**vipw**), and set up group files (**vigr**). **vigr** is the best choice for editing the group file and **vipw** for editing the password file.

Getting Familiar With The Command And Input Modes

The **vi** text editor has a command mode and an input mode. Although text cannot be entered in the command mode, you can switch to the input mode easily to enter text. To return to the command mode from the input mode, press Esc.

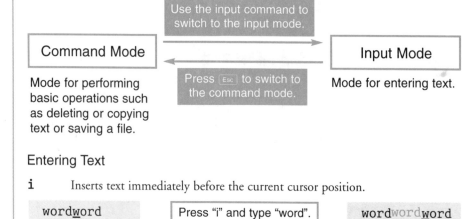

Use the input command to switch to the input mode.

Command Mode		Input Mode

Press Esc to switch to the command mode.

Mode for performing basic operations such as deleting or copying text or saving a file.

Mode for entering text.

Entering Text

i   Inserts text immediately before the current cursor position.

word<u>w</u>ord tango	Press "i" and type "word".	word<u>word</u><u>w</u>ord tango

a   Appends text immediately to the right of the cursor.

word<u>w</u>ord tango	Press "a" and type "word".	wordw<u>word</u><u>o</u>rd tango

o   Opens a new line directly below the current line.

word<u>w</u>ord tango	Press "o" and type "word".	wordword word_ tango

5.8

Deleting Text

x   Deletes the current character.

| wordw̲ord tango | Press "x" once. → | wordo̲rd tango |

Searching For Text

/word Searches for the text "word"

| w̲ordword tango | Specify /word → | wordw̲ord tango |

To repeat the same search, enter "n".

The search begins after the current cursor position, and the cursor moves to the beginning of the next match.

Basic **vi** Text Editor

1 Start the vigr text editor.

Specify the name of the configuration file to be edited as an argument when you start the **vigr** text editor.

Enter the command.

```
[root@server /root]# vigr /etc/group⏎
```

The **vigr** text editor starts, and the group registration file is opened.

```
root::0:root
bin::1:root,bin,daemon
daemon::2:root,bin,daemon
sys::3:root,bin,adm
adm::4:root,adm,daemon
tty::5:
disk::6:root
lp::7:daemon,lp
mem::8:
kmem::9:
wheel::10:root
mail::12:mail
news::13:news
uucp::14:uucp
man::15:
games::20:
gopher::30:
dip::40:
ftp::50:
nobody::99:
users::100:
floppy:x:19:
console:x:101:
utmp:x:102:
"/etc/group" 29 lines, 404 characters
```

② Switch to the input mode.

Press ⒤.

```
floppy:x:19:
console:x:101:
utmp:x:102:
"/etc/group" 29 lines, 404 characters
```

```
floppy:x:19:
console:x:101:
utmp:x:102:
-- INSERT --
```

INSERT, which indicates the command mode, is displayed at the bottom of the screen. The **vigr** text editor is switched to the command mode.

③ Switch to the command mode.

Press ⒠ˢᶜ.

```
floppy:x:19:
console:x:101:
utmp:x:102:
-- INSERT --
```

```
floppy:x:19:
console:x:101:
utmp:x:102:
```

INSERT disappears. The **vigr** text editor is switched to the input mode.

④ Exit the **vigr** text editor.

Press ⒥ and ⓠ.

```
floppy:x:19:
console:x:101:
utmp:x:102:
:q
```

```
floppy:x:19:
console:x:101:
utmp:x:102:
[root@server /root]# _
```

The **vigr** text editor terminates, and the command prompt appears.

If :q does not terminate the **vigr** text editor, use the :q! command to exit.

List Of **vigr** Commands

Basic Operations

Command Mode R Input Mode

a   Appends text immediately to the right of the cursor.
A   Appends text to the end of the line.
i   Inserts text immediately before the current cursor position.
I   Inserts text at the beginning of the current line.
o   Opens a new line directly below the current line.
O   Opens a new line directly above the current line.

Command Mode

x   Deletes the current character.
dd   Deletes the current line and places it into the paste buffer.
yy   Copies (yanks) the current line into the paste buffer.
p   Pastes onto the end of the line directly below the current line.
P   Pastes onto the end of the line directly above the current line.
        (The last deleted or copied text is pasted)
/word⏎   Finds the next occurrence of the string "word". (Press "n" to repeat the search.)
?word⏎   Searches backward for the previous occurrence of the string "word".
        (Use n to repeat the search.)
:$s/old/new/g⏎   Replaces the string "old" with the string "new "(without asking for confirmation).
:$s/old/new/cg⏎   Replaces the string "old" with the string "new" (asks for confirmation).

Saving Files And Quitting The **vigr** Text Editor

:w⏎   Saves (writes) the entire work buffer to the current file name if the file doesn't already exist.
:q⏎   Quits **vigr**.
:w!⏎   Forces a write; will overwrite an existing file.
:q!⏎   Quits without saving.

Cursor Movement

j   Down one line.
k   Up one line.
h   Left (backward) one character.
l   Right (forward) one character.
w   Right (forward) to the first letter of the next word.
b   Left (backward) to the first letter of the previous word.
$ Move to end of the line.
0 (zero)   Move to beginning of the line.
:$⏎   Move to end of the file.
:n⏎   Move to the nth line (1 indicates the first line of the file).
[Ctrl] f   Scroll forward one screen.
[Ctrl] b   Scroll backward one screen.

The **vigr** text editor allows you to combine commands and cursor operations in the command mode.

c   Replace existing text with new text from the cursor position to the specified location.
d   Delete text from the cursor position to the specified location.
(A Few Examples)
cw   Overwrite text from the cursor position to the end of the word (switches to input mode).
dw   Delete text from the cursor position to the end of the word.
c$ Overwrite text from the cursor position to the end of the line (switches to input mode).
d$ Delete text from the cursor position to the end of the line.

STEP UP

Using The **man** Command

In Linux, you can search the online system reference manuals for help about commands and other aspects of the system by using the **man** command.

Basic **man** Command Syntax

man [options] [sections] keyword

Example

```
[root@server /root]# man ls⏎
```
(handwritten: man vr)

> Search the manual for pages on the **ls** command.

man Command Options

If you're not sure of the exact command you're looking for, use the -k option to retrieve a list of related items.

man Command Sections

The **man** command has a feature known as *sections*. Sections categorize the manual pages by use. Specify a section by including the section number before the keyword. Section numbers run from 1 to 9. For example, commands are 1, file formats are 5, and system administration commands are 8.

Examples Of Specifying A Section

> Explanation of **passwd** command.

```
[root@server /root]# man 1 passwd⏎
[root@server /root]# man 5 passwd⏎
```

> /etc/passwd file format.

Chapter 6
Creating A DNS Server

One of the basic services of the Internet is provided by domain name service (DNS) servers that associate hostnames and IP addresses. If you take the time to create a DNS server, you can decide what your hostnames will be and put your domain name to better practical use. This chapter describes how to configure a DNS server.

Contents Of This Chapter

How A DNS Server Works

DNS

When using the Internet, there are very few times when you use an IP address directly. A mechanism called a domain name service (DNS) converts the hostname format, which humans find easier to work with, to the IP address format.

Because the DNS associates Internet hostnames and IP addresses, you may think that the DNS mechanism is extremely complicated and difficult. If you have a basic understanding of domains, however, it is not so difficult. This section describes the basic parts of the DNS mechanism.

The DNS Is A Service That Associates Hostnames And IP Addresses

The DNS is a service that maps hostnames to IP addresses and vice versa. It can find an IP address from a hostname (forward lookup) or a hostname from an IP address (reverse lookup). Mapping a hostname to an IP address is called *name resolution.*

Hostname   **Forward lookup**
(name resolution)   **IP address**

server.dekiru.gr.jp   ⟶   **210.248.12.98**

Reverse lookup

A DNS server has tables that are used to associate hostnames and IP addresses. Because the Internet is expanding so rapidly, however, managing the mapping tables for all hostnames and IP addresses in one place would be extremely difficult. Moreover, because the correspondences between hostnames and IP addresses are frequently updated throughout the world, managing all the updates in a single place would be impossible. Instead, the DNS server of each domain restricts itself to maintaining the mapping tables for the hostnames and IP addresses of the domain that it manages. Name resolution for all other hostnames is achieved through the mutual exchange of information with the DNS servers of other domains throughout the Internet.

Searching For The IP Address Of **www.impress.co.jp**
From The **dekiru.gr.jp** Domain

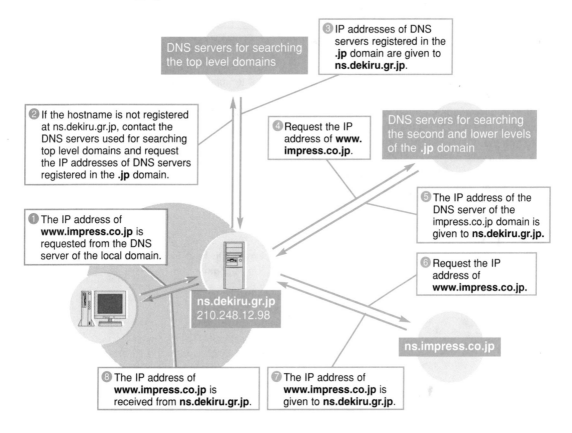

Primary And Secondary DNS Servers

The DNS is the basic service for managing information related to domains or individual hosts. To have a domain, you must have two DNS servers because DNS must operate continuously. Therefore, if you have your own domain, for the sake of redundancy, you must provide two computers as DNS servers. In most case, your Internet service provider (ISP) will provide you with a second server. From the standpoint of reliability, this is usually a better solution than having both DNS name servers at your location.

The two DNS servers must maintain the same content. The DNS server that manages and updates information is the *primary DNS server*. The DNS server that copies and saves the contents of the primary DNS server automatically is the *secondary DNS server*.

Creating A DNS Server, Part 1

Configuration File Preparations

To create a DNS server, you must have several configuration files. Among these are three files that you must configure yourself.

The named.conf file is the configuration file on which the entire DNS server is based. This file contains basic settings, such as the kind of server to be configured and the locations and file names of the other configuration files.

The template and template.rev files contain information about your domain. These files contain the configuration for the forward lookup data and reverse lookup data, respectively.

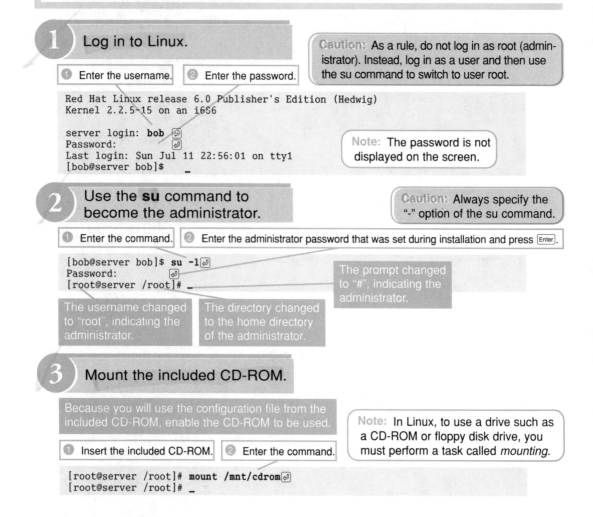

1 Log in to Linux.

Caution: As a rule, do not log in as root (administrator). Instead, log in as a user and then use the su command to switch to user root.

❶ Enter the username.   ❷ Enter the password.

```
Red Hat Linux release 6.0 Publisher's Edition (Hedwig)
Kernel 2.2.5-15 on an i686

server login: bob ↵
Password:         ↵
Last login: Sun Jul 11 22:56:01 on tty1
[bob@server bob]$ _
```

Note: The password is not displayed on the screen.

2 Use the **su** command to become the administrator.

Caution: Always specify the "-" option of the su command.

❶ Enter the command.   ❷ Enter the administrator password that was set during installation and press Enter.

```
[bob@server bob]$ su -1↵
Password:          ↵
[root@server /root]# _
```

The prompt changed to "#", indicating the administrator.

The username changed to "root", indicating the administrator.

The directory changed to the home directory of the administrator.

3 Mount the included CD-ROM.

Because you will use the configuration file from the included CD-ROM, enable the CD-ROM to be used.

❶ Insert the included CD-ROM.   ❷ Enter the command.

Note: In Linux, to use a drive such as a CD-ROM or floppy disk drive, you must perform a task called *mounting*.

```
[root@server /root]# mount /mnt/cdrom↵
[root@server /root]# _
```

4 Change to the directory.

Change to the directory.

Note: Change to the directory used to unpack the files from the archive.

```
[root@server /root]# mount /mnt/cdrom↵
[root@server /root]# cd /etc↵
[root@server /etc]#
```

5 Unpack the configuration files.

Enter the command.

```
[root@server /root]# cd /etc
[root@server /etc]# tar xvzf /mnt/cdrom/dekiru/conf/namedb.tar.gz↵
named.conf
namedb/
namedb/template
namedb/localhost
namedb/localhost.rev
namedb/named.conf
namedb/named.root
namedb/template.rev
[root@server /etc]# _
```

The names of the unpacked files are listed on the screen.

The configuration files are unpacked into the /etc directory.

Using BIND To Create A DNS Server

This book uses software called *Berkeley Internet Name Domain* (BIND) for a DNS server. Either version 4.x or 8.x, is usually used, especially the latter. The syntax of the configuration files differs slightly for these versions. BIND 8.2 is provided with Red Hat Linux.

The BIND configuration files are divided as follows.

• Overall configuration such as the directories and file names of the other configuration files (named.conf)
• Root name server configuration (named.root)
• Forward lookup database for finding IP addresses from hostnames (template)
• Reverse lookup database for finding hostnames from IP addresses (template.rev)
• Local host forward lookup (localhost)
• Local host reverse lookup (localhost.rev)

Creating A DNS Server, Part 2

Editing named.conf

The named.conf configuration file defines the overall configuration of the DNS server and determines the directory organization of the configuration files and the like. This file also sets zone information and the file names of the associated configuration files. A *zone* is a subdivision used for managing domains.

The domain name is used as it is usually written for the name of the forward lookup zone, and the network address, written in reverse order with ".in-addr.arpa" appended to it, is used for the name of the reverse lookup zone. One configuration file is allocated for each zone.

1 Open the configuration file.

① Change to the directory.

```
[root@server /etc]# cd namedb⏎
[root@server namedb]# vigr named.conf⏎
```

② Enter the command.

The vigr text editor is started and the configuration file is opened.

Modify this configuration file to match your environment.

Note: For **vigr** text editor commands, see page 95.

```
//
//      /etc/named.conf -- Dekiru Linux, July 1999
//
options {
     directory "/etc/namedb";
     allow-transfer{
        203.139.160.104;
        };
     };

zone "." {
     type hint;
     file "named.root";
     };

//      localhost
//
zone "localhost" {
     type master;
     file "localhost";
     };

zone "0.0.127.in-addr.arpa" {
     type master;
"named.conf" 38 lines, 528 characters
```

② Modify the configuration file.

```
//
//      /etc/named.conf -- Dekiru Linux, July 1999
//
options {
    directory "/etc/namedb";
    allow-transfer{
        203.139.160.104;
        };
    };

zone "." {
    type hint;
    file "named.root";
    };

//      localhost
//
zone "localhost" {
    type master;
    file "localhost";
    };

zone "0.0.127.in-addr.arpa" {
    type master;
    file "localhost.rev";
    };

//      primary
//
zone "dekiru.gr.jp" {
    type master;
    file "template";
    };

zone "96.12.248.210.in-addr.arpa" {
    type master;
    file "template.rev";
    };
```

① Use the absolute path to specify the directory in which the configuration file resides. (If you are directly using the configuration described in this book, you need not change this path.)

② Enter the IP address of the secondary DNS server.

Caution: Be careful not to make any mistakes when specifying the domain name or network address.

③ Enter your domain name.

④ Enter the network address with the numbers in reverse order.

Enter the names of the IP address forward and reverse lookup configuration files.

Note:
Forward lookup = Look up the IP address from the hostname
Reverse lookup = Look up the hostname from the IP address

```
//      primary
//
zone "dekiru.gr.jp" {
    type master;
    file "dekiru.gr.jp";
    };

zone "96.12.248.210.in-addr.arpa" {
    type master;
    file "dekiru.gr.jp.rev";
    };
```

⑤ Enter your domain name.

The names of configuration files are differentiated by appending the domain name being configured.

⑥ Enter the name with ".rev" appended to the domain name.

⑦ After modifying the file, save it by overwriting the original file and then quit.

﹍ﾉ a DNS Server, Part 3

BIND Configuration File

Prepare a configuration file by entering host or domain information for each zone that was configured in the named.conf file. The DNS server uses this configuration file to associate hostnames and IP addresses. Because the syntax of this configuration file is somewhat peculiar, we will discuss it.

Basically, one record or *resource record* (RR) is written on one line. There are several types of records, and each plays a different role.

1 Change the file names.

Note: Change the files names of the forward and reverse lookup configuration files.

Change the file names that were set in the configuration file.

① Change the name of the forward lookup configuration file.

Caution: Make sure that you enter the file names that were set in step 2 of Section 6.3.

```
[root@server namedb]# mv template dekiru.gr.jp⏎
[root@server namedb]# mv template.rev dekiru.gr.jp.rev⏎
[root@server namedb]# _
```

② Change the name of the reverse lookup configuration file.

2 Open the forward lookup configuration file.

Enter the command.

```
[root@server namedb]# mv template.rev dekiru.gr.jp.rev
[root@server namedb]# vigr dekiru.gr.jp⏎
```

TIP!

The Comment Character Is The Semicolon

In the configuration files for DNS forward or reverse lookup, all text following a semicolon (;) is considered a comment, and anything written there is ignored. Creating a comment by placing a semicolon (;) at the beginning of a line that was formerly meaningful is referred to as "*commenting out*" the line.

Basic Structure Of Records

Each record has the following structure:

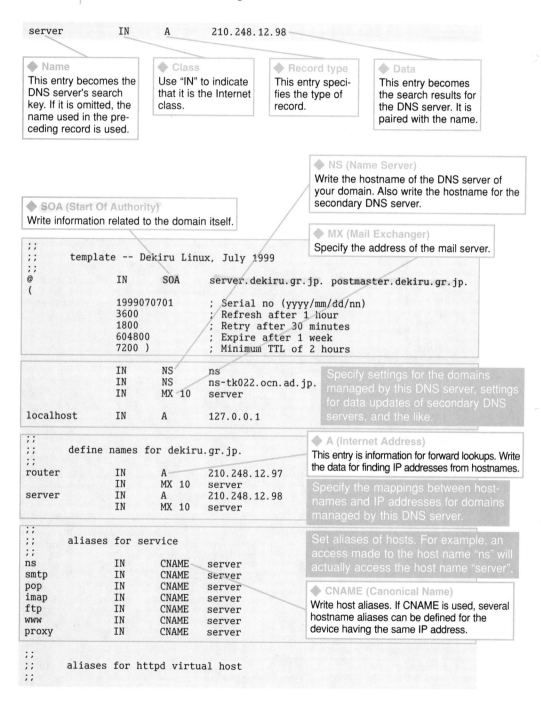

```
server          IN      A       210.248.12.98
```

◆ Name
This entry becomes the DNS server's search key. If it is omitted, the name used in the preceding record is used.

◆ Class
Use "IN" to indicate that it is the Internet class.

◆ Record type
This entry specifies the type of record.

◆ Data
This entry becomes the search results for the DNS server. It is paired with the name.

◆ NS (Name Server)
Write the hostname of the DNS server of your domain. Also write the hostname for the secondary DNS server.

◆ SOA (Start Of Authority)
Write information related to the domain itself.

◆ MX (Mail Exchanger)
Specify the address of the mail server.

```
;;
;;      template -- Dekiru Linux, July 1999
;;
@               IN      SOA     server.dekiru.gr.jp. postmaster.dekiru.gr.jp.
(
                1999070701      ; Serial no (yyyy/mm/dd/nn)
                3600            ; Refresh after 1 hour
                1800            ; Retry after 30 minutes
                604800          ; Expire after 1 week
                7200 )          ; Minimum TTL of 2 hours

                IN      NS      ns
                IN      NS      ns-tk022.ocn.ad.jp.
                IN      MX 10   server
localhost       IN      A       127.0.0.1
```

Specify settings for the domains managed by this DNS server, settings for data updates of secondary DNS servers, and the like.

```
;;
;;      define names for dekiru.gr.jp.
;;
router          IN      A       210.248.12.97
                IN      MX 10   server
server          IN      A       210.248.12.98
                IN      MX 10   server
```

◆ A (Internet Address)
This entry is information for forward lookups. Write the data for finding IP addresses from hostnames.

Specify the mappings between hostnames and IP addresses for domains managed by this DNS server.

```
;;
;;      aliases for service
;;
ns              IN      CNAME   server
smtp            IN      CNAME   server
pop             IN      CNAME   server
imap            IN      CNAME   server
ftp             IN      CNAME   server
www             IN      CNAME   server
proxy           IN      CNAME   server
```

Set aliases of hosts. For example, an access made to the host name "ns" will actually access the host name "server".

◆ CNAME (Canonical Name)
Write host aliases. If CNAME is used, several hostname aliases can be defined for the device having the same IP address.

```
;;
;;      aliases for httpd virtual host
;;
```

Creating A DNS Server, Part 4

Configuring Forward Lookup Information

Write records such as the SOA, NS, A, MX, and CNAME records in the configuration file for forward lookup data. The forward lookup data settings need to be modified when you want to add equipment with new hostnames, when the secondary DNS server address is changed, or when you want to set host aliases.

When you modify this file, always increase the serial number of the SOA record. If you do not increase the serial number, the changes may not become effective for a long time.

forward and reverse cannot have the same serial #

1 Set the domain name.

Caution: If you make a mistake when specifying the contents of the configuration file, the DNS server will not operate normally. Change only one character at a time so that you do not make a mistake.

TIP!

Do Not Forget The Final Period

Do not omit the period (.) at the end of the hostname in the DNS server configuration files. All hostnames that do not have the final period are treated as if the domain portion were omitted. Forgetting to append the final period is one of the careless mistakes that occur relatively often in the BIND configuration file.

For the serial number, use a combination of the date the file was modified and the revision count for that day.

❶ Change the serial number.

❷ Enter the host name of the server machine. (Be sure to add the final period.)

❸ Enter "postmaster", with the domain name appended to it. (Be sure to add the final period.)

```
;;
;;      template -- Dekiru Linux, July 1999
;;
@           IN      SOA     server.dekiru.gr.jp. postmaster.dekiru.gr.jp. (
            1999070701      ; Serial no (yyyy/mm/dd/nn)
            3600            ; Refresh after 1 hour
            1800            ; Retry after 30 minutes
            604800          ; Expire after 1 week
            7200 )          ; Minimum TTL of 2 hours

            IN      NS      ns
            IN      NS      ns-tk022.ocn.ad.jp.
            IN      MX 10   server

localhost   IN      A       127.0.0.1
```

Note: Usually, the *at* sign (@) is included in a mail address. Here, however, because this symbol represents the zone name in the DNS server's configuration file, it is replaced with a period (.).

❺ Enter the hostname of the secondary DNS server. (Be sure to add the final period.)

❹ Enter the primary DNS server hostname that you used when you obtained your domain name from InterNIC. (The domain portion may be omitted here.)

❻ Enter the hostname of the server machine. (The domain portion may be omitted.)

Note: This must be the same hostname you gave to your ISP.

Note: For **vigr** text editor commands, see page 95.

2 Specify the forward lookup settings.

Set the mapping between hostnames and IP addresses.

❶ Enter the IP address that was set for the router.

```
;;
;;      define names for dekiru.gr.jp.
;;
router          IN      A       210.248.12.97
                IN      MX 10   server
server          IN      A       210.248.12.98
                IN      MX 10   server
```

❸ Enter the hostname of the server machine. (The domain portion may be omitted.)

❹ Enter the IP address of the server machine.

❷ Enter the hostname of the server machine. (The domain portion may be omitted.)

❺ Enter the hostname of the server machine. (The domain portion may be omitted.)

TIP!

The MX Record Indicates The Destination For Incoming Mail

The MX record is used to find the mail server that you will use as the destination when mail is sent addressed to that domain. Set an MX record for the entire domain and for each host. An alias defined in a CNAME record cannot be used for the hostname that is used in an MX record. Likewise, an MX record cannot be defined for an alias that is defined in a CNAME record.

3 Set host aliases.

Because general aliases are already set, no particular settings are required here.

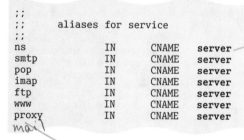

```
;;
;;      aliases for service
;;
ns              IN      CNAME   server
smtp            IN      CNAME   server
pop             IN      CNAME   server
imap            IN      CNAME   server
ftp             IN      CNAME   server
www             IN      CNAME   server
proxy           IN      CNAME   server
mail
```

❶ Enter the hostname of the server machine. (The domain portion may be omitted.)

Define a host alias for each service.

❷ Save the file and quit.

TIP!

Use CNAME To Associate Multiple Hostnames With One IP Address

The CNAME record defines a host alias. If you use CNAME, you can define several hostnames for the same IP address such as **ns.dekiru.gr.jp** or **www.dekiru.gr.jp** for the IP address of **server.dekiru.gr.jp**.

Creating A DNS Server, Part 5

Configuring Reverse Lookup Information   *reverse* PIR *has*

Write SOA, NS, and PTR records in the config-uration file for reverse lookup information.
When you add a device that uses a new IP address, make sure that a reverse lookup can also be performed when you modify the forward lookup data.
When you modify this file, always increase the serial number of the SOA record. Because the

forward and reverse lookup serial numbers are independent, this number doesn't need to match the serial number of the SOA record of the forward lookup configuration file.

---

1 Modify the reverse lookup configuration file.

test by ns lookup

Open the reverse lookup configuration file.

① Enter the command.

Note: For **vigr** text editor commands, see page 95.

```
[root@server namedb]# vigr dekiru.gr.jp.rev⏎
```

Caution: If you make a mistake when specifying the contents of the configuration file, the DNS server will not operate normally. Carefully change one character at a time so that you do not make a mistake.

Modify this configuration file to match your environment.

For the serial number, use a combination of the date the file was modified and the revision count for that day.

② Change the serial number.

③ Enter the hostname of the server machine (Be sure to add the final period.)

④ Enter the name "postmaster" with the domain name appended to it. (Be sure to add the final period.)

```
;;
;;      template.rev -- Dekiru Linux, July 1999
;;
@          IN    SOA   server.dekiru.gr.jp. postmaster.dekiru.gr.jp. (
           1999070701        ; Serial no (yyyy/mm/dd/nn)
           3600              ; Refresh after 1 hour
           1800              ; Retry after 30 minutes
           604800            ; Expire after 1 week
           7200 )            ; Minimum TTL of 2 hours

           IN    NS    ns.dekiru.gr.jp.
           IN    NS    ns-tk022.ocn.ad.jp.
```

⑤ Enter the hostname of the server machine (Be sure to add the final period).

⑥ Enter the hostname of the secondary DNS server (Be sure to add the final period.)

108

2 Specify the reverse lookup settings.

1 Enter the last number of the IP address. For example, if the IP address is 210.248.12.97, enter 97.

2 Enter the hostname corresponding to the IP address (Be sure to add the final period.)

3 Save the file and quit.

```
;;
;;      define addresses for dekiru.gr.jp.
;;
97              IN      PTR     router.dekiru.gr.jp.
98              IN      PTR     server.dekiru.gr.jp.
```

◆ PTR (Pointer)

This is information for performing a reverse lookup. Write data for finding the hostname from the IP address. Because the name of the zone differs from the domain name, you must write the hostname without omitting the final period (.).

3 Reload BIND.

The configuration is finished. Rerun BIND.

Enter the command.

Note: The **ndc** command specifies the stopping, starting, or restarting of BIND, the reading of a configuration file, and so on.

```
[root@server namedb]# ndc reload⏎
[root@server namedb]# _
```

TIP!

List of Records

SOA	Information related to the domain itself
NS	DNS server information
A	Forward lookup information
MX	Mail server information
CNAME	Host alias
PTR	Reverse lookup information

TIP!

Report The Configuration When It Is Completed

After you are finished configuring the DNS server and have started it up, notify your ISP.

test ?

π5

ng The DNS Server, Part 1

nslookup

The **nslookup** utility can be used to test your DNS server. You can use **nslookup** to issue requests to the DNS server.

This section uses the **nslookup** command to confirm the DNS server configuration. If the DNS server configuration is invalid, check the configuration file again. Most configuration failures are due to simple typing mistakes, such as forgetting to add a final period.

Look Up An IP Address From A Hostname

Verify that you can look up an IP address from a hostname.

Enter the command.

Verify that you can look up the IP address for the hostname of the DNS server you created.

Be sure to add the final period to the hostname that you want to look up.

```
[root@server namedb]# nslookup ns.dekiru.gr.jp.⏎
```

```
[root@server namedb]# nslookup ns.dekiru.gr.jp.
Server:    server.dekiru.gr.jp
Address:   210.248.12.98
Aliases:   98.12.248.210.in-addr.arpa
```
The DNS server that was used for the hostname search is listed.

```
Name:      server.dekiru.gr.jp
Address:   210.248.12.98
Aliases:   ns.dekiru.gr.jp
```
The hostname search results are listed.

```
[root@server namedb]# _
```

```
Name:      server.dekiru.gr.jp
Address:   210.248.12.98
Aliases:   ns.dekiru.gr.jp
```
Hostname that was found.

IP address that was found.

When the hostname that was found has an alias, that name is listed.

Caution: If the listed information is incorrect, return to Sections 6.3 and 6.6 and check the forward lookup data configuration file.

TIP!
Strange Hostname Display

If you use **nslookup** for a search and an excess character string is appended to the end of the IP address (such as xxx.xxx.xxx.xxx.in-addr.arpa), the reverse lookup data configuration file may be invalid. Verify again that you appended the period to the end of the hostname. After the configuration is changed, you must reload the configuration by running **ndc reload**.

You always have to up the secondary not primary

Look Up A Hostname From An IP Address

Verify that you can look up a hostname from an IP address.

Enter the command.

Verify that you can look up the hostname for the IP address of the DNS server you created.

```
[root@server namedb]# nslookup 210.248.12.98.⏎
```

```
[root@server namedb]# nslookup 210.248.12.98
Server:    server.dekiru.gr.jp
Address:   210.248.12.98
Aliases:   98.12.248.210.in-addr.arpa
```
The DNS server that was used for the IP address search is listed.

```
Name:      server.dekiru.gr.jp
Address:   210.248.12.98
Aliases:   98.12.248.210.in-addr.arpa
```
The IP address search results are listed.

```
[root@server namedb]# _
```

```
Name:      server.dekiru.gr.jp
Address:   210.248.12.98
Aliases:   98.12.248.210.in-addr.arpa
```

Hostname that was found.

IP address that was found.

Alias for a reverse lookup (this may not be displayed).

Caution: If the listed information is incorrect, return to Sections 6.3 and 6.6 and check the reverse lookup data configuration file.

TIP!

Reverse Lookup Fails, Part 1

The reverse lookup settings are also specified in the named.conf file. If the zone information of the named.conf file is invalid, a reverse lookup will only be possible locally. The reverse lookup zone information consists of ".in-addr.arpa" appended to the end of the IP address for the network address that has been written in reverse order.

TIP!

Reverse Lookup Fails, Part 2

When a new address is added to the reverse lookup configuration, you may not be able to find the reverse lookup data immediately. In some cases, changes are not propagated externally until a considerable amount of time has passed since the last update. Check again after a few days.

Always Increase The Serial Number When You Change A Configuration File

When you change the forward or reverse lookup configuration file, be sure to increase the serial number of the modified file and reload the file by running **ndc reload**. If you do not increase this number, the secondary DNS server will not be informed that the file was updated. This may lengthen the time that transpires before your changes are reflected.

Testing The DNS Server, Part 2

Confirming The Connection With A Remote Site

By default, **nslookup** will search only the A and PTR records. If you use a slightly more complicated method, however, you can specify the records to be searched and which DNS server you want to use for the search.

In this section we introduce the use of **nslookup** to test MX records and whether an external DNS server can be used to reference the domain information that you set yourself.

Confirming Whether Host For Exchanging Mail Is Defined

Enter **nslookup** interactive mode.

❶ Enter the command.

```
[root@server namedb]# nslookup↵
Default Server: server.dekiru.gr.jp
Address:   210.248.12.98
Aliases:   98.12.248.210.in-addr.arpa

> _
```

The DNS server to be used for the search is listed.

The interactive mode command input prompt appears.

❷ Enter the command. ❸ Enter the domain name.

Be sure to add the final period to the domain name that you want to look up.

❹ Confirm that this message is displayed.

```
> set type=mx↵
> dekiru.gr.jp.↵
Server:    server.dekiru.gr.jp
Address:   210.248.12.98
Aliases:   98.12.248.210.in-addr.arpa

dekiru.gr.jp       preference = 10, mail exchanger = server.dekiru.gr.jp
dekiru.gr.jp       nameserver = ns-tk022.ocn.ad.jp
dekiru.gr.jp       nameserver = ns.dekiru.gr.jp
server.dekiru.gr.jp     internet address = 210.248.12.98
ns-tk022.ocn.ad.jp      internet address = 203.139.160.104
> _
```

The DNS server to be used for the search is listed.

Verify that the server name for exchanging mail is correct.

❺ Enter the command.

```
> exit↵
[root@server namedb]# _
```

Exit **nslookup** interactive mode.

Caution: If the listed information is incorrect, return to Sections 6.3 and 6.6 and check the forward lookup data configuration file.

Look Up The IP Address Of A Remote Host

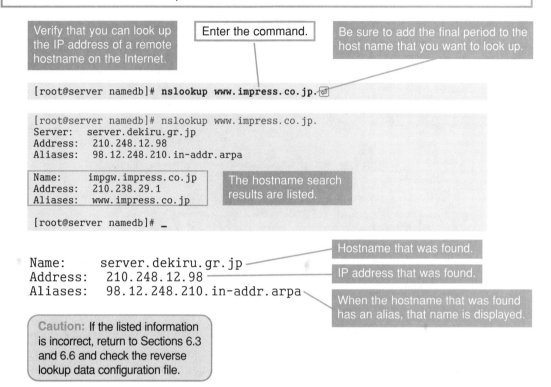

Verify that you can look up the IP address of a remote hostname on the Internet.

Enter the command.

Be sure to add the final period to the host name that you want to look up.

```
[root@server namedb]# nslookup www.impress.co.jp.⏎
```

```
[root@server namedb]# nslookup www.impress.co.jp.
Server:    server.dekiru.gr.jp
Address:   210.248.12.98
Aliases:   98.12.248.210.in-addr.arpa

Name:      impgw.impress.co.jp
Address:   210.238.29.1
Aliases:   www.impress.co.jp
```

The hostname search results are listed.

```
[root@server namedb]# _
```

```
Name:      server.dekiru.gr.jp
Address:   210.248.12.98
Aliases:   98.12.248.210.in-addr.arpa
```

Hostname that was found.

IP address that was found.

When the hostname that was found has an alias, that name is displayed.

Caution: If the listed information is incorrect, return to Sections 6.3 and 6.6 and check the reverse lookup data configuration file.

Use A Remote DNS Server To Look Up The Address Of A Hostname

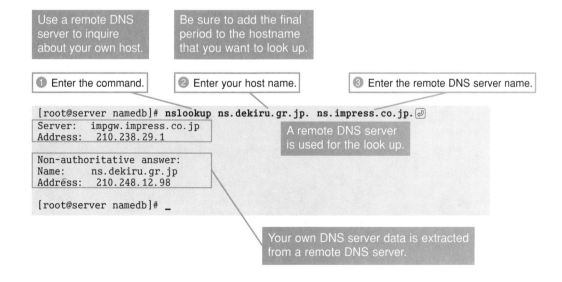

Use a remote DNS server to inquire about your own host.

Be sure to add the final period to the hostname that you want to look up.

❶ Enter the command.   ❷ Enter your host name.   ❸ Enter the remote DNS server name.

```
[root@server namedb]# nslookup ns.dekiru.gr.jp. ns.impress.co.jp.⏎
Server:    impgw.impress.co.jp
Address:   210.238.29.1
```

A remote DNS server is used for the look up.

```
Non-authoritative answer:
Name:    ns.dekiru.gr.jp
Address:   210.248.12.98
```

```
[root@server namedb]# _
```

Your own DNS server data is extracted from a remote DNS server.

S TEP UP

DNS Server Caching Function

Although a DNS server maps hostnames to IP addresses and IP addresses to host-names, each DNS server only has information for the domains for which it has been configured. As a result, a DNS server operates by querying other DNS servers for data that it does not have. Because the same operation reoccurs each time another search for the same address is performed, however, this approach quickly becomes extremely inefficient.

The DNS server has a caching function that locally stores addresses for which a search has been performed. This cached data not only speeds up a second or subsequent search, but also reduces unnecessary Internet traffic. Because the latest changes to data on authoritative name servers would not reach the rest of the network if the cached data were kept forever, it is erased after a fixed period is known as the *time to live* (TTL). Because the data is stored by the BIND program, not on the disk, it becomes invalid when BIND is stopped and restarted.

Restarting BIND When Settings Have Not Properly Changed

Although the DNS server cache provides several benefits, it may also cause the DNS service not to operate as expected. The information for which settings were changed may not be reflected properly. Usually, when the DNS server settings are changed, you should reload the settings. If this does not cause the information to be reflected properly, try restarting BIND. Use the **ndc** command to reload the settings as well as to restart BIND.

Reload the settings.

```
[root@server /root]# ndc reload↵
```

Restart BIND.

```
[root@server /root]# ndc restart↵
```

Chapter 7
Creating A Mail Server

Mail is a typical Internet service. If you set up your own mail server, you can take advantage of such enjoyable benefits as being able to create mail addresses and set up mailing lists. This chapter describes how to set up a mail server.

Contents Of This Chapter

Mail Works

send mail
Fetchmail

Sendmail And qpopper

→test

A mail server is not a single program. It is implemented by two programs: an simple mail transfer protocol (SMTP) server and a post office protocol (POP) server. Each is responsible for part of the job.

IMAP is the latest version

The SMTP server is a *transport agent*. It receives all of the mail destined for your domain and delivers your outgoing mail to other mail servers across the Internet. This book uses Sendmail for the SMTP server.

The POP server is a *delivery agent*. It distributes incoming mail that has been stored by the SMTP server. This book uses qpopper for the POP server. This section describes the role and functions of each of these servers.

Role Of The Mail Server

The mail server provides functions for receiving and storing mail addressed to your domain, and delivering outgoing mail (SMTP server), and for distributing incoming mail (POP server).

Role Of The Mail Server
• Receiving incoming mail and delivering outgoing mail
• Storing mail
• Distributing incoming mail

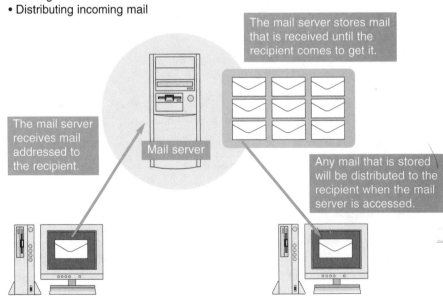

The mail server stores mail that is received until the recipient comes to get it.

The mail server receives mail addressed to the recipient.

Mail server

Any mail that is stored will be distributed to the recipient when the mail server is accessed.

send mail
mail basball@hatmail.com

Functions Of Sendmail And qpopper

Sendmail is the server (transport agent) used for sending outgoing and receiving incoming mail. qpopper is the server (delivery agent) that distributes the mail that has been received and stored by Sendmail. Building these two servers will enable mail to be used freely.

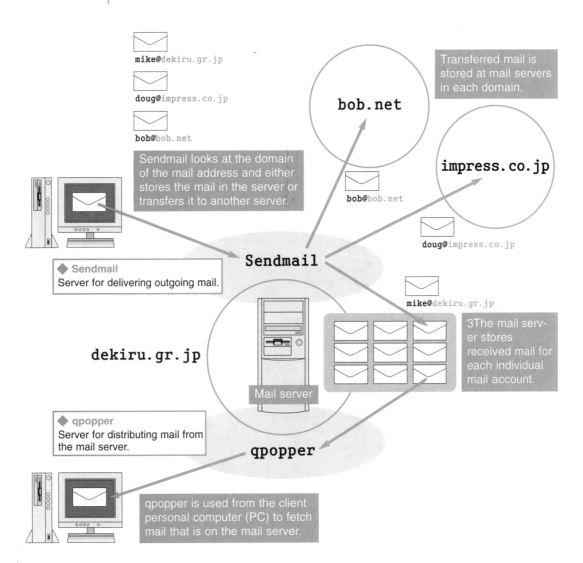

mike@dekiru.gr.jp

doug@impress.co.jp

bob@bob.net

bob.net

Transferred mail is stored at mail servers in each domain.

bob@bob.net

impress.co.jp

Sendmail looks at the domain of the mail address and either stores the mail in the server or transfers it to another server.

doug@impress.co.jp

Sendmail

◆ Sendmail
Server for delivering outgoing mail.

mike@dekiru.gr.jp

3The mail server stores received mail for each individual mail account.

dekiru.gr.jp

Mail server

◆ qpopper
Server for distributing mail from the mail server.

qpopper

qpopper is used from the client personal computer (PC) to fetch mail that is on the mail server.

Names Of Mail Servers Used In This Book
Server for sending outgoing mail (SMTP)   smtp.dekiru.gr.jp
Server for distributing received mail (POP)   pop.dekiru.gr.jp

Installing Mail Server Software

Installing Sendmail

To ensure security, you should obtain the most recent version of Sendmail yourself and compile and install it. You should also update Sendmail whenever a new version is released. This section briefly describes how to compile (convert the program's source file to an executable file) and install Sendmail.

Although the **make** command is normally used to compile a program, the **Build** command is specifically provided for the current version of Sendmail. This enables Sendmail to be created to accommodate a variety of environments.

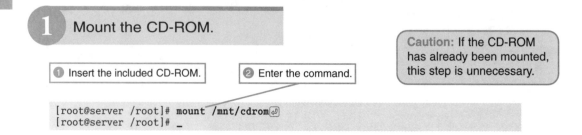

1 Mount the CD-ROM.

① Insert the included CD-ROM.   **②** Enter the command.

Caution: If the CD-ROM has already been mounted, this step is unnecessary.

```
[root@server /root]# mount /mnt/cdrom↵
[root@server /root]# _
```

2 Change to the directory for unpacking files.

Change directory.

```
[root@server /root]# mount /mnt/cdrom
[root@server /root]# cd /usr/local/src↵
[root@server src]# _
```

TIP!
Use The Latest Version For Your Mail Server
This book uses Sendmail 8.9.3 and CF 3.7Wp12. If a newer Sendmail or CF [jb1] has been released by the time you are building your server, be sure to use it.

TIP!
Addresses For Obtaining Sendmail And CF
Sendmail
www.sendmail.org/
CF
ftp.kyoto.wide.ad.jp/pub/mail/CF

3 Unpack the source files.

Enter the command.

```
[root@server /root]# cd /usr/local/src
[root@server src]# tar xvzf /mnt/cdrom/dekiru/src/sendmail.8.9.3.tar.gz⏎
sendmail-8.9.3/FAQ
sendmail-8.9.3/KNOWNBUGS
```

```
sendmail-8.9.3/doc/usenix/Makefile
sendmail-8.9.3/doc/usenix/usenix.me
sendmail-8.9.3/doc/usenix/usenix.ps
[root@server src]# _
```

The names of files that are unpacked are listed.

The source files are unpacked.

4 Compile Sendmail.

Note: Compiling converts a source listing to a form that can be used as a program.

① Change directory.

```
sendmail-8.9.3/doc/usenix/usenix.ps
[root@server src]# cd sendmail-8.9.3/src⏎
[root@server src]# sh Build⏎
Configuration obj.Linux.2.2.5-15.i586 using ../BuildTools/OS/Linux
Maling dependencies in obj.Linux.2.2.5-15.i686
```

```
groff -Tascii -mandoc newaliases.1 > newaliases.0
groff -Tascii -mandoc sendmail.8 > sendmail.0
[root@server src]# _
```

Compilation may take a long time to complete.

② Enter the command.

5 Install Sendmail.

Note: Installing integrates the program with the operating system (OS) so that it can actually be used.

Enter the command.

```
groff -Tascii -mandoc sendmail.8 > sendmail.0
[root@server src]# sh Build install⏎
Configuration: os=Linux, rel=2.2.5-15, rbase=2, rroot=2.2, arch=i586, sfx=
Making in obj.Linux.2.2.5-15.i686
```

```
install -c -o bin -g bin -m 444 mailq.0 /usr/man/man1/mailq.1
install -c -o bin -g bin -m 444 newalias.0 /usr/man/man1/newaliases.1
[root@server src]# _
```

Sendmail is installed.

Creating A Mail Server, Part 1

Configuring Sendmail

You cannot properly use Sendmail just by installing it. You must create a configuration file that is suited to your specific network environment.

Although the Sendmail configuration file is located in /etc/sendmail.cf, modifying this file yourself is extremely difficult. A useful tool called *CF* enables you to create a Sendmail configuration file with relative ease.

This section describes how to use *CF* to create sendmail.cf.

1 Change to the directory for unpacking the files.

Change directory.

```
install -c -o bin -g bin -m 444 newalias.0 /usr/man/man1/newaliases.1
[root@server src]# cd /usr/local/src↵
[root@server src]# _
```

2 Unpack the CF files.

This book uses the tool called *CF* to create the Sendmail configuration file.

Caution: If the attached CD-ROM has not been mounted, see step 1 in Section 7.2 and mount it.

Enter the command.

```
[root@server src]# cd /usr/local/src
[root@server src]# tar xvzf /mnt/cdrom/dekiru/src/CF-3.7Wp12.tar.gz↵
CF-3.7Wp12/
CF-3.7Wp12/ChangeLog
```

```
CF-3.7Wp12/support/README
CF-3.7Wp12/README
[root@server src]# _
```

The names of files that are unpacked are listed.

3) Copy the configuration file.

Copy the configuration
file to be used by *CF*.

Enter the
command.

```
CF-3.7Wp12/README
[root@server src]# cp /mnt/cdrom/dekiru/conf/sendmail.def /usr/local/src/CF-3.7Wp12↵
[root@server src]# _
```

4) Modify and save the configuration file.

① Change directory.   ② Enter the command.

```
[root@server src]# cp /mnt/cdrom/dekiru/conf/sendmail.def /usr/local/src/CF-3.7Wp12
[root@server src]# cd CF-3.7Wp12↵
[root@server CF-3.7Wp12]# vigr sendmail.def↵
```

Modify the file to match your
own network environment.

Note: See page 95 for information
about the **vigr** text editor.

```
##
##      sendmail.def -- Dekiru Linux, July 1999
##

##
CF_TYPE=R8V8

##
DEF_ID='Dekiru Linux, July 1999'

##
VERSION=3.7Wp12
VERSION_SEPARATOR=/
LOCAL_VERSION=DEKIRU1.00
```

③ Enter the first three
numbers of the
network address.

```
##
MAIL_RELAY_RESTRICTION=yes
LOCAL_HOST_IPADDR='210.248.12'
LOCAL_HOST_DOMAIN='dekiru.gr.jp'
```

④ Enter your
domain name.

Outgoing mail will not be
accepted unless it is from
the network set here.

```
##
DONT_BLAME_SENDMAIL='GroupWritableDirPathSafe GroupWritableIncludeFileSafe'
```

⑤ Save the modified file and quit.

TIP!

Added Settings For NAT

If you use NAT (described in Chapter 9), you will be
able to use Sendmail even from a local area network
(LAN) inside of NAT. To use NAT, add the IP
addresses that are used by the LAN (such as
192.168.1), separated by spaces, to the
LOCAL_HOST_IPADDR line of the sendmail.def file.

test

...te the configuration file.

Enter the command.

```
[root@server CF-3.7Wp12]# make sendmail.cf⏎
MASTERDIR=./Master TOOLDIR=./Tools
./Tools/Configure sendmail.def > sendmail.cf.tmp
mv -f sendmail.cf.tmp sendmail.cf
[root@server CF-3.7Wp12]# _
```

6 Start Sendmail in test mode.

Note: The -**bt** option specifies test mode, and the -**C** option specifies the configuration file.

Enter the command.

```
[root@server CF-3.7Wp12]# /usr/sbin/sendmail -bt -C./sendmail.cf⏎
Cannot open hash database /etc/aliases.db: Invalid argument
WARNING: cannot open alias database /etc/aliases; reading text version

ADDRESS TEST MODE (ruleset 3 NOT automatically invoked)
Enter <ruleset> <address>
> _
```

7 Test mail transmission.

Enter "3,0" and the administrator's mail address.

Note: This tests mail delivery to your domain.

```
> 3,0 root@dekiru.gr.jp⏎
rewrite: ruleset   3    input: root @ dekiru . gr . jp
rewrite: ruleset  96    input: root < @ dekiru . gr . jp >
rewrite: ruleset  96  returns: root < @ dekiru . gr . jp >
rewrite: ruleset   3  returns: root < @ dekiru . gr . jp >
rewrite: ruleset   0    input: root < @ dekiru . gr . jp >
rewrite: ruleset  97    input: root
rewrite: ruleset   3    input: root
rewrite: ruleset   3  returns: root
rewrite: ruleset   0    input: root
rewrite: ruleset   0  returns: $# local $: root
rewrite: ruleset  97  returns: $# local $: root
rewrite: ruleset   0  returns: $# local $: root
> _
```

If "returns" is shown for the specified administrator's mail address, the file is configured properly.

If "local' is shown, it means that this server received the mail.

The user name to which the mail was sent is shown here.

TIP!

What Is 3,0?

The numbers written in the first line represent the type of object to be tested. Because you are testing a mail address, we specify the 3,0 rule.

8 Test mail delivery to an external domain.

Enter "3,0" and a mail address outside of your own domain.

```
> 3,0 bob@bob.net⏎
rewrite: ruleset   3    input: bob @ bob . net
rewrite: ruleset  96    input: bob < @ bob . net >
rewrite: ruleset  96  returns: bob < @ bob . net >
rewrite: ruleset   3  returns: bob < @ bob . net >
rewrite: ruleset   0    input: bob < @ bob . net >
rewrite: ruleset  88    input: < smtp  bob . net > . bob < @ bob . net >
rewrite: ruleset  88  returns: $# smtp $@ bob . net . $: bob < @ bob . net >
rewrite: ruleset   0  returns: $# smtp $@ bob . net . $: bob < @ bob . net >
> _
```

If "returns" is shown for the specified mail address, the file is configured properly.

If "smtp" is shown, it means that the mail is sent to another SMTP server.

9 Quit test mode.

how do you get out of mail (ctrl D)
→ test ?

When the prompt appears, press Ctrl + D.

```
rewrite: ruleset  97  returns: $# smtp $@ bob . net . $: bob < @ bob . net >
rewrite: ruleset   0  returns: $# smtp $@ bob . net . $: bob < @ bob . net >
> Ctrl + D
```

```
rewrite: ruleset  97  returns: $# smtp $@ bob . net . $: bob < @ bob . net >
rewrite: ruleset   0  returns: $# smtp $@ bob . net . $: bob < @ bob . net >
> [root@server CF-3.7Wp12]# _
```

The normal prompt appears.

10 Save the original configuration file.

To be safe, save the current configuration file now.

Enter the command.

```
> [root@server CF-3.7Wp12]# mv /etc/sendmail.cf /etc/sendmail.cf.orig⏎
[root@server CF-3.7Wp12]# _
```

11 Copy the configuration file.

Copy the sendmail.cf file that you created.

Enter the command.

```
> [root@server CF-3.7Wp12]# mv /etc/sendmail.cf /etc/sendmail.cf.orig
[root@server CF-3.7Wp12]# cp sendmail.cf /etc⏎
[root@server CF-3.7Wp12]# _
```

12 Restart Sendmail.

Enter the command.

```
[root@server CF-3.7Wp12]# cp sendmail.cf /etc
[root@server CF-3.7Wp12]# /etc/rc.d/init.d/sendmail restart⏎
Shutting down sendmail:                              [  OK  ]
Starting sendmail:                                   [  OK  ]
[root@server CF-3.7Wp12]# _
```

Sendmail is restarted with the new settings.

This completes the procedure for creating the mail server for delivering outgoing mail.

How Mail Delivery Works

When a user sends mail, the mail server looks at the destination address and decides whether to receive the mail by its own domain or to send the mail to another mail server of another domain. If the mail address is within its own domain, the mail server stores it in a spool until the recipient retrieves it. If the mail address is in another domain, the mail server determines to which mail server the mail should be sent to and forwards it.

When the user requests mail delivery, the mail server sends the mail that is stored in the spool.

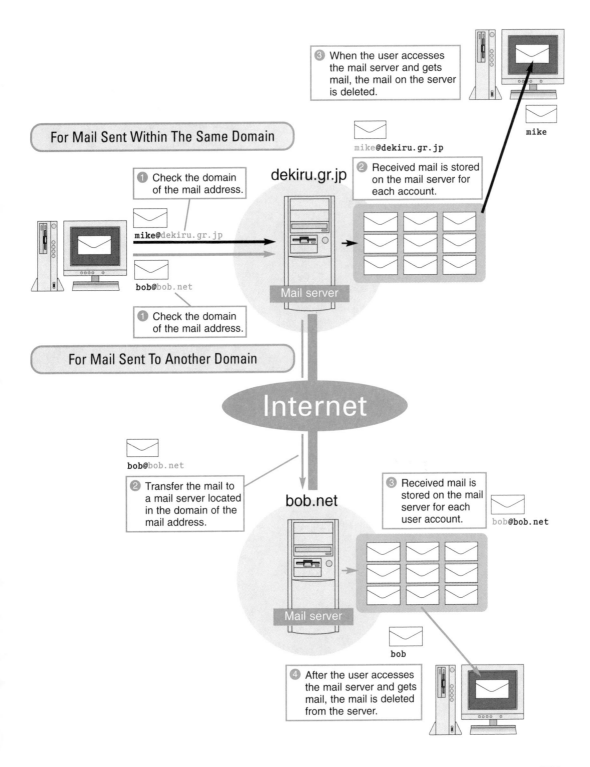

③ When the user accesses the mail server and gets mail, the mail on the server is deleted.

mike

For Mail Sent Within The Same Domain

mike@dekiru.gr.jp

❶ Check the domain of the mail address.

dekiru.gr.jp

② Received mail is stored on the mail server for each account.

mike@dekiru.gr.jp

bob@bob.net

Mail server

❶ Check the domain of the mail address.

For Mail Sent To Another Domain

Internet

bob@bob.net

② Transfer the mail to a mail server located in the domain of the mail address.

bob.net

③ Received mail is stored on the mail server for each user account.

bob@bob.net

Mail server

bob

❹ After the user accesses the mail server and gets mail, the mail is deleted from the server.

Creating A Mail Server, Part 2

Installing qpopper

Incoming mail addressed to a user is stored on the mail server by the SMTP server. The user accesses the POP server to request mail delivery from the server and to have the mail turned over to the user's mail client. The POP server then deletes this mail from the mail server, completing mail delivery.

This section describes how to compile and install the POP server program qpopper that enables the Linux mail server to provide POP server functions.

1 Change to the directory for unpacking files.

Change directory.

```
[root@server CF-3.7Wp12]# cd /usr/local/src⏎
[root@server src]# _
```

2 Unpack the source files.

Unpack the qpopper source files.

Enter the command.

Caution: If the included CD-ROM has not been mounted, see step 1 in Section 7.2 and mount it.

```
[root@server CF-3.7Wp12]# cd /usr/local/src
[root@server src]# tar xvfz /mnt/cdrom/dekiru/src/qpopper3.0b18.tar.Z⏎
qpopper3.0/
qpopper3.0/INSTALL

qpopper3.0/test/tgen
qpopper3.0/test/tscript
[root@server src]# _
```

TIP!

An Address For Obtaining qpopper

The URL for obtaining mail servers such as qpopper is **http://eudora.qualcomm.com/free/servers.html**.

3 Prepare for compiling qpopper.

Configure qpopper so that it supports APOP.

① Change directory.   ② Enter the command.

```
[root@server src]# cd qpopper3.0⏎
[root@server qpopper3.0]# ./configure --enable-apop --with-popuid=mail --enable-specialauth⏎
creating cache ./config.cache
checking whether make sets ${MAKE}... yes
```

```
creating mmangle/Makefile
creating config.h
[root@server qpopper3.0]# _
```

4 Compile qpopper.

Enter the command.

```
[root@server qpopper3.0]# --enable-apop --with-popuid=mail --enable-specialauth
[root@server qpopper3.0]# make⏎
cd ./popper  && make all
make[1]: Entering directory '/usr/local/src/qpopper3.0/popper'
gcc -c -I.. -I.. -I. -I../mmangle -g -O2 -fstrength-reduce -fpcc-struct-return
```

It may take a long time before the last line appears. Be patient.

```
gcc  -o popauth flock.o base64.o scram.o md5.o hmac.o popauth.o -lresolv -lgdbm
make[1]: Leaving directory '/usr/local/src/qpopper3.0/popper'
[root@server qpopper3.0]# _
```

5 Install qpopper.

① Change directory.

```
make[1]: Leaving directory '/usr/local/src/qpopper3.0/popper f
[root@server qpopper3.0]# cd popper⏎
[root@server popper]# install -s -m 4755 -o mail -g mail popauth /usr/bin⏎
[root@server popper]# install -s popper /usr/sbin⏎
[root@server popper]# _
```

② Enter the command.   ③ Enter the command.

6 Initialize the APOP password data file.

Enter the command.

```
[root@server popper]# install -s -m 4755 -o mail -g mail popauth /usr/bin
[root@server popper]# popauth -init↵
[root@server popper]# _
```

7 Edit the configuration file.

❶ Enter the command.

Note: The inetd.conf file is the Linux network service configuration file.

```
[root@server popper]# popauth -init
[root@server popper]# vigr /etc/inetd.conf↵
```

The configuration file is opened.

Note: See page 95 for information about the **vigr** text editor.

```
#
# Pop and imap mail services et al
#
#pop-2    stream   tcp      nowait   root     /usr/sbin/tcpd       ipop2d
#pop-3    stream   tcp      nowait   root     /usr/sbin/tcpd       ipop3d
#imap     stream   tcp      nowait   root     /usr/sbin/tcpd       imapd
#
# The Internet UUCP service.
```

Change the ipop3d daemon to popper.

Because the pop-3 line is commented out, make it effective.

❷ Type "popper -s".

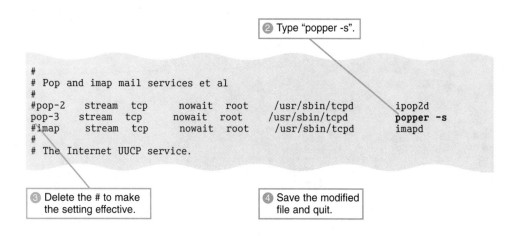

```
#
# Pop and imap mail services et al
#
#pop-2    stream   tcp      nowait   root     /usr/sbin/tcpd       ipop2d
pop-3     stream   tcp      nowait   root     /usr/sbin/tcpd       popper -s
#imap     stream   tcp      nowait   root     /usr/sbin/tcpd       imapd
#
# The Internet UUCP service.
```

❸ Delete the # to make the setting effective.

❹ Save the modified file and quit.

8 Implement the settings.

Enter the command.

```
[root@server popper]# /etc/rc.d/init.d/inet reload⏎
[root@server popper]# _
```

The new configuration file is loaded.

This completes the mail server installation.

IMAP Can Be Used Instead Of POP

The Internet message access protocol (IMAP) instead of POP can be used to read mail. IMAP gives the impression that a mailbox has been placed on the server. When POP is used, mail is deleted from the server after it has been retrieved by a client. As a result, the mail can be read only from that client. If IMAP is used, the same mailbox can be accessed from another client or from another machine.

To make your Linux mail server support IMAP, use the **rpm** command to install the IMAP server, and then uncomment the imap line of the /etc/inetd.conf file.

❶ Enter the command.

```
[root@server /root]# rpm -i /mnt/cdrom/RedHat/RPMS/imap-4.5-3.i386.rpm⏎
[root@server /root]# vigr /etc/inetd.conf⏎
```

❷ Enter the command.

❸ Remove the # to make the setting effective.

```
#imap    stream  tcp    nowait  root    /usr/sbin/tcpd  imapd
```

```
imap     stream  tcp    nowait  root    /usr/sbin/tcpd  imapd
```

❹ Save the modified file and quit.

❺ Enter the command.

```
[root@server /root]# /etc/rc.d/init.d/inet reload⏎
[root@server /root]# _
```

To use IMAP, the client side must also support IMAP. Various mail clients, such as Netscape Messenger and Outlook Express, support IMAP.

Creating A Shared Mail Account

aliases

The /etc/aliases file is a Sendmail configuration file that associates mail accounts with mail addresses. If the /etc/aliases file is used, mail addressed to a specific account can be delivered to a user with a different name, or a simple mailing list can be created.

This section describes how to configure the /etc/aliases file so that incoming mail addressed to the administrative account root is delivered to your account and how to create a simple mailing list.

Transferring Mail Addressed To root To Another User

1 Edit the /etc/aliases file.

Transfer mail addressed to root to mike.

① Enter the command.

```
[root@server /root]# vigr /etc/aliases
```

The configuration file is opened.

Note: See page 95 for information about the **vigr** text editor.

```
#
#       @(#)aliases     8.2 (Berkeley) 3/5/94
#
#   Aliases in this file will NOT be expanded in the header from
#   Mail, but WILL be visible over networks or from /bin/mail.
```

```
# Person who should get root's mail
#root:          marc
root:           mike
```

② Type "root:" at the end of the file.

③ Enter the mail address.

④ Save the modified file and quit.

Specify the mail account from which mail is to be transferred.

Specify the mail address to which mail is to be transferred.

If the mail address is at the local server, the @ symbol and subsequent portion can be omitted.

Warning: If you forget the colon (:) after the source mail account, this file will not be configured correctly.

2 Implement the changes.

Implement the changes you made to the aliases in the file.

Enter the command.

Note: The modified aliases do not take effect until **newaliases** is executed. Be sure to rerun newaliases whenever you modify the aliases.

```
[root@server /root]# newaliases
/etc/aliases: 15 aliases, longest 10 bytes, 164 bytes total
[root@server /root]# _
```

The /etc/aliases File Links A Set Of Mail Addresses To One Another

The /etc/aliases file links together the mail account on the left side of the colon (:) and the list of mail addresses and other entries on the right side of the colon. Depending on the contents on the right side of the colon, you can configure the /etc/aliases file so that mail is transferred, or you can create a simple mailing list.

Transferring Mail Addressed To root To Users Who Perform Administrative Duties

Because information related to system errors and mail sent from users or external administrators may be delivered to the root-addressed mailbox, the administrator should always read mail addressed to root.

By using the /etc/aliases file to transfer root-addressed mail to your own mailbox, you can always read root-addressed mail using your regular account and regular mail client.

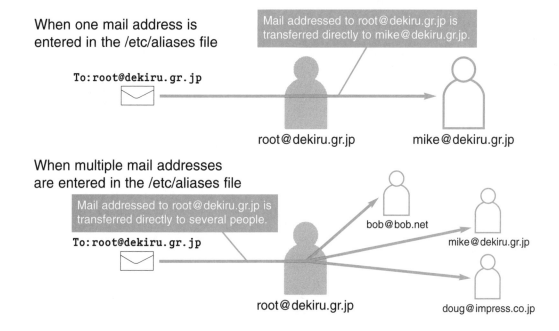

When one mail address is entered in the /etc/aliases file

Mail addressed to root@dekiru.gr.jp is transferred directly to mike@dekiru.gr.jp.

To: root@dekiru.gr.jp

root@dekiru.gr.jp   mike@dekiru.gr.jp

When multiple mail addresses are entered in the /etc/aliases file

Mail addressed to root@dekiru.gr.jp is transferred directly to several people.

To: root@dekiru.gr.jp

bob@bob.net

mike@dekiru.gr.jp

root@dekiru.gr.jp   doug@impress.co.jp

Simultaneously Sending The Same Mail To Multiple Recipients

The mechanism used to send the same mail to multiple recipients simultaneously is called a *mailing list*. You can create a mailing list by using the /etc/aliases file. To use a mailing list to send mail to multiple recipients, create a mail address for submissions to the mailing list. Then, when mail is sent to that address, the same mail will be sent to all of the members of the list.

Creating A Mailing List

1 Edit the /etc/alias file.

Transfer mail addressed to root to mike.

① Enter the command.

```
[root@server /root]# vigr /etc/aliases↵
```

The configuration file is opened.

Note: See page 95 for information about the **vigr** text editor.

```
#
#       @(#)aliases      8.2 (Berkeley) 3/5/94
#
#   Aliases in this file will NOT be expanded in the header from
#   Mail, but WILL be visible over networks or from /bin/mail.
```

```
# Person who should get root's mail
root:           mike
project:        mike, mika, bob@bob.net, doug@impress.co.jp
```

② Type "project:" at the end of the file.

③ Enter the mail address of each list member.

④ Save the modified file and quit.

If the mail address is at the local server, the @ symbol and subsequent portion can be omitted.

Specify the mail account for the mailing list.

Enter the mail addresses separated by commas.

Warning: If you forget the colon (:) after the mail account of the mailing list, this file will not be configured correctly.

2 Implement the changes.

Implement the changes you made to the /etc/aliases file.

Enter the command.

Note: Even if the /etc/aliases file is modified, the modifications do not take effect until **newaliases** is rerun. Be sure to rerun **newaliases** whenever you modify the aliases.

```
[root@server /root]# newaliases↵
/etc/aliases: 16 aliases, longest 52 bytes, 223 bytes total
[root@server /root]# _
```

If The Mailing List Gets Too Big

As the size of the mailing list increases, modifying the /etc/aliases file and running **newaliases** each time members are added can become timeconsuming. Also, the /etc/aliases file can become difficult to edit because of the length of the line corresponding to the mailing list. To avoid these problems, you can collect all of the mail addresses of list members in a separate file and configure the /etc/aliases file to read that file. As a result, whenever you want to add or delete members, all you have to do is modify that separate file; you will not have to rerun **newaliases** each time.

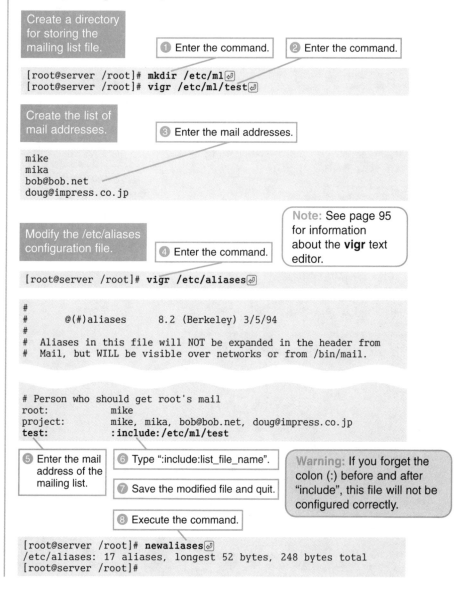

Create a directory for storing the mailing list file.

① Enter the command. ② Enter the command.

```
[root@server /root]# mkdir /etc/ml⏎
[root@server /root]# vigr /etc/ml/test⏎
```

Create the list of mail addresses.

③ Enter the mail addresses.

```
mike
mika
bob@bob.net
doug@impress.co.jp
```

Note: See page 95 for information about the **vigr** text editor.

Modify the /etc/aliases configuration file.

④ Enter the command.

```
[root@server /root]# vigr /etc/aliases⏎
```

```
#
#       @(#)aliases        8.2 (Berkeley) 3/5/94
#
#  Aliases in this file will NOT be expanded in the header from
#  Mail, but WILL be visible over networks or from /bin/mail.


# Person who should get root's mail
root:           mike
project:        mike, mika, bob@bob.net, doug@impress.co.jp
test:           :include:/etc/ml/test
```

⑤ Enter the mail address of the mailing list.

⑥ Type ":include:list_file_name".

⑦ Save the modified file and quit.

Warning: If you forget the colon (:) before and after "include", this file will not be configured correctly.

⑧ Execute the command.

```
[root@server /root]# newaliases⏎
/etc/aliases: 17 aliases, longest 52 bytes, 248 bytes total
[root@server /root]#
```

Enhancing Mail Security

APOP

APOP can be used instead of POP to read email. Because APOP sends encrypted passwords, it's safer and more security-conscious than the ordinary POP protocol, which sends passwords in clear text (not encrypted).

To use APOP, you must use a mail client that supports APOP.
Not every mail client supports APOP. First, determine whether your mail client can support APOP.

Setting An APOP Password

1 Log in under the username that you want changed.

● Enter the username.

Note: To use APOP, a password must be registered beforehand in a database.

```
Red Hat Linux release 6.0 (Hedwig)
Kernel 2.2.5-15 on an i586

server login:bob⏎
Password:
Last login: Sun Jul 11 22:59:22 on tty1
[bob@server bob]$ _
```

❷ Enter the password.

2 Change the password.

● Enter the command.

```
Red Hat Linux release 6.0 (Hedwig)
Kernel 2.2.5-15 on an i586

server login:bob
Password:
Last login: Sun Jul 11 22:59:22 on tty1
[bob@server bob]$ popauth⏎
Changing only APOP password for bob.
New password:
Retype new password:
[bob@server bob]$ _
```

❷ Enter the APOP password.

❸ Re-enter the APOP password.

Warning: The password for a non-administrator user account should be entered by the actual user.

134

Required Settings For The Mail Client

To use APOP, you must use a mail client that supports APOP and you must configure that mail client for APOP.

For Becky! Internet Mail

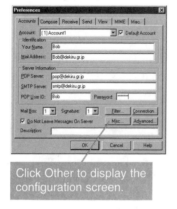 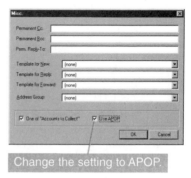

Change the setting to APOP.

Click Other to display the configuration screen.

For Eudora Pro (Windows version)

Select Incoming Mail tab.

Change the setting to APOP.

Deleting An APOP Password

After a user account is set up to use APOP, mail can no longer be read by using the ordinary POP protocol. If APOP is set by mistake, even though that user is using a mail client that does not support APOP, the root account must be used to delete that user's APOP password.

Enter the command.

Specify the user for which the APOP password is to be deleted.

```
[root@server /root]# popauth -delete bob⏎
[root@server /root]# _
```

STEP UP

Beware Of Relay Abuse

Sendmail operates by storing received mail on disk or by relaying it according to the Sendmail configuration. Unless Sendmail is specifically configured otherwise, it makes no difference from where the received mail orginated. This kind of configuration leaves your mail server vulnerable to abuse because a completely unrelated third party could freely use your mail server to relay mail.

Mail can be sent to many people simultaneously by specifying multiple addresses. Before this mail is relayed, only one mail message in which multiple addresses are written needs be sent. The mail server that actually delivers the mail, on the other hand, sends mail individually to the mail server of every domain specified in the list of addresses. If your mail server is abused as a relay point, the Sendmail program of your domain is used as the mail server for actually delivering the mail. The malicious third party will have increased the load on your network. Therefore, as a rule, you should restrict the relaying of mail.

MAIL_RELAY_RESTRICTION in the sendmail.def file is used to assign relay restrictions by checking the IP addresses of the mail senders. If this is set to "yes", only mail from the network specified by LOCAL_HOST_IPADDR and LOCAL_HOST_DOMAIN will be relayed. To permit relaying for other specific networks, change these specifications.

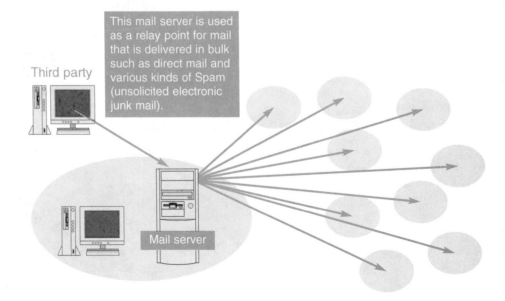

Third party

This mail server is used as a relay point for mail that is delivered in bulk such as direct mail and various kinds of Spam (unsolicited electronic junk mail).

Mail server

Chapter 8
Creating A Web Server

If you create a Web server, you can present information to the entire world through your own Web pages. This chapter describes how to install and configure Apache, the most popular Web server on the Internet.

Contents Of This Chapter

How Web Pages Are Displayed

Apache

Various Web browsers such as Netscape Communicator or Internet Explorer are available for displaying Web pages. All of these browsers display the contents of pages they receive from Web servers.
This chapter describes Apache, the most widely used Web server on the Internet today.

Apache sets a specific directory in Linux as the document root (a root directory for Web pages) and exhibits the directory tree within the document root as the Web page directory tree.

How Web Pages Are Displayed

When a Uniform Resource Locator (URL) is specified in a Web browser, the Web browser accesses the Web server specified by the URL, asks the Web server to transfer the Web page, and displays the page on the screen. If images or other items are embedded in the Web page, the Web browser displays those images by having them transferred one at a time in the same way as it did the Web page.

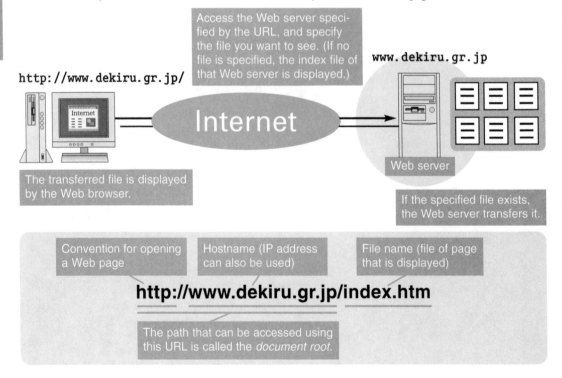

Access the Web server specified by the URL, and specify the file you want to see. (If no file is specified, the index file of that Web server is displayed.)

`http://www.dekiru.gr.jp/`

www.dekiru.gr.jp

Internet

Web server

The transferred file is displayed by the Web browser.

If the specified file exists, the Web server transfers it.

Convention for opening a Web page

Hostname (IP address can also be used)

File name (file of page that is displayed)

http://www.dekiru.gr.jp/index.htm

The path that can be accessed using this URL is called the *document root*.

Role Of Apache

Apache has a mechanism that makes a part of the Linux directory tree publicly available so that it can be read by a client browser. If the client only specified the directory without specifying a file, the file that was specified as the index file on the server side will be loaded.

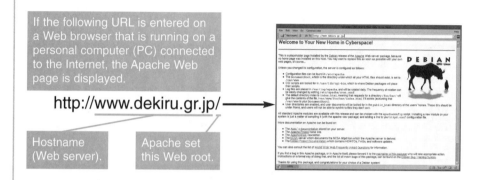

If the following URL is entered on a Web browser that is running on a personal computer (PC) connected to the Internet, the Apache Web page is displayed.

http://www.dekiru.gr.jp/

Hostname (Web server).

Apache set this Web root.

Apache Document Root

The URL for opening the file named /usr/local/www/htdocs/manual/index.html, for example, is as follows.

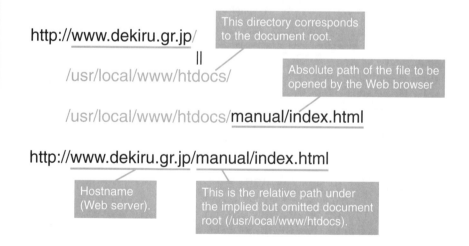

http://www.dekiru.gr.jp/

This directory corresponds to the document root.

||

/usr/local/www/htdocs/

Absolute path of the file to be opened by the Web browser

/usr/local/www/htdocs/manual/index.html

http://www.dekiru.gr.jp/manual/index.html

Hostname (Web server).

This is the relative path under the implied but omitted document root (/usr/local/www/htdocs).

To upload Web pages by using an FTP server, you must first install the FTP server. See page 189 for information about installing an FTP server.

Installing Your Web Server

Installing Apache

A Web server receives hits very frequently, These accesses from external sources may be concentrated at certain times; therefore, it is essential that you install the very latest, enhanced version.

This section explains how to compile and install Apache, how to specify the basic configuration, and how to configure Apache so that it starts up during the boot process. If a version of Apache was installed previously, we will delete it, then compile and install a more recent version.

1 Delete the version of Apache that was included in the package.

Note: The **-e** option specifies the uninstall operation.

Delete Apache to make sure there is no previous version of Apache installed.

Enter the command.

This message informs you that no previous version of Apache is installed.

```
[root@server /root]# rpm -e apache⏎
error: package apache is not installed
[root@server /root]# _
```

2 Mount the CD-ROM.

① Insert the included CD-ROM. ② Enter the command.

Caution: If the CD-ROM has already been mounted, this step is unnecessary.

```
[root@server /root]# mount /mnt/cdrom⏎
[root@server /root]# _
```

3 Change to the directory for unpacking files.

Change directory.

```
[root@server /root]# mount /mnt/cdrom
[root@server /root]# cd /usr/local/src⏎
[root@server src]# _
```

TIP!

Address For Obtaining Apache

The Apache Software Foundation's address is **www.apache.org.**

140

4 Unpack the source files.

Unpack the Apache
source files.

Enter the command.

```
[root@server /root]# cd /usr/local/src
[root@server src]# tar xvzf /mnt/cdrom/dekiru/src/apache_1.3.6.tar.gz⏎
apache_1.3.6/
apache_1.3.6/src
```

```
apache_1.3.6/icons/small/uu.gif
apache_1.3.6/logs/
[root@server src]# _
```

5 Prepare to compile Apache.

Note: The configuration settings
for compiling Apache have been
written in the conf-apache file.

Use the conf-apache
file to configure Apache.

1 Change directory.   2 Enter the command.

```
[root@server src]# tar xvzf /mnt/cdrom/dekiru/src/apache_1.3.6.tar.gz⏎
[root@server src]# cd apache_1.3.6⏎
[root@server apache_1.3.6]# sh /mnt/cdrom/dekiru/conf/conf-apache⏎
Configuring for Apache, Version 1.3.6
 + using installation path layout: GNU (config.layout)
```

```
Creating Makefile in src/os/unix
Creating Makefile in src/modules/standard
[root@server apache_1.3.6]# _
```

6 Compile Apache.

Enter the command.

```
Creating Makefile in src/modules/standard
[root@server apache_1.3.6]# make⏎
===> src
make[1]: Entering directory `/usr/local/src/apache_1.3.6 f
```

```
make[1]: Leaving directory `/usr/local/src/apache_1.3.6 f
<=== src
[root@server apache_1.3.6]# _
```

Apache compilation
is complete.

Install Apache.

> Enter the command.

```
<=== src
[root@server apache_1.3.6]# make install⏎
make[1]: Entering directory `/usr/local/src/apache_1.3.6 f
===> [mktree: Creating Apache installation tree]
```

```
make[1]: Leaving directory `/usr/local/src/apache_1.3.6 f
+---------------------------------------------------------+
| You now have successfully built and installed the       |
| Apache 1.3 HTTP server. To verify that Apache actually  |
| works correctly you now should first check the          |
| (initially created or preserved) configuration files    |
|                                                         |
|    /usr/local/etc/apache/httpd.conf                     |
|                                                         |
| and then you should be able to immediately fire up      |
| Apache the first time by running:                       |
|                                                         |
|    /usr/local/sbin/apachectl start                      |
|                                                         |
| Thanks for using Apache.        The Apache Group        |
|                                 http://www.apache.org/  |
+---------------------------------------------------------+
[root@server apache_1.3.6]# _
```

8 **Copy the Apache startup file.**

> Enter the command.

```
| Thanks for using Apache.        The Apache Group        |
|                                 http://www.apache.org/  |
+---------------------------------------------------------+
[root@server apache_1.3.6]# cp /mnt/cdrom/dekiru/conf/httpd /etc/rc.d/init.d⏎
[root@server apache_1.3.6]# _
```

9 **Change the permissions.**

> Enter the command.

```
[root@server apache_1.3.6]# cp /mnt/cdrom/dekiru/conf/httpd /etc/rc.d/init.d
[root@server apache_1.3.6]# chmod 755 /etc/rc.d/init.d/httpd⏎
[root@server apache_1.3.6]# _
```

10 **Specify the Apache configuration settings.**

> Enter the command.

```
[root@server apache_1.3.6]# chmod 755 /etc/rc.d/init.d/httpd
[root@server apache_1.3.6]# vigr /usr/local/etc/apache/httpd.conf⏎
```

11 Save the modified settings.

Note: See page 95 for information about the **vigr** text editor.

```
##
## httpd.conf -- Apache HTTP server configuration file
##



# as error documents.
#
ServerAdmin webmaster@dekiru.gr.jp



# anyway, and this will make redirections work in a sensible way.
#
ServerName www.dekiru.gr.jp
```

❶ Enter the mail address of the administrator.

Caution: See page 142, and add the alias address "webmaster".

❷ Delete the #, and enter the hostname of the Web server.

❸ Save the modified file and quit.

12 Start Apache.

Enter the command.

```
[root@server apache_1.3.6]# /etc/rc.d/init.d/httpd start⏎
/usr/local/sbin/apachectl start: httpd started
[root@server apache_1.3.6]# _
```

13 Configure Apache to start automatically.

Enter the command.

Configure Apache to start automatically when Linux is booted.

```
[root@server apache_1.3.6]# /etc/rc.d/init.d/httpd start
/usr/local/sbin/apachectl start: httpd started
[root@server apache_1.3.6]# ln -s /etc/rc.d/init.d/httpd /etc/rc.d/rc3.d/S85httpd⏎
[root@server apache_1.3.6]# _
```

14 Configure Apache to stop automatically.

Enter the command.

Configure Apache to stop automatically when Linux is shut down.

```
[root@server apache_1.3.6]# ln -s /etc/rc.d/init.d/httpd /etc/rc.d/rc3.d/S85httpd
[root@server apache_1.3.6]# ln -s /etc/rc.d/init.d/httpd /etc/rc.d/rc0.d/K15httpd⏎
[root@server apache_1.3.6]# _
```

15 Create the administrative user.

Create an administrative user of the Web server named www.

❶ Enter the command.

Specify the password.

```
[root@server apache_1.3.6]# ln -s /etc/rc.d/init.d/httpd /etc/rc.d/rc0.d/K15httpd
[root@server apache_1.3.6]# useradd -d /usr/local/www -p '********' -g users www⏎
[root@server apache_1.3.6]# chown -R www /usr/local/www⏎
```

❷ Enter the command.

Customizing Your Web Server

Modifying Configuration Files

Most Apache configuration settings are specified using the httpd.conf file located in the /usr/local/etc/apache directory. You can change the Apache configuration freely by the editing httpd.conf file.

In this section, we will add an index file with a different name, change the directory name for user Web pages, and make sure that Apache is running properly.
Each time the configuration is changed, Apache must be restarted.

8.3

You Can Freely Set How A Browser Will Be Able To See Your Site

To Display A Specific Directory
/usr/local/www/htdocs/manual ➤ http://www.dekiru.gr.jp/Apache/
Change The Name Of The File That Is Displayed By Default
Before customization, only ➤ Enable this file to be displayed
"index.html" will be displayed.   with "index.htm" also.
Configure Apache So That Each User Can Create Their Own Home Page
/home/bob/WWW/ ➤ http://www.dekiru.gr.jp/~bob/
Redirect A URL
http://www.dekiru.gr.jp/harry/ ➤ http://www.dekiru.gr.jp/~bob/

Transferring Mail Addressed To root To Another User

1 Open the httpd.conf file.

Enter the command.

```
[root@server /root]# vigr /usr/local/etc/apache/httpd.conf↵
```

```
# Note that if you include a trailing / on fakename then the server will
# require it to be present in the URL.  So  g/icons h isn ft aliased in this
# example, only "/icons/"..
#
Alias /icons/ "/usr/local/www/icons/"
```

A directory is added to the Web server in accordance with the settings written in an Alias line.

Alias /icons/ /usr/local/www/icons/

Name of subdirectory under Web root that will be associated with the other directory.

Linux directory.

Note: See page 95 for information about the **vigr** text editor.

144

2 Modify the httpd.conf file.

Note: The /home/www/htdocs/manual/ directory contains the Apache manual.

```
# Note that if you include a trailing / on fakename then the server will
# require it to be present in the URL.  So g/icons h isn ft aliased in this
# example, only "/icons/"..
#
Alias /icons/ "/usr/local/www/icons/"
Alias /Apache/ "/usr/local/www/htdocs/manual/"
```

❶ Add a line and type "Alias".

❷ Enter the directory name to be used on the Web.

❸ Enter the Linux directory that you want to display.

❹ Save the modified file and quit.

3 Restart Apache.

Enter the command.

```
[root@server /root]# /etc/rc.d/init.d/httpd restart⏎
/usr/local/sbin/apachectl restart: httpd restarted
[root@server /root]# _
```

Adding A New Index File

1 Modify the httpd.conf file.

❶ Enter a command.

Note: See page 95 for information about the **vigr** text editor.

```
[root@server /root]# vigr /usr/local/etc/apache/httpd.conf⏎
```

```
# DirectoryIndex: Name of the file or files to use as a pre-written HTML
# directory index.  Separate multiple entries with spaces.
#
DirectoryIndex index.html index.htm
```

The file specified on the DirectoryIndex line will be the index file.

❷ Add the name of the file you will use as the index file.

❸ Save the modified file and quit.

TIP!

Index File

An index file is the file that is displayed if only the directory name with no file name is specified in the URL. If you use a Windows-based Web authoring tool, you should add an index file with a three-letter extension, such as index.htm.

2 Restart Apache.

Enter the command.

```
[root@server /root]# /etc/rc.d/init.d/httpd restart⏎
/usr/local/sbin/apachectl restart: httpd restarted
[root@server /root]# _
```

Changing The Name Of The Directory That Will Be Used For A User's Web Pages

1 Modify the httpd.conf file.

Enter the command.

```
[root@server /root]# vigr /usr/local/etc/apache/httpd.conf⏎
```

If the directory name written in the UserDir line exists in the user's home directory, that directory will be used for the user's Web pages.

```
# UserDir: The name of the directory which is appended onto a user fs home
# directory if a ~user request is recieved.
#
UserDir WWW
```

❶ Enter the directory name to be set for the user's Web pages.

❷ Save the modified file and quit.

Note: See page 95 for information about the **vigr** text editor.

2 Restart Apache.

Enter the command.

```
[root@server /root]# /etc/rc.d/init.d/httpd restart⏎
/usr/local/sbin/apachectl restart: httpd restarted
[root@server /root]# _
```

Creating A Web Page For Each Linux User

1 Change the permissions of the home directory.

Change the permissions so that people other than the user can access this directory.

Enter the command.

```
[root@server /root]# chmod 755 /home/bob⏎
[root@server /root]#
```

2 Log in again as the user.

Note: You can also change to the user by using "su user_name".

❶ Log out.

❷ Log in as the user.

```
Red Hat Linux release 6.0 (Hedwig)
Kernel 2.2.5-15 on an i686

server login: bob⏎
Password:        ⏎
Last login: Mon Jul 12 00:22:24 on tty1
[bob@server bob]$ _
```

3 Create a directory for Web pages.

Caution: Enter the same directory name that was set in the httpd.conf file for the user's Web pages directory.

Enter the command.

```
Last login: Mon Jul 12 00:22:24 on tty1
[bob@server bob]$ mkdir WWW⏎
[bob@server bob]$ _
```

Create the directory (WWW) for Web pages.

Save the Web page files in the created directory.

Redirecting A Specific URL

1 Modify the httpd.conf file.

❶ Enter the command.

```
[root@server /root]# vigr /usr/local/etc/apache/httpd.conf⏎
```

Enter the redirection source and destination URLs on the last line.

Note: See page 95 for information about the **vigr** text editor.

```
#<VirtulaHost>
Redirect /harry/ http://www.dekiru.gr.jp/~bob/
```

❷ Type "Redirect".

❸ Enter the URL to be redirected (the portion up to the hostname of the URL is omitted).

❹ Enter the redirection destination URL.

❺ Save the modified file and quit.

2 Restart Apache.

Enter the command.

```
[root@server /root]# /etc/rc.d/init.d/httpd restart⏎
/usr/local/sbin/apachectl restart: httpd restarted
[root@server /root]# _
```

Using Hostnames Other Than www With The Web Server

Virtual Host

If a DNS alias (CNAME) is used, the Web server will also be able to be accessed by using a URL with a different hostname. With no other specific settings, the only result will be that there will appear to be multiple Web sites with the same contents. If you configure your Web server for virtual hosts, however, you can change the Web page that is displayed according to the hostname used for access.

Using virtual hosts enables you to create multiple Web sites easily and inexpensively. This section describes how to use virtual hosts.

8.4

Make it possible to access the home page of the user "bob" by using **bob.dekiru.gr.jp.**

---

1 Modify the BIND configuration file.

Add a virtual host to the DNS forward lookup data configuration file.

① Enter the command.

Note: Use the file name that was set in Section 6.3.

```
[root@server /root]# vigr /etc/namedb/dekiru.gr.jp⏎

;;
;;       template -- Dekiru Linux, July 1999
;;
@               IN      SOA     server.dekiru.gr.jp
                1999070702              ; Serial no (yyyy/m
                3600                    ; Refresh after 1 hour
                1800                    ; Retry after 30 minutes


proxy           IN      CNAME   server

;;
;;       aliases for httpd virtual host
;;
bob             IN      CNAME   server
```

② Enter a combination of the date and the revision count for the serial number. "1999070702" means that the second revision was made on July 7, 1999.

③ Enter the hostname.

④ Enter this in the same way as it was entered for setting an alias.

Note: See page 95 for information about the **vigr** text editor.

2 Refresh the settings.

Enter the command.

```
[root@server /root]# ndc reload⏎
[root@server /root]#
```

3 Configure Apache.

① Enter the command.

```
[root@server /root]# vigr /usr/local/etc/apache/httpd.conf⏎
```

```
# least one IP address (and port number) for them.
#
#NameVirtualHost 12.34.56.78:80
NameVirtualHost 210.248.12.98
```

② Delete the # at the beginning, and enter the IP address of the Web server.

```
# Almost any Apache directive may go into a VirtualHost container.

<VirtualHost 210.248.12.98>
    DocumentRoot /usr/local/www/htdocs
    ServerName www.dekiru.gr.jp
</VirtualHost>
```

③ Set the Web hostname that is normally used.

```
<VirtualHost 210.248.12.98>
    DocumentRoot /usr/local/www/htdocs/hide/www
    ServerName hide.dekiru.gr.jp
</VirtualHost>
```

④ Set the hostname of the virtual host.

⑤ Save the modified file and quit.

4 Restart Apache.

Enter the command.

```
[root@server /root]# /etc/rc.d/init.d/httpd restart⏎
/usr/local/sbin/apachectl restart: httpd restarted
[root@server /root]# _
```

5 Access Web page.

Use the Web browser to access **bob.dekiru.gr.jp**.

Use the Web browser to access **www.dekiru.gr.jp**.

STEP UP

Be Aware Of The Limitations Of Your Connection

Besides being able to configure a Web server freely on the Internet server that you have constructed yourself, you can also run various programs by means of a common gateway Interface (CGI) or small scale integrated (SSI) circuit and provide as much content as your disk capacity allows. Instead of thinking that you have a completely unrestricted Web server, however, keep in mind that there are limitations to the amount of data your line can handle.

For example, consider the case of a 128Kbps fractional T1 leased line. With a line speed of 128Kbps, the maximum amount of data that can be transferred per second is 16K (=128Kbps/8 bits). If an image that is 1MB (=1024K) in size is placed on the Web site and someone on the Internet tries to view it, it takes at least 64 seconds (=1024K/16K) to transfer the image. Moreover, if this image is accessed by many people simultaneously, the transfer time increases relative to the time for a single person by the number of accesses. Of course, not all of your Web pages will be as big as 1MB. On the other hand, there will often be more than one person accessing the pages simultaneously. As a result, if you want to operate a serious Web site that will receive large numbers of hits, it may prove difficult at a bandwidth of only 128Kbps. One advantage of a fractional T1 leased line is the ease at which it can be scaled up to greater bandwidth. You may increase your 128Kbps bandwidth as much as 12 times before reaching the limits of a T1 line without changing your digital service unit (DSU) or routing equipment. Increased bandwidth will cost more per month, of course.

You must consider two important factors with regard to bandwidth: the size of the Web pages, including images and other items used within them, and the number of accesses. Small Web page files can be accessed reasonably often without a problem, but large files are acceptable only if they are accessed infrequently. If they are accessed frequently, the line bandwidth may have to increase. If you are thinking about producing a serious Web site, a permanent connection such as those provided by an Imtegrated Services Digital Network (ISDN) line or a 128Kbps fractional T1 may be acceptable only as a first step. If your site is successful in generating a great number of hits or if your content files are usually large, you probably will need to increase the bandwidth of your permanent connection before long. Unless you require full, hands-on control over the configuration of your Web server and the content that it serves, you may consider renting your Web server services from an Internet service provider (ISP).

Chapter 9
Using An Internet Server
From A Client PC

In the previous chapters, you configured a server that is accessed from the Internet. Now you will configure a server for clients using a local area network (LAN). This chapter describes how to use your LAN to connect numerous personal computers (PCs) to the Internet by using a limited number of IP addresses.

Contents Of This Chapter

Connecting A LAN To The Internet

Private And Global IP Addresses

A range of IP addresses that can be safely used in a LAN have been defined. These IP addresses, which are called *private IP addresses*, cannot be used on the Internet. The IP addresses that are used on the Internet are called *global IP addresses*.

In previous chapters, you configured a network that used eight global IP addresses. A network can also be built using private IP addresses within the LAN. This book assumes that there are two networks, which are referred to as the Internet side and the LAN side.

**Range of Internet-side IP addresses
210.248.12.96/255.255.255.248**
(210.248.12.96 to 210.248.12.103)

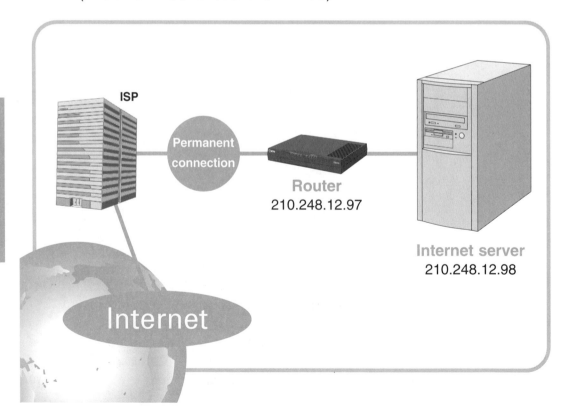

ISP

Permanent connection

Router
210.248.12.97

Internet server
210.248.12.98

Internet

Range Of Private IP Addresses

The range of private IP addresses that can be used for the LAN are:

10.0.0.0/255.0.0.0
(Up to 16,777,216 IP addresses are available.)
172.16.0.0/255.255.0.0 to **172.31.0.0/255.255.0.0**
(Up to 65,536 IP addresses are available.)
192.168.0.0/255.255.255.0 to **192.168.255.0/255.255.255.0**
(Up to 256 IP addresses are available.)

This book uses the 256 private IP addresses of 192.168.1.0/255.255.255.0.

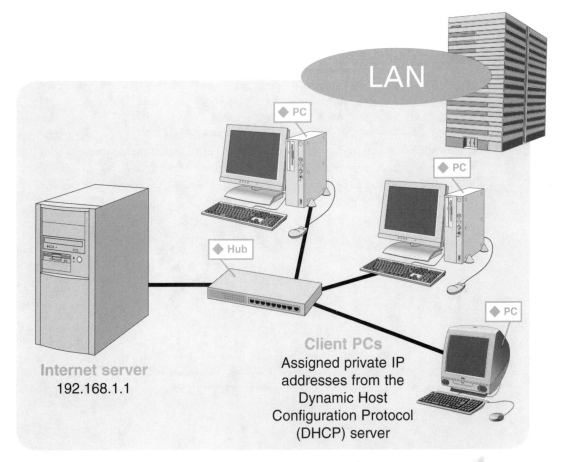

Internet server
192.168.1.1

Client PCs
Assigned private IP
addresses from the
Dynamic Host
Configuration Protocol
(DHCP) server

Range of LAN-side IP addresses
192.168.1.0/255.255.255.0
(192.168.1.0 to 192.168.1.255)

How To Connect Client PCs To The Internet

Network Address Translator (NAT)

Network address translator (NAT) is a means of converting IP addresses. Using NAT to convert between private and global IP addresses enables clients within a LAN to access the Internet easily.
Although Linux has NAT installed by default, two network cards are required to configure

NAT in Linux, because a single Linux machine must be connected to networks on both the LAN side and the Internet side.

How NAT Works

A global IP address is required to identify a particular host on the Internet. To access a server located on the Internet and receive a reply, a client must also have a global IP address.

When NAT is used, each time the Internet is accessed from the LAN, the originating IP address is converted to an Internet-side IP address. From the viewpoint of the accessed server, it appears as if it were being accessed from an Internet-side IP address, regardless of which client in the LAN initiated the access. That is, by running NAT, a single PC can impersonate any of the PCs on the LAN.

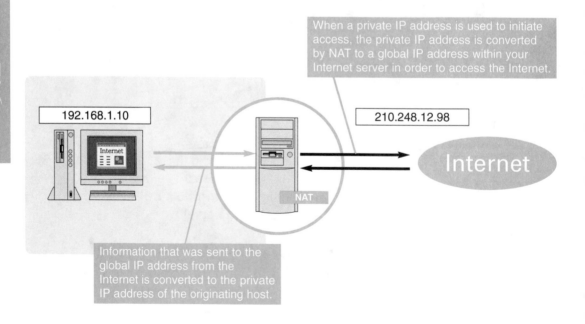

When a private IP address is used to initiate access, the private IP address is converted by NAT to a global IP address within your Internet server in order to access the Internet.

192.168.1.10

210.248.12.98

Internet

NAT

Information that was sent to the global IP address from the Internet is converted to the private IP address of the originating host.

Two Network Cards Are Required

To use NAT, two network cards are required. Connect one to the Internet side (router side), and connect the other to the LAN side (hub attached to the LAN). Assign a private IP address to the LAN-side network card, and assign a global IP address that is valid on the Internet to the Internet-side network card.

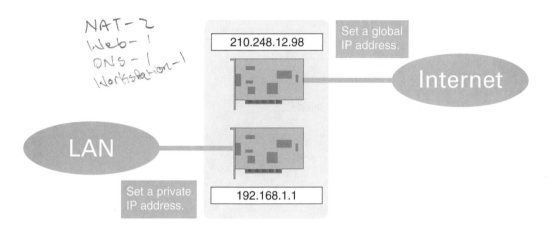

IP Addresses Are Assigned To Each Network Card

An IP address that identifies a particular device on the Internet is actually assigned to the network card, not the PC. NAT requires two network cards because completely different IP addresses are associated with a single Linux PC.

NAT And IP Masquerading

NAT is often called *IP Masquerading* in Linux documents. IP Masquerading is the name of the software that implements the NAT feature on Linux. Its functions have been extended slightly beyond the strict meaning of NAT. This book uses the IP Masquerading that is installed on Linux by default.

Using An Internet Server From A LAN, Part 1

Adding A Network Card

The following steps must be taken before NAT can be used.
• Install a second network card.
• Configure each network card.
• Configure NAT.
This book also covers configuring a DHCP server for NAT to reduce the work required for configuring the client network.

This section explains how to install the second network card.

---

1 Shut down your Internet server.

To install a network card, power down the server.

Enter the command.

Note: The **shutdown** command halts Linux.

```
[root@server /root]# shutdown -h now⏎
```

```
The system is halted
System halted
```

2 Install another network card.

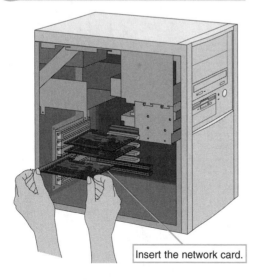

Insert the network card.

> **TIP!**
>
> ### Attach A Sticker To Each Network Card
>
> If you use two identical network cards, you will not be able to tell merely by looking at them which is used for the LAN side and which is used for the Internet side. After you install and configure them, attach identifying stickers to each card so that you do not mistake one for the other.

3 Start up the server.

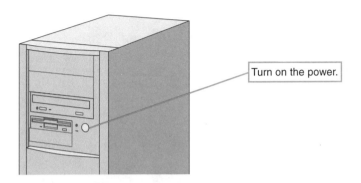

Turn on the power.

```
LILO boot:
Loading linux............
Uncompressing Linux... Ok, booting the kernel.
Linux version 2.2.5-15 (root@porky.devel.redhat.com) (gcc version egcs-2.91.66 1
990314/Linux (egcs-1.1.2 release)) #1 Mon Apr 19 21:39:28 EDT 1999
Detected 398526331 Hz processor.
Console: colour VGA+ 80x25
Calibrating delay loop... 397.31 BogoMIPS
Memory: 63016k/65472k available (1060k kernel code, 412k reserved, 924k data, 60
k init)
VFS: Diskquotas version dquot_6.4.0 initialized
CPU: Intel Celeron (Mendocino) stepping 05
Checking 386/387 coupling... OK, FPU using exception 16 error reporting.
Checking 'hlt' instruction... OK.
Checking for popad bug... OK.
POSIX conformance testing by UNIFIX
mtr: v1.2b (19981001) Richard Gooch (rgooch@atnf.csiro.au)
PCI: PCI BIOS revision 2.10 entry at 0xfd9c4
PCI: Using configuration type 1
PCI: Probing PCI hardware
PCI: Enabling memory for device 00:50
PCI: Enabling I/O for device 00:90
PCI: Enabling I/O for device 00:a0
PCI: Enabling memory for memory for device 00:a0
```

```
Red Hat Linux release 6.0 Publisher's Edition (Hedwig)
Kernel 2.2.5-15 on an i686

server login: _
```

Linux boots.

Use The Same Kind Of Card For The Second Network Card

Use a second network card that you know will operate properly. If you select the same kind of network card as the first card you installed, it will use the same driver.

Using An Internet Server From A LAN, Part 2

Configuring The Network Card

Under Linux, names are assigned to network cards. These names are used to configure Linux networks.

The names "eth0" and "eth1" are normally used for network cards. This book follows suit and sets the name "eth0" for the Internet-side network card and the name "eth1" for the LAN-side network card.

1 Assign a name to the second card.

① Enter the command.

```
[root@server /root]# vigr /etc/conf.modules⏎
```

The configuration file is opened.

```
alias eth0 ne2k-pci
alias parport_lowlevel parport_pc
pre-install pcmcia_core /etc/rc.d/init.d/pcmcia start
```

Modify the configuration file.   Enter the same line, changing "eth0" to "eth1".

```
alias eth0 ne2k-pci
alias eth1 ne2k-pci
alias parport_lowlevel parport_pc
pre-install pcmcia_core /etc/rc.d/init.d/pcmcia start
```

② Enter the name of the network card and the driver name.

③ Save the modified file and quit.

Connect the network card corresponding to eth1 to the LAN side and the network card corresponding to eth0 to the Internet side.

2 Create the configuration file for eth1.

Create the configuration file for eth1 by copying the configuration file for eth0.

① Change directory.   ② Enter the command.

```
[root@server /root]# cd /etc/sysconfig/network-scripts⏎
[root@server network-scripts]# cp ifcfg-eth0 ifcfg-eth1⏎
[root@server network-scripts]# _
```

9.4

3 Verify the configuration file for eth0.

Enter the command.

```
[root@server network-scripts]# cp ifcfg-eth0 ifcfg-eth1
[root@server network-scripts]# vigr ifcfg-eth0⏎
```

Verify that this is eth0.

Verify that this is the IP address of the server on which NAT is configured.

```
DEVICE=eth0
IPADDRESS=210.248.12.98
NETMASK=255.255.255.248
NETWORK=210.248.12.96
BROADCAST=210.248.12.103
ONBOOT=yes
```

Verify the net mask.

Verify the network address.

Verify the broadcast address.

4 Modify the network configuration.

① Enter the command.

```
[root@server network-scripts]# vigr /etc/sysconfig/network⏎
```

② Type "true".

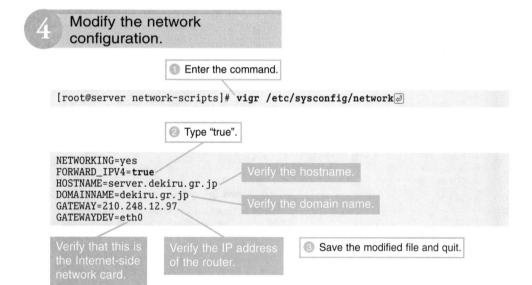

```
NETWORKING=yes
FORWARD_IPV4=true
HOSTNAME=server.dekiru.gr.jp
DOMAINNAME=dekiru.gr.jp
GATEWAY=210.248.12.97
GATEWAYDEV=eth0
```

Verify the hostname.

Verify the domain name.

Verify that this is the Internet-side network card.

Verify the IP address of the router.

③ Save the modified file and quit.

5 Modify and save the configuration file for eth1.

Enter the command.

```
[root@server network-scripts]# vigr ifcfg-eth1↵
```

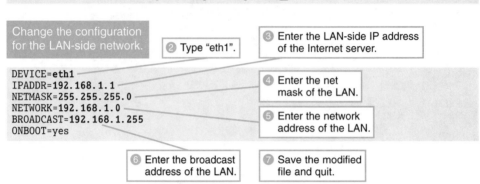

Change the configuration for the LAN-side network.

② Type "eth1".

③ Enter the LAN-side IP address of the Internet server.

```
DEVICE=eth1
IPADDR=192.168.1.1
NETMASK=255.255.255.0
NETWORK=192.168.1.0
BROADCAST=192.168.1.255
ONBOOT=yes
```

④ Enter the net mask of the LAN.

⑤ Enter the network address of the LAN.

⑥ Enter the broadcast address of the LAN.

⑦ Save the modified file and quit.

6 Reinitialize the settings.

Because the network configuration was modified, reinitialize the settings.

Enter the command.

```
[root@server network-scripts]# /etc/rc.d/init.d/network reload↵
Enabling IPv4 packet forwarding                        [  OK  ]
Bringing up device eth1                                [  OK  ]
[root@server network-scripts]# _
```

TIP!

How To Check The eth0 Card

When both network cards use the same driver, the original network card will not necessarily remain the Internet-side card (eth0).
To determine which card is which, first set each IP address and net mask. Then, use a cable to connect either one of the network cards to the router. If the router or a host on the Internet replies to a **ping** command when using this setup, that card is for external communications. If the **ping** command doesn't receive a reply like those shown in this book, try reconnecting the cable to the other network card.

7 Verify the network configuration.

Caution: If the network is not configured correctly, check the steps beginning with step 4, and re-edit the configuration files.

Use the **ifconfig** command to verify the network configuration.

Enter the command.

Verify that the global IP address and net mask are assigned to the eth0 network card.

```
[root@server network-scripts]# ifconfig⏎
eth0      Link encap:Ethernet  HWaddr 00:60:97:AC:0F:D2
          inet addr:210.248.12.98  Bcast:210.248.12.103  Mask:255.255.255.248
          UP BROADCAST RUNNING MULTICAST  MTU:1500  Metric:1
          RX packets:0 errors:0 dropped:0 overruns:0 frame:0
          TX packets:7622 errors:0 dropped:0 overruns:0 carrier:7622
          collisions:0 txqueuelen:100
          Interrupt:9 Base address:0x6c00

eth1      Link encap:Ethernet  HWaddr 00:00:E8:73:D7:2E
          inet addr:192.168.1.1  Bcast:192.168.1.255  Mask:255.255.255.0
          UP BROADCAST RUNNING MULTICAST  MTU:1500  Metric:1
          RX packets:0 errors:0 dropped:0 overruns:0 frame:0
          TX packets:0 errors:0 dropped:0 overruns:0 carrier:0
          collisions:0 txqueuelen:100
          Interrupt:10 Base address:0x6800

lo        Link encap:Local Loopback
          inet addr:127.0.0.1  Mask:255.0.0.0
          UP LOOPBACK RUNNING  MTU:3924  Metric:1
          RX packets:2565 errors:0 dropped:0 overruns:0 frame:0
          TX packets:2565 errors:0 dropped:0 overruns:0 carrier:0
          collisions:0 txqueuelen:0
[root@server network-scripts]# _
```

Verify the IP address and net mask of eth1, which is connected to the other PCs via the hub.

The configurations of the networks that are currently running are displayed.

8 Verify that the network card is connected.

Note: The **ping** command is used to verify a network connection.

Verify the status of the connection to the Internet.

① Enter the command.

Verify that the network card is connected to the Internet.

```
          collisions:0 txqueuelen:0
[root@server network-scripts]# ping www.impress.co.jp⏎
PING impgw.impress.co.jp(210.238.29.1): 56 data bytes
64 bytes from 210.238.29.1: icmp_seq=0 ttl=244 time=47.8 ms
64 bytes from 210.238.29.1: icmp_seq=1 ttl=244 time=39.0 ms
64 bytes from 210.238.29.1: icmp_seq=2 ttl=244 time=39.8 ms
```

② Press Ctrl + C.

Note: If you can't communicate with the network card, connect the network cable that is attached to the router to the network card that was added, and execute the command again.

```
64 bytes from 210.238.29.1: icmp_seq=2 ttl=244 time=39.8 ms

--- impgw.impress.co.jp ping statistics ---
3 packets transmitted, 3 packets received, 0% packet loss
round-trip min/avg/max = 39.0/42.2/47.8 ms
[root@server network-scripts]# _
```

Using An Internet Server From A LAN, Part 3

Configuring NAT

NAT is included in the Linux kernel when you first install Linux. You can use it directly just by configuring it. No special software is needed. If you are using private network addresses for your LAN than differ from the ones used in this book, be sure to change the relevant part of the configuration script.

Linux (PC where NAT is implemented) acts as a gateway for the LAN on the private side of the NAT. Therefore, set the LAN-side IP address of Linux for the gateway address.

1 Connect the server to the LAN.

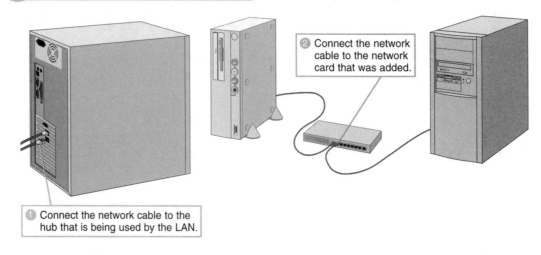

❷ Connect the network cable to the network card that was added.

❶ Connect the network cable to the hub that is being used by the LAN.

2 Mount the included CD-ROM.

❶ Insert the included CD-ROM.

❷ Enter the command.

```
[root@server network-scripts]# mount /mnt/cdrom⏎
[root@server network-scripts]#
```

3 Copy the configuration file.

Enter the command.

```
[root@server network-scripts]# mount /mnt/cdrom
[root@server network-scripts]# cp /mnt/cdrom/dekiru/conf/ipmasq /etc/rc.d/init.d⏎
[root@server network-scripts]#
```

4 Change the permissions.

① Change directory.

Note: The **chmod** command changes file permissions.

```
[root@server network-scripts]# cp /mnt/cdrom/dekiru/conf/ipmasq /etc/rc.d/init.d
[root@server network-scripts]# cd /etc/rc.d/init.d⏎
[root@server init.d]# chmod 755 ipmasq⏎
[root@server init.d]#
```

② Enter the command.

5 Modify the configuration file.

① Enter the command.

```
[root@server init.d]# chmod 755 ipmasq
[root@server init.d]# vigr ipmasq⏎
```

```
ROTO="ftp cuseeme irc quake raudio vdolive"
LOCALNET=192.168.1.0/255.255.255.0
```

② Enter the LAN-side network address and net mask.

6 Start NAT.

Enter the command.

TIP!

If You Are Using Another Network Range

If you are using a network address other than the 192.168.1.0 used in this book, enter that network address and net mask.

```
[root@server init.d]# ./ipmasq start⏎
Starting IP Masquerade: ftp cuseeme irc quake raudio vdoliv[  OK  ]
[root@server init.d]# _
```

7 Configure NAT so that it starts automatically on boot.

① Change directory.

Configure NAT so that it is starts automatically when you boot Linux.

```
[root@server init.d]# cd /etc/rc.d/rc3.d⏎
[root@server rc3.d]# ln -s ../init.d/ipmasq S11ipmasq⏎
[root@server rc3.d]# _
```

② Enter the command.

Automatically Assigning IP Addresses

Configuring The DHCP Server

DHCP is a service that configures a network automatically. It reduces administrative time because you do not have to configure the network for each client machine nor be concerned with duplicate IP addresses. Using DHCP enables you to configure the network correctly for a client just by connecting the cable.

In this section, you configure the DHCP server in Linux for LAN-side clients. A network configuration for each client is made automatically.

1 Mount the included CD-ROM.

❶ Insert the included CD-ROM.

❷ Enter the command.

Caution: If the CD-ROM has already been mounted, this step is unnecessary.

```
[root@server /root]# mount /mnt/cdrom⏎
[root@server /root]# _
```

2 Install the DHCP server.

Enter the command.

```
[root@server /root]# mount /mnt/cdrom
[root@server /root]# rpm -i /mnt/cdrom/RedHat/RPMS/dhcp-2.0b1pl6-6.i386.rpm⏎
[root@server /root]# _
```

The DHCP server is installed.

3 Copy the configuration file.

Copy the configuration file that is provided on the included CD-ROM.

Enter the command.

```
[root@server /root]# rpm -i /mnt/cdrom/RedHat/RPMS/dhcp-2.0b1pl6-6.i386.rpm
[root@server /root]# cp /mnt/cdrom/dekiru/conf/dhcpd.conf /etc⏎
[root@server /root]# _
```

Edit the configuration file.

① Enter the command.

```
[root@server /root]# cp /mnt/cdrom/dekiru/conf/dhcpd.conf /etc
[root@server /root]# vigr /etc/dhcpd.conf⏎
```

② Specify the range of IP addresses to be assigned automatically by DHCP.

Enter the first and last numbers of the IP addresses to be assigned.

③ Enter the network address and net mask of the LAN.

```
server-identifier server;

shared-network DHCP {
    option subnet-mask 255.255.255.0;

    subnet 192.168.1.0 netmask 255.255.255.0 {
        range 192.168.1.10 192.168.1.250;
        option broadcast-address 192.168.1.255;
        option routers 192.168.1.1;
        option domain-name "dekiru.gr.jp";
        option domain-name-servers 210.248.12.98;
        default-lease-time 21600;
        max-lease-time 43200;
    }
}
```

④ Enter the broadcast address of the LAN.

⑤ Enter the IP address of the LAN-side network card.

⑥ Enter the domain name.

⑦ Enter the IP address of the Domain Name Service (DNS) server.

5 **Create a backup of the original DHCP startup script.**

Enter the command.

```
[root@server /root]# mv /etc/rc.d/init.d/dhcpd /etc/rc.d/init.d/dhcpd.bak⏎
[root@server /root]# _
```

6 **Copy the DHCP startup script for NAT.**

Enter the command.

```
[root@server /root]# mv /etc/rc.d/init.d/dhcpd /etc/rc.d/init.d/dhcpd.bak
[root@server /root]# cp /mnt/cdrom/dekiru/conf/dhcpd /etc/rc.d/init.d⏎
[root@server /root]# _
```

7 Change the permissions.

Enter the command.

```
[root@server /root]# cp /mnt/cdrom/hogehoge/dhcpd /etc/rc.d/init.d
[root@server /root]# chmod 755 /etc/rc.d/init.d/dhcpd⏎
[root@server /root]# _
```

8 Create an empty file.

Create a file to be used by DHCP.

Enter the command.

Note: You can use the **touch** command to create a file in which nothing is specified.

```
[root@server /root]# chmod 755 /etc/rc.d/init.d/dhcpd
[root@server /root]# touch /etc/dhcpd.leases⏎
[root@server /root]# _
```

9 Start the DHCP daemon.

Enter the command.

```
[root@server /root]# touch /etc/dhcpd.leases
[root@server /root]# /etc/rc.d/init.d/dhcpd start⏎
Starting dhcpd:                                              [  OK  ]
[root@server /root]# _
```

If The Internet Cannot Be Accessed From A Client

If a Windows client cannot access the Internet even though it is connected and configured, you must determine and eliminate the cause. Try to verify the connection by using the **ping** command, which is included in both Linux and Windows.

From A Windows Client, Pinging The Linux Machine Where NAT Is Running

Select Start|Programs|MS-DOS Prompt, and enter the following command.

Enter the command.

```
C:\WINDOWS>ping 192.168.1.1⏎
```

```
C:\WINDOWS>ping 192.168.1.1

Pinging 192.168.1.1 with 32 bytes of data:

Reply from 192.168.1.1: bytes=32 time=0ms TTL=255
Reply from 192.168.1.1: bytes=32 time<10ms TTL=255
Reply from 192.168.1.1: bytes=32 time<10ms TTL=255
Reply from 192.168.1.1: bytes=32 time<10ms TTL=255

Ping statistics for 192.168.1.1:
    Packets: Sent = 4, Received = 4, Lost = 0 (0% loss),
Approximate round trip times in milli-seconds:
    Minimum = 0ms, Maximum =  1ms, Average =  0ms

C:\WINDOWS>
```

If you cannot connect:

• Verify that the network cable is connected properly
  (see Section 9.5).

Verify that you have not inadvertently used a crossover cable, nor connected the PC to the Up-Link port of the hub, and the like. If everything is connected correctly, the network card or hub LED should be lit.

• Verify that Linux has not mixed up the LAN-side and Internet-side network cards (see Section 9.3).

Try connecting the LAN-side cable that is connected to Linux to the other network card.

• Verify that a valid IP address has been assigned to the client.

Select Start|Run, and type "winipcfg" to verify that an address was set by DHCP on Linux.

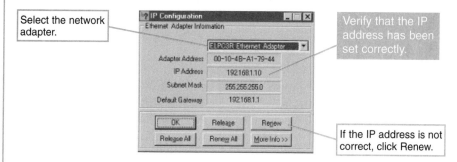

Select the network adapter.

Verify that the IP address has been set correctly.

If the IP address is not correct, click Renew.

• Verify that the NAT DHCP startup script is being used
  (see steps 6 and 7 on pages 165-166).

You must use a different DHCP startup script for NAT than the one that was installed by the **rpm** command.

• Verify the Linux dhcpd.conf file and restart dhcpd.
  (See step 4 on page 165).

If any value (such as the range of IP addresses to be used by DHCP, the network address, or the net mask) has not been set correctly, reset it and restart dhcpd.

Pinging An Internet-Side Host From Linux

Packet internet gopher (ping)

Execute the **ping** command on Linux.

❶ Enter the command.

```
[root@server /root]# ping www.impress.co.jp↵
PING impgw.impress.co.jp (210.238.29.1): 56 data bytes
64 bytes from 210.238.29.1: icmp_seq=0 ttl=243 time=50.3 ms
64 bytes from 210.238.29.1: icmp_seq=1 ttl=244 time=41.9 ms
64 bytes from 210.238.29.1: icmp_seq=2 ttl=244 time=45.8 ms
64 bytes from 210.238.29.1: icmp_seq=3 ttl=244 time=40.0 ms

--- impgw.impress.co.jp ping statistics ---
4 packets transmitted, 4 packets received, 0% packet loss
round-trip min/avg/max = 40.0/44.5/50.3 ms
[root@server /root]# _
```

❷ Press Ctrl + C.

If you cannot connect:

- **Verify that the network cable is connected properly (see Section 9.5).**

    Verify that a crossover cable has not been used, that the PC has been connected correctly to the Ethernet port of the router, and so on.

- **Verify the Linux network configuration (see Section 9.4).**

    Verify that the IP address and net mask settings of the Linux network card are correct. If they are not set correctly, modify the following configuration files and then reinitialize with the new values.

    /etc/conf.modules
    /etc/sysconfig/network
    /etc/sysconfig/network-script/ifcfg-eth0
    /etc/sysconfig/network-script/ifcfg-eth1

Enter the command.

```
[root@server /root]# /etc/rc.d/init.d/network restart↵
Shutting down interface eth0                              [  OK  ]
Shutting down interface eth1                              [  OK  ]
Disabling IPv4 packet forwarding                          [  OK  ]
Enabling IPv4 packet forwarding                           [  OK  ]
Bringing up interface lo                                  [  OK  ]
Bringing up interface eth0                                [  OK  ]
Bringing up interface eth1                                [  OK  ]
[root@server /root]# _
```

Pinging An Internet-Side Host From Windows

Select Start|Programs|MS-DOS Prompt, and enter the following command.

Enter the command.

```
C:\WINDOWS>ping www.impress.co.jp⏎

Pinging impgw.impress.co.jp [210.238.29.1] with 32 bytes of data:

Reply from 210.238.29.1: bytes=32 time=60ms TTL=241
Reply from 210.238.29.1: bytes=32 time=40ms TTL=244
Reply from 210.238.29.1: bytes=32 time=40ms TTL=244
Reply from 210.238.29.1: bytes=32 time=40ms TTL=244

Ping statistics for 210.238.29.1:
    Packets: Sent = 4, Received = 4, Lost = 0 (0% loss),
Approximate round trip times in milli-seconds:
    Minimum = 40ms, Maximum =  60ms, Average =  45ms

C:\WINDOWS>
```

If you cannot connect:

• Reconfigure NAT on Linux (see step 5 on page 163).

If the ping to Linux from Windows and the ping to an Internet host from Linux receive replies, but the ping to an Internet host from Windows does not, NAT on Linux may not be configured properly.

How A Proxy Server Works

Squid

If you use a proxy server (called *Squid*), whenever multiple users within a LAN view the same Web page, access speed can be increased by means of the effective use of cached data. Most of the data exchanged on the Internet is Web data. By using Squid, the number of external accesses for Web data can be reduced.

This will, in turn, lighten the load on the line that connects your LAN to the Internet and make surfing the Web more enjoyable.

Role Of A Proxy

If you use a proxy server when viewing Web pages, if the Web page you want to access has recently been accessed by someone using the same proxy server, it will be served up immediately from the cache. A cache is an area for temporarily storing data to increase access speed. Because an internal network is normally much faster than an external connection, the response will be much faster. Additionally, the load on your line to your ISP will be reduced.

For example, if the speed of the connection provided by your fractional T1 is 128Kbps, internal communications will be significantly faster than external communications, because the speed of an internal network is 10Mbps or 100Mbps.

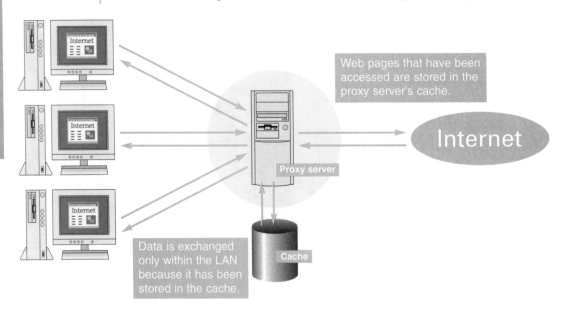

Web pages that have been accessed are stored in the proxy server's cache.

Internet

Proxy server

Data is exchanged only within the LAN because it has been stored in the cache.

Cache

If The Data Is Not Stored In The Cache

If the data requested by the client is not stored in the cache, Squid accesses the Web server located on the Internet, downloads the Web page, and delivers it to the client. Squid also stores the downloaded data in the cache automatically at this time.

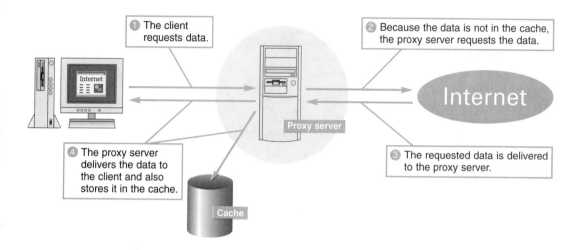

① The client requests data.

② Because the data is not in the cache, the proxy server requests the data.

Proxy server

Internet

④ The proxy server delivers the data to the client and also stores it in the cache.

③ The requested data is delivered to the proxy server.

Cache

If The Data Is Stored In The Cache

If the data requested by the client is stored in the cache, Squid delivers it to the client.

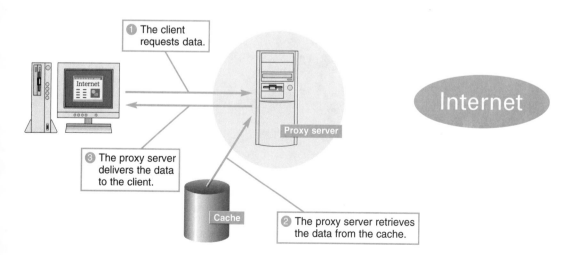

① The client requests data.

Proxy server

Internet

③ The proxy server delivers the data to the client.

Cache

② The proxy server retrieves the data from the cache.

Creating A Proxy Server

Installing Squid

Squid's large number of configuration settings
may be disconcerting at first, but only a limited
number of items need editing.
This book follows the standard configuration,
using port number 8080 and limiting access to
internal clients.

1 Mount the included CD-ROM.

1 Insert the included CD-ROM.

2 Enter the command.

Note: If the CD-ROM has already been mounted, this step is unnecessary.

```
[root@server /root]# mount /mnt/cdrom⏎
[root@server /root]# _
```

2 Install Squid.

Enter the command.

```
[root@server /root]# mount /mnt/cdrom
[root@server /root]# rpm -i /mnt/cdrom/RedHat/RPMS/squid-2.2.STABLE1-1.i386.rpm⏎
[root@server /root]# _
```

Squid is installed.

3 Open the configuration file.

1 Change directory.

```
[root@server /root]# cd /etc/squid⏎
[root@server squid]# vigr squid.conf⏎
```

2 Enter the command.

TIP!

vi Searches

To search in **vi** or **vigr**, specify "/" or "?" followed by the search string. To repeat the search, use "n" or "N".

 Modify the configuration file.

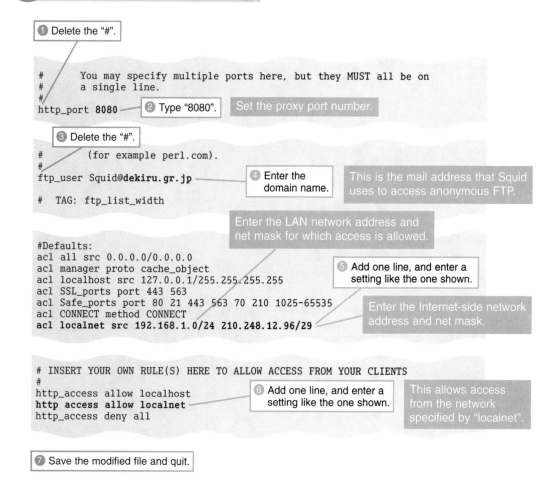

❶ Delete the "#".

```
#        You may specify multiple ports here, but they MUST all be on
#        a single line.
#
http_port 8080
```
❷ Type "8080". — Set the proxy port number.

❸ Delete the "#".
```
#          (for example perl.com).
#
ftp_user Squid@dekiru.gr.jp

#  TAG: ftp_list_width
```
❹ Enter the domain name. — This is the mail address that Squid uses to access anonymous FTP.

Enter the LAN network address and net mask for which access is allowed.

```
#Defaults:
acl all src 0.0.0.0/0.0.0.0
acl manager proto cache_object
acl localhost src 127.0.0.1/255.255.255.255
acl SSL_ports port 443 563
acl Safe_ports port 80 21 443 563 70 210 1025-65535
acl CONNECT method CONNECT
acl localnet src 192.168.1.0/24 210.248.12.96/29
```
❺ Add one line, and enter a setting like the one shown.

Enter the Internet-side network address and net mask.

```
# INSERT YOUR OWN RULE(S) HERE TO ALLOW ACCESS FROM YOUR CLIENTS
#
http_access allow localhost
http access allow localnet
http_access deny all
```
❻ Add one line, and enter a setting like the one shown.

This allows access from the network specified by "localnet".

❼ Save the modified file and quit.

TIP!

What Is Port Number 8080?

An IP address and a port number are used when accessing something in TCP/IP. The port number is a 16-bit integer. Each service in TCP/IP uses a different port number. Number 8080 is often used for a Web proxy server.

5 Start Squid.

① Enter the command.   ② Press [Enter].

```
[root@server squid]# /etc/rc.d/init.d/squid start↵
Starting squid: init_cache_dir /var/spool/squid... squid
[root@server squid]# squid[656]: Squid Parent: child process 657 started

[root@server squid]# _
```

The proxy server is now installed.

6 Configure Squid to boot automatically.

① Enter the command.

Configure Squid so that it starts automatically when you boot Linux.

```
[root@server squid]# squid[656]: Squid Parent: child process 657 started
[root@server squid]# cd /etc/rc.d/rc3.d↵
[root@server rc3.d]# ln -s ../init.d/squid S90squid↵
[root@server rc3.d]# _
```

② Enter the command.

To get all of the details about Squid or Apache, including the latest news and latest stable version of the program, visit their Web page:

www.squid-cache.org

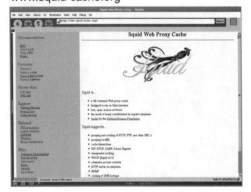

www.apache.org

TIP!

LAN Cache Server

If you are considering operating a LAN with more than a dozen or so PCs, consider using a cache server. For low-cost and moderate performance, consider the Squid cache or Apache caching server on a PC running Linux.

Configuring The Client

1 Configure the Web browser.

❸ Enter your proxy server hostname.

❹ Enter "8080".

❶ Select the Connections tab.

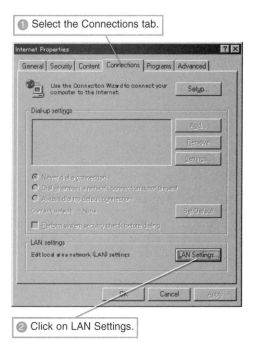

❷ Click on LAN Settings.

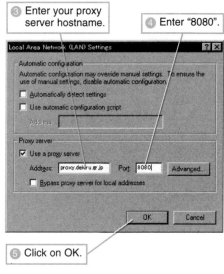

❺ Click on OK.

2 View a Web page.

The Web page is displayed.

TIP!

LAN Cache Server Minimum requiremets

A Pentium or 486 PC with a 1GB disk (monitor not required) is recommended as the minimum hardware configuration for a cache server.

STEP UP

Advantages Of Using NAT

Computers or other devices within a LAN that have not been assigned global IP addresses on the Internet can, nevertheless, access the Internet by using NAT. Does this mean that the computers or devices within the LAN also can be accessed from the Internet?

NAT accesses the Internet by temporarily substituting the IP address of the host on which NAT is running for the private IP address of each computer or device within the LAN that is not directly connected to the Internet. Even if the LAN contains multiple computers, all accesses to the Internet from them will be carried out by substituting the single IP address of the host on which NAT is running. Because NAT keeps track of all accesses from within the LAN, whenever a response to an access is returned from anywhere on the Internet, NAT searches its memory to determine the private IP address of the computer within the LAN that initiated the contact and routes the returning data to that computer. The different private addresses of all of the machines on the LAN are replaced by the one global IP address of the NAT host. Because only the IP address of the host on which NAT is running is visible from the Internet, the computers or devices within the LAN cannot be identified from the Internet side. Therefore, access to a device within the LAN cannot normally occur from the Internet side.

Enabling free access to your computer on the Internet means that your machine is vulnerable to hacker attacks. On the other hand, a server cannot provide services unless it can be accessed freely from external locations. Because a user's PC is not normally used as an Internet server, however, external locations need not be given free access to it. NAT is appropriate for such machines because it allows free access to outside locations, but not vice versa.

Chapter 10
Operating A Secure Internet Server

The job isn't over after the Internet server is built. To operate the Internet server the administrator must focus on security issues and take the proper measures to correct any problems that arise. This chapter describes the minimum that an administrator must know.

Contents Of This Chapter

Protecting Your Internet Server From Unauthorized Access

Security

Because an Internet server is always connected to the Internet, it is exposed to attacks by *crackers* (people who access computers illegally). In particular, if you are not careful enough concerning security (because remote operations are easily performed in Linux), your machine may be used as a stepping stone for attacking another site.

This section covers a variety of topics, ranging from general background information to methods of actually restricting access to protect your Internet server from attacks by crackers.

What Is Security?

Whenever you have a computer or device connected to the Internet, you must think about security. An Internet server is exposed to serious danger because it can always be accessed from anywhere on the Internet. Attacks on servers come in a variety of types and gradations:

Intrusion

This type of attack includes stealing private or confidential information, arbitrarily changing or deleting data, and changing configuration settings. An intrusion attack may also prevent you from being able to configure security measures by rewriting configuration programs to facilitate the next intrusion.

Using A Site As A Stepping Stone For Attacking Another Site

To protect their identities, crackers often plan an attack on one site via multiple other sites they have penetrated so that either no trail remains or the trail is too complex to follow.

Denial Of Service

This type of attack halts service. There are various types of Denial Of Service (DoS) attacks. Usually, a DoS attack produces an unnatural condition, and there seem to be many elaborate ones that probe for weaknesses to exploit.

Security Holes

A cracker can launch an attack by striking at a weak point in a server's security setup. This weak point is called a *security hole*.

Security holes can be broadly divided into two main types: holes caused by administrator negligence or mis-configuration, and holes caused by problems in the server.

● Administration- or configuration-related security holes

    Actions: Check the configuration files again, and do not run services that are not needed.

● Software-related security holes

    Actions: Pay attention to update information and upgrade the software version immediately if any problems are detected.

Remember not to run servers or services that you are not using. This is just plain common sense. It would be a waste of time and effort to worry about the security of these unused servers and services. You probably would not want to upgrade the versions of these servers constantly even if a security hole were known. You may not need to use all of the servers described in this book.

The server administrator should institute security measures in the following ways.

• Restrict access (prevents access before reaching the server).

• Encrypt passwords (prevents access by someone impersonating a user).

• Upgrade software versions (eliminates security holes due to software bugs).

• Check logs (monitors suspicious accesses).

When A Server Is Not Protected By Security   When A Server Is Protected By Security

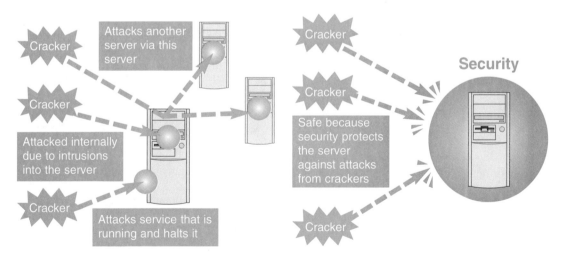

Restricting Access By Using tcpd

Restricting the computers or networks that can access each server is an effective security measure. Servers that use inetd (such as qpopper, ftpd, and telnetd) are configured by the inetd.conf file, so that software for restricting access, called *tcpd* (tcp_wrapers), is made to intervene. Therefore, tcpd functions should be used to restrict access. The tcpd software has two configuration files named /etc/hosts.allow and etc/hosts.deny. For security, let's try to configure these files so that all accesses are denied by default and accesses from the local area network (LAN) are specifically permitted.

① Enter the command.

```
[root@server /root]# vi /etc/hosts.deny⏎
```

```
# you should know that NFS uses portmap!
ALL: ALL
```

Setting this denies all accesses by default.

② Type "ALL: ALL".

③ Enter the command.

```
[root@server /root]# vi /etc/hosts.allow⏎
```

Setting this allows all accesses from your own network.

```
#                    by the '/usr/sbin/tcpd' server.
#
ALL: LOCAL
ALL: 192.168.1.0/255.255.255.0 210.248.12.96/255.255.255.248
```

④ Enter the specifications as shown.

On the left side of the colon (:) is a word that is at the end of a line in the inetd.conf file. For example, the setting for a post office protocol (POP) server would be "popper" and the setting for telnet would be "in.telnetd". The command file name of the server program is "popper" or "in.telnetd". Use the entry that follows /usr/sbin/tcpd on each line of the /etc/inetd.conf file.

Use the entry written here.

```
# These are standard services.
#
ftp     stream  tcp  nowait  root  /usr/sbin/tcpd  in.ftpd -l -a
telnet  stream  tcp  nowait  root  /usr/sbin/tcpd  in.telnetd
```

If "ALL" is specified here, the setting is for all servers. On the right side of the colon (:), you can write a hostname or IP address, a notation representing a network, or the like.

Entries That Can Be Written Before The Colon

Server name (word at the end of each line of the inetd.conf file)
    "ALL"   This indicates all servers.
    "EXCEPT"   Entries following this keyword are excluded.

Entries That Can Be Written After The Colon

Address (hostname or IP address) of destination client:

"ALL"	This indicates all addresses.
"LOCAL"	This can be used when the domain name is the same.
Network specification	(210.248.12.96/255.255.255.248)
Network abbreviation	(192/168.1.)
Domain name specification	(.dekiru.gr.jp)
"EXCEPT"	Entries following this keyword are excluded.

Use the **tcpdchk** and **tcpdmatch** commands to verify the settings. If you use **tcpdchk**, you can find syntax mistakes in the hosts.allow and hosts.deny files.

```
[root@server /root]# tcpdchk⏎
warning: /etc/hosts.allow, line 7: 192.168.1.0/255.255.0: bad net/mask pattern
[root@server /root]# _
```

This tells you that the netmask is invalid.

Correct the net mask in the hosts.allow file to "255.255.255.0".

This message indicates that line 7 of the /etc/hosts.allow file is invalid. If the syntax is correct, nothing will be displayed when **tcpdchk** is executed.

```
[root@server /root]# tcpdmatch popper 192.168.1.1⏎
client:    address   192.168.1.1
server:    process   popper
matched:   /etc/hosts.allow line 7
access:    granted
[root@server /root]# _
```

This is a test for when the POP server is accessed from 192.168.1.1.

"granted" indicates that access is allowed.

```
[root@server /root]# tcpdmatch in.ftpd 192.168.2.1⏎
client:    address   192.168.2.1
server:    process   in.ftpd
matched:   /etc/hosts.deny line 9
access:    denied
[root@server /root]# _
```

This is a test for when the FTP server is accessed from 192.168.2.1.

"denied" indicates that access is denied.

Encrypting Passwords

Reason For Passwords

A *password* is an important key for proving the identity of a user. If the password is stolen, a cracker can do anything that the user is able to do. Therefore, it is extremely important to prevent passwords from being disclosed to outside sources.

Password data is sent through the network at various times. First, let's learn where password data goes when certain actions are taken. When we know this, we can think about security and decide what measures must be taken.

Services That Use Passwords And Services That Do Not

Among the servers described in this book, most of those that use passwords (such as FTP or POP) send usernames and passwords as clear text (not encrypted). Therefore, these servers should be restricted to access from clients inside the LAN.

Telnet or File Transfer Protocol (FTP)

The username and password are sent as clear text. Because entered commands and displayed characters are also sent unchanged, the use of these services from an external site is dangerous. You should restrict access so that it is limited to connections from internal clients.

Anonymous FTP

The username and password are sent as clear text. Because the username is "anonymous" and the password is your own mail address, however, no problem will occur even if they are stolen. Although commands (such as **cd** or **ls**) and file data that are transferred are also sent as clear text, no problem will occur as long as you are using a server that is publicly available via anonymous FTP.

POP or Internet Message Access Protocol (IMAP)

The username and password are sent as clear text. Mail is sent in a form in which the contents can be read directly. The use of these services from an external site is dangerous. You should restrict access so that it is limited to connections from internal clients.

APOP

The username is sent in clear text, but the password is encrypted. Mail is sent in a form in which the contents can be read directly. Usually, this is better than using POP.

Simple Mail Transfer Protocol (SMTP)

SMTP doesn't use usernames or passwords. Mail is sent and received in a form in which the contents can be read directly.

Hypertext Transfer Protocol (HTTP)

Normally, HTTP doesn't use usernames or passwords. If a Web page is created with an access restriction whereby passwords must be entered, all passwords are sent directly in clear text. Therefore, HTTP password authentication should only be used when this limitation is clearly understood.

Domain Name Service (DNS)

The information that is exchanged is not encrypted. However, this is safe because no usernames or passwords are exchanged.

Upgrading The Software Version

You cannot rectify a security hole due to a problem with the software itself merely by paying attention to the configuration settings. To eliminate this kind of security hole, you must make it a top priority to check software information everyday.

A security hole in the software itself is rarely discovered at the time of an attack on your system. Most attacks actually occur after the security hole has been announced and before the administrator of each site is able to take measures to correct it.

You can prevent these attacks by upgrading your software quickly to the latest version that includes a fix for the announced security holes.

How To Use ncftp

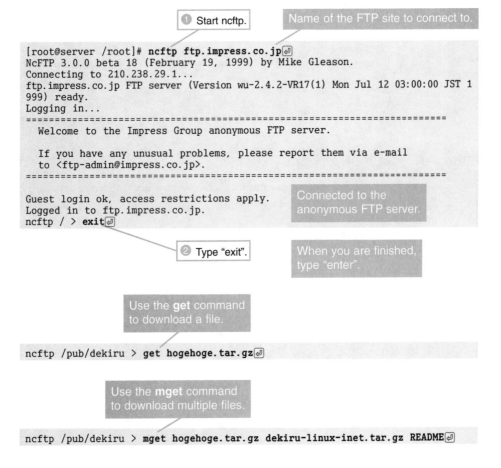

❶ Start ncftp.

Name of the FTP site to connect to.

```
[root@server /root]# ncftp ftp.impress.co.jp⏎
NcFTP 3.0.0 beta 18 (February 19, 1999) by Mike Gleason.
Connecting to 210.238.29.1...
ftp.impress.co.jp FTP server (Version wu-2.4.2-VR17(1) Mon Jul 12 03:00:00 JST 1
999) ready.
Logging in...
=========================================================================
  Welcome to the Impress Group anonymous FTP server.

  If you have any unusual problems, please report them via e-mail
  to <ftp-admin@impress.co.jp>.
=========================================================================

Guest login ok, access restrictions apply.
Logged in to ftp.impress.co.jp.
ncftp / > exit⏎
```

Connected to the anonymous FTP server.

❷ Type "exit".

When you are finished, type "enter".

Use the **get** command to download a file.

```
ncftp /pub/dekiru > get hogehoge.tar.gz⏎
```

Use the **mget** command to download multiple files.

```
ncftp /pub/dekiru > mget hogehoge.tar.gz dekiru-linux-inet.tar.gz README⏎
```

---
ncftp Command Reference

Startup Methods ————————————

ncftp	Starts ncftp.
ncftp host_name	Starts ncftp, and specifies an FTP site.
ncftp -u user_name host_name	Logs in by using the specified username.

open Commands ————————————

open host_name	Connects to an FTP site.
open -u user_name host_name	Logs in by using the specified username.

Changing The Mode ————————————

ascii	Changes to text mode.
binary	Changes to binary mode.

Changing Or Confirming The Directory ——

cd	Changes the directory.
ls	Displays a list of files.
dir	Displays a detailed list of files.
pwd	Displays the current (present working) directory.

Changing Or Confirming The Local Directory

lcd	Changes the directory.
lls	Displays a list of files.
lpwd	Displays the current (present working) directory.

Changing Or Inspecting A File ————————

get	Downloads a file.
mget	Downloads multiple files.
page	Inspects a text file.
put	Uploads a file.
mput	Uploads multiple files.

help Commands ————————————

help	Displays a list of available commands.
help command	Displays help for the specified command.

Exiting ————————————

quit, **exit**, or **bye**	Exits ncftp.
close	Closes the connection.

Discovering An Unauthorized Entry

Looking at logs isn't a definitive means of discovering unauthorized access. If an intrusion has really occurred and the root authority has been taken over, the intruder will probably have destroyed all traces. There will be nothing remaining to be discovered, even if you inspect the logs. Looking at logs, however, is effective in discovering illegal access, which precedes unauthorized intrusion and occurs before the root authority has been usurped. If anything seems suspicious, check the access logs first.

/var/log/boot.log	Log of the starting and stopping of daemons.
/var/log/cron	Log of crond (daemon for routinely executing commands).
/var/log/dmesg	Kernel messages.
/var/log/maillog	Log of Sendmail or imapd.
var/log/messages	Log of Berkeley Internet name domain (BIND), the kernel, su, or the like.
/var/log/secure	Login records or log of tcpd.

/var/log/xferlog	Log of ftpd.
/usr/local/www/logs/access_log	Access log of Apache.
/usr/local/www/logs/error_log	Error log of Apache.
/var/log/squid/access.log	Access log of Squid.
/var/log/squid/cache.log	Log related to Squid operations.
/var/log/squid/store.log	Log related to Squid cache preservation.

You can also use the **last** command to check the user login records.

```
[root@server /root]# last⏎
watanabe tty1              Mon Jul 12 04:03    still logged in
watanabe pts/5             Mon Jul 12 04:03 - 04:03  (00:00)
watanabe pts/3             Mon Jul 12 04:03 - 04:03  (00:00)

wtmp begins Thu Jul  1 04:03:36 1999
[root@server /root]# _
```

Useful Server Security Web Sites

Red Hat, Inc.
www.redhat.com
This site has errata (bug) information announced by Red Hat, Inc. and links to update information. The errata information describes ways to deal with security holes.

CERT/CC
www.cert.org
Besides publishing various kinds of security information, this site accepts reports of actual attacks and enables you to participate in discussions.

Linux Online
www.linux.org
This site has links to reference sites related to Linux.

FreeBSD
www.freebsd.org
This is a site for FreeBSD, which is another PC-Unix operating system(OS). Even though the OS differs, because many of the software packages used with Unix are the same, there is a lot of information in common.

Minimizing Internet Server Problems

Backups

If a problem that causes your Internet server to stop working occurs, a backup can be a lifesaver.

If you routinely make backups of the configuration files, they will come in handy when you reinstall Linux or when you must reconfigure a configuration file that was inadvertently overwritten, rendering your Internet server inopera-

ble. Also, if you back up user data or the contents of a Web server in advance, you can limit the loss if the server is damaged.

How To Verify The Size Of The File System

Use the **df** command to check the amount of free space remaining in a mounted filesystem.

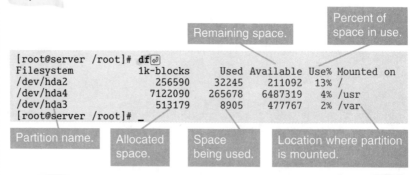

Remaining space.

Percent of space in use.

```
[root@server /root]# df⏎
Filesystem          1k-blocks      Used  Available  Use% Mounted on
/dev/hda2              256590     32245     211092   13% /
/dev/hda4             7122090    265678    6487319    4% /usr
/dev/hda3              513179      8905     477767    2% /var
[root@server /root]# _
```

Partition name.

Allocated space.

Space being used.

Location where partition is mounted.

If the **df** command indicates to you that you are running out of space, you should delete unnecessary files first. Use the **du** command to check which directories are using space.

Enter the command.

Sorts the values by size, in ascending order.

```
[root@server /root]# du -xS /var | sort -n⏎
1       /var
1       /var/catman
```

```
324     /var/spool/squid/00/00
4085    /var/lib/rpm
[root@server /root]# _
```

Sizes and directory names are displayed.

Backing Up Configuration Files

A convenient method of backing up configuration files is to create a list of the configuration files, and then use the **tar** command to consolidate them in a single file.

1 Create a backup file list.

① Enter the command.

```
[root@server /root]# vi etc-list⏎
```

② Enter the file names for which a backup is to be made.

The files in this list are backed up.

Note: Be sure to enter the absolute path for each file name.

```
/etc/passwd
/etc/group
/etc/shadow
/etc/inetd.conf
/etc/sendmail.cf
/usr/local/src/CF-3.7Wpl2/sendmail.def
/etc/aliases
/etc/pop.auth
/etc/dhcpd.conf
/etc/hosts.allow
/etc/hosts.deny
/etc/named.conf
/etc/namedb
/etc/conf.modules
/etc/sysconfig/network-scripts/ifcfg-eth0
/etc/sysconfig/network-scripts/ifcfg-eth1
/etc/squid/squid.conf
/usr/local/etc/apache/httpd.conf
/etc/rc.d/init.d/httpd
/etc/rc.d/init.d/ipmasq
```

③ Save the file and quit.

2 Compress the files.

Note: Depending on the number of files to be backed up and their sizes, it may take some time to complete this step.

Enter the command.　Enter the name of the backup file.　The created list file is read.

```
[root@server /root]# tar cvfzT /tmp/bakup-etc.tar.gz etc-list⏎
tar: Removing leading '/' from absolute path names in the archive
etc/passwd
etc/group
```

```
etc/rc.d/init.d/ipmasq
[root@server /root]# _
```

The configuration files are backed up.

WARNING! This file contains some files that could only be read by a limited number of users originally. Store it carefully in a location that can only be read only by the administrator.

Restoring Configuration Files

To restore configuration files that have been saved, expand the configuration files and then copy them. If a problem occurs and you have to build the server again, using the configuration files that had been backed up enables you to build the server with the same configuration that you used previously.

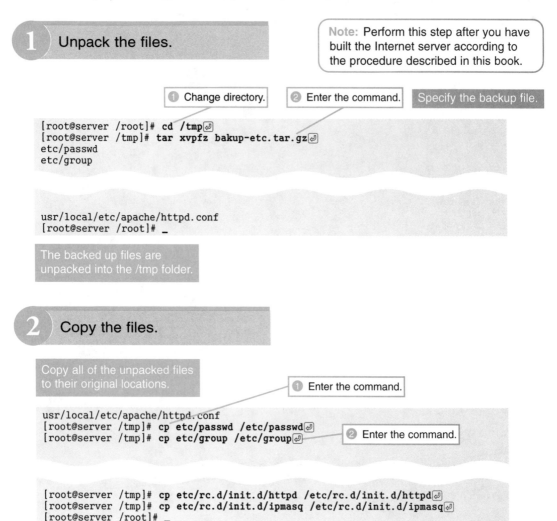

1 Unpack the files.

Note: Perform this step after you have built the Internet server according to the procedure described in this book.

① Change directory. ② Enter the command. Specify the backup file.

```
[root@server /root]# cd /tmp⏎
[root@server /tmp]# tar xvpfz bakup-etc.tar.gz⏎
etc/passwd
etc/group
```

```
usr/local/etc/apache/httpd.conf
[root@server /root]# _
```

The backed up files are unpacked into the /tmp folder.

2 Copy the files.

Copy all of the unpacked files to their original locations.

① Enter the command.

```
usr/local/etc/apache/httpd.conf
[root@server /tmp]# cp etc/passwd /etc/passwd⏎
[root@server /tmp]# cp etc/group /etc/group⏎
```

② Enter the command.

```
[root@server /tmp]# cp etc/rc.d/init.d/httpd /etc/rc.d/init.d/httpd⏎
[root@server /tmp]# cp etc/rc.d/init.d/ipmasq /etc/rc.d/init.d/ipmasq⏎
[root@server /root]# _
```

Backing Up Data Files

The home directory data and the Web data of users is placed in the /home or /usr/local/www directory, respectively. Saving all of the data in these directories will create data backups.

```
[root@server /root]# cd /usr/local/src⏎
[root@server src]# tar cvfz home-bak.tar.gz /home⏎
tar : Removing leading '/' from absolute path names in the archive
home/
```

```
home/hide/.bashrc
[root@server src]# cd /usr/local⏎
[root@server local]# tar cvfz src/www-bak.tar.gz www⏎
www/
```

```
www/proxy
[root@server local]# _
```

With the commands given previously, the data in the /home and in /usr/local/www
directories is saved in the backup files home-bak.tar.gz and www-bak.tar.gz under
/usr/local/src. You can copy these backup files to another location for safe keeping.
Any location is fine as long as the files can be extracted if the server is damaged.
However, these files should probably be transferred off the server to a client PC using
the FTP server.

Installing The FTP Server

If the FTP server hasn't been installed yet, it is difficult to transfer the backup files to
another location. Use the **rpm** command to install the FTP server on Linux.

| Enter the command. | Install the server called "wu-ftpd". |

```
[root@server /root]# rpm -i /mnt/cdrom/RedHat/RPMS/wu-ftpd-2.4.2vr17-3.i386.rpm⏎
[root@server /root]#
```

To log in to the FTP server, use the username and password of a Linux user. You cannot log in as root, so use your usual username and password.

Restoring Data Files

When restoring files that had been backed up, if you directly expand the backed-up
data, new data may be overwritten. To prevent this, rename the original directory
before using the **tar** command to expand the files.

| Change the name of the existing /home directory to make a backup. | Unpack the backup file. |

```
[root@server /root]# cd /⏎
[root@server /]# mv home home.old⏎
[root@server /]# tar xvpfz /usr/local/src/home-bak.tar.gz⏎
```

189

Managing Mail So That
It Can Be Used Without Worry

Mail

When an Internet server is used, various problems can arise. The server has a feature that sends mail to a special account (root or postmaster) automatically to report an incident if a problem occurs.

Also, the root or postmaster account is used as a service center for complaints or requests from external administrators or users.

Therefore, configure the mail server so that mail addressed to its special account will be transferred to the regular account of the administrator so that problems can be dealt with as soon as they occur.

Mail Not Reaching Its Destination

If you use the sendmail.cf settings to over-restrict a network that is using a mail server, mail may not be able to be delivered to its external destination. In this case, an error message is displayed in the user's mail client. Return to Chapter 7 and recheck the configuration settings.

In a different case, when Sendmail cannot deliver the mail to its intended destination, Sendmail sends an error message to the sender with some explanation of the delivery failure. Error messages that occur relatively often are "User Unknown" or "Host Unknown." These indicate that an invalid destination address was used in the mail that was sent.

The error message that is mailed to the sender includes the full text of the mail that was sent. An error message that omits the text of the original mail is also mailed to the postmaster mail account at the same time. Therefore, if the administrator sets up the mail server so that postmaster-addressed mail is, by default, sent to the address that the administrator ordinarily uses, the administrator can keep track of mail server errors.

Not Receiving Mail From Someone Outside Your LAN

There are several reasons why mail cannot be received from someone outside your LAN.

The Spool Is Full

Mail is temporarily stored in a spool file at /var/spool/mail. If the **df** command tells you that the /var filesystem is full, use the **du** command to find unnecessary files in /var and delete them. (See Section 10.2.)

Also, if a large volume of mail is accumulated in the spool file causing the mail spool to become extremely large, delete any totally unused user accounts. If a user wants to retain only the address of an unused mail account, you can transfer the mail to his normal account by using /etc/aliases.

A Remote Site Cannot Specify The SMTP Server Of Your Local Domain

If the MX record of the DNS server is invalid, a remote server cannot identify your local mail server, and the mail cannot be sent. Use the **nslookup** command (see Chapter 6) to verify the MX record.

The Sendmail Configuration Is Invalid

This condition results in the inability to receive mail. Return to Chapter 7 and check the sendmail.cf configuration settings to see if Sendmail has been configured to receive mail addressed to your own domain.

Mail Addressed To Special Accounts

Mail that is addressed to the special accounts named postmaster, Webmaster, root, and MAILER-DAEMON may contain important information. This mail should be transferred to the administrator's actual account by using /etc/aliases so the administrator will read it. See Chapter 7 for information about /etc/aliases.

Mail From Other Administrators Or Users

If you are managing a server, you will be sent mail addressed to postmaster or Webmaster from other administrators or users. This mail may contain complaints or ongoing discussions. Dealing with this kind of mail is an important role of an administrator. Try to respond to everything other than SPAM or other questionable mail.

Dealing With Problems

Network Problems

If the server or network connections seem to be acting strangely, the administrator must do something to rectify the situation. The following section describes techniques for dealing with some network problems.
Try to avoid rebooting the server unless there is absolutely no other choice. Restart only the program wherein you think there is a problem (such as the DNS or Web server) without rebooting the Linux OS.

When You Cannot Connect To The Network

If you cannot connect to the network, the hardware may be at fault. Check the connections on the cables, hub, and router.

- **Is the cable loose?**
  Insert the cable firmly until you hear a click. Check the hub, router, or network card LEDs.

- **Is the hub or router turned on?**
  Check the power LED of the hub and router.

- **Is a hub port that cannot be used at the same time as a cascade port being used?**
  If the cable is connected to a port that cannot be used at the same time as a cascade port, the network will not be able to use any equipment that is connected to that hub.

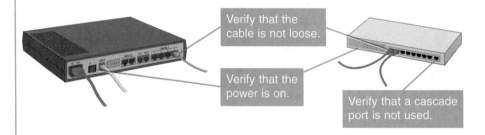

Verify that the cable is not loose.

Verify that the power is on.

Verify that a cascade port is not used.

- **Is a crossover cable being used?**
  A crossover cable is used to connect two network cards directly in a one-to-one fashion. Use a straight cable when connecting to the hub.

Verifying That The Network Is Connected

The **ping** command determines whether you are able to communicate with another host on the network by means of IP. Executing the **ping** command to discover if you can reach another machine is called *pinging* that machine.

To verify that the networks are connected, ping various locations from Linux. You can also ping another machine from a Windows or Unix client, not just from Linux.

When you ping a machine, you can check to see that the LED of the related hub or router is blinking at fixed intervals.

Pinging The Internet Side

Execute **ping** from the Windows client.

Enter the command.

```
C:\WINDOWS>ping www.impress.co.jp↵

Pinging impgw.impress.co.jp [210.238.29.1] with 32 bytes of data:

Reply from 210.238.29.1: bytes=32 time=39ms TTL=242
Reply from 210.238.29.1: bytes=32 time=36ms TTL=243
Reply from 210.238.29.1: bytes=32 time=36ms TTL=243
Reply from 210.238.29.1: bytes=32 time=36ms TTL=243

Ping statistics for 210.238.29.1:
    Packets: Sent = 4, Received = 4, Lost = 0 (0% loss),
Approximate round trip times in milli-seconds:
    Minimum = 36ms, Maximum = 39ms, Average = 36ms

C:\WINDOWS> _
```

If you get a response, the client is connected to the Internet.

Pinging The LAN Side

Enter the command.

```
C:\WINDOWS>ping 192.168.1.1↵

Pinging 192.168.1.1 with 32 bytes of data:

Reply from 192.168.1.1: bytes=32 time=1ms TTL=255
Reply from 192.168.1.1: bytes=32 time<10ms TTL=255
Reply from 192.168.1.1: bytes=32 time<10ms TTL=255
Reply from 192.168.1.1: bytes=32 time<10ms TTL=255

Ping statistics for 192.168.1.1:
    Packets: Sent = 4, Received = 4, Lost = 0 (0% loss),
Approximate round trip times in milli-seconds:
    Minimum = 0ms, Maximum = 1ms, Average = 0ms

C:\WINDOWS> _
```

If you get a response, the client is connected to the LAN.

If The ping Results Are Odd

If the ping results make you think Linux is acting strangely, return to Chapter 9 and check the following files:

/etc/conf.modules
/etc/sysconfig/network
/etc/sysconfig/network-scripts/ifcfg-eth0
/etc/sysconfig/network-scripts/ifcfg-eth1

Reinitialize any changes you have made.

```
[root@server /root]# /etc/rc.d/init.d/network restart↵
Shutting down interface eth0                              [  OK  ]
Shutting down interface eth1                              [  OK  ]
Disabling IPv4 packet forwarding                          [  OK  ]
Enabling IPv4 packet forwarding                           [  OK  ]
Bringing up interface lo                                  [  OK  ]
Bringing up interface eth0                                [  OK  ]
Bringing up interface eth1                                [  OK  ]
[root@server /root]# _
```

If a ping doesn't pass from the LAN side to the Internet side, the network address translator (NAT) configuration may be incorrect. Reconfigure NAT.

```
[root@server /root]# /etc/rc.d/init.d/ipmasq restart↵
```

Restarting Daemons

If a service isn't acting properly even though the network connection checks out, try restarting each server. If you changed the configuration, the changes may not go into effect until the service is restarted.

Service	Restart Method
BIND	ndc restart
Apache	/etc/rc.d/init.d/httpd restart
Sendmail	/etc/rc.d/init.d/sendmail restart
qpopper	/etc/rc.d/init.d/inet restart
FTP	/etc/rc.d/init.d/inet restart
dhcpd	/etc/rc.d/init.d/dhcpd restart
Squid	/etc/rc.d/init.d/squid restart
NAT	/etc/rc.d/init.d/ipmasq restart

How To Check For Active Programs

Use the **ps** command to determine which programs are running on your Linux system. The **ps** command enables you to determine whether each server is running.

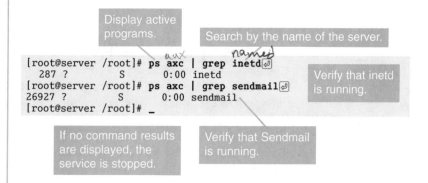

This method enables you to see servers that are started up from inetd (such as qpopper or ftpd) only while they are connected. Because NAT is implemented differently than the other servers, it is not listed when you run **ps**.

Search for ftpd.

```
[root@server /root]# ps axc | grep ftpd⏎
[root@server /root]# _
```

Because ftpd is started up by
a call from inetd, it is not listed.

STEP UP

Who Decides How The Internet Works?

The Internet relies on various protocols, conventions, and mechanisms, several of which were introduced in this book. Who decides how these are implemented? A committee called the Internet Engineering Task Force (IETF) decides the various protocols, conventions, and mechanisms the Internet uses. Anyone interested can participate in IETF meetings, and the results are consolidated in documents known as *Internet Drafts*.

If an Internet Draft is approved by a committee called the *Internet Architecture Board (IAB)*, it becomes a formal document called a *Request for Comments (RFC)*. Anyone can download both Internet Drafts and RFCs by anonymous FTP or HTTP. Serial numbers are assigned to RFCs. If you look for RFC #2068, for example, you will find the protocol specifications for HTTP version 1.1, currently in use on the Web.

Besides various kinds of Internet specifications, RFCs include summaries of other documents and introductory information called *FYIs (For Your Information)* that provide explanations, questions and answers (Q&As), and a history of the Internet. RFCs also include specific standards (STD) that have been approved for the Internet. Serial numbers are also assigned to STDs. If you have any questions concerning the Internet or if there is anything you specifically want to know, you should read the appropriate RFC first.

The most significant factor in RFCs and STDs being approved as formal specifications on the Internet is that programs or devices are actually operating according to these specifications, not whether the specifications seem logically correct. A standard is really just something that is commonly used and operates correctly. This is illustrated by the frequently used line, "It is a de facto standard on the Internet."

IAB   www.iab.org
IETF   www.ietf.org

How To Configure A Windows Client PC

Adding A Network Card To A Desktop Personal Computer

1 Insert the network card into the Windows PC.

Insert the network card into the client PC.

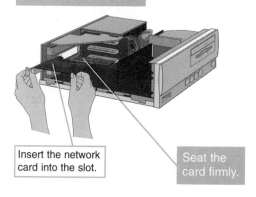

Insert the network card into the slot.

Seat the card firmly.

2 Connect the network cable to the PC.

◆ Network card connector

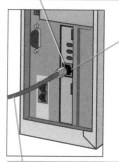

Connect the network cable to the network card in the PC.

After connecting the cable, turn on the computer.

The network cable connects to the router.

3 Turn on the PC.

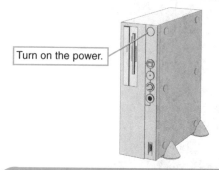

Turn on the power.

4 The network card is recognized.

When Windows is booted, the network card is recognized automatically.

New Hardware

PCI Ethernet DEC 21041 Based Adapter

Window is installing the software for your new hardware.

5 Install the driver.

Caution: Each different network card has its own dedicated driver disk. Prepare the driver disk that was packaged with the network card and follow the instructions.

The driver is installed as necessary.

Copying Files...

Source:
Windows 98 CD-ROM
Destination:
C:\WINDOWS\SYSTEM\MSWSOSP.DLL

66%

Cancel

Reboot Windows.

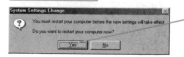

System Settings Change

You must restart your computer before the new settings will take effect.

Do you want to restart your computer now?

Yes   No

Click on Yes.

Adding A Network Card To A Notebook PC

1 Insert the network card into the notebook PC.

Prepare a PCMCIA-type network card.

Insert the card into the PCMCIA card slot.

2 The network adapter is recognized.

When Windows is booted, the network card is recognized automatically.

New Hardware

PCI Ethernet DEC 21041 Based Adapter

Windows is installing the software for your new hardware.

The driver is installed as necessary.

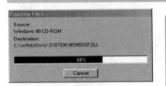

Copying Files...

Source:
Windows 98 CD-ROM
Destination:
C:\WINDOWS\SYSTEM\MSWSOSP.DLL

66%

Cancel

Caution:
A dedicated driver disk is required for the network card.

Reboot Windows.

System Settings Change

You must restart your computer before the new settings will take effect.
Do you want to restart your computer now?

Yes   No

Click on Yes.

Configuring The Network

1 Display the network properties.

Open items in the following order.

- Start menu
  - Settings
    - Control Panel
      - Network

2 Verify TCP/IP protocol.

Verify that TCP/IP is present.

Network

Configuration | Identification | Access Control

The following network components are installed:
Client for Microsoft Networks
3Com EtherLink 10/100 PCI NIC (3C905-TX)
NetBEUI
TCP/IP

Add...   Remove   Properties

Primary Network Logon:
Client for Microsoft Networks

File and Print Sharing

Description

OK   Cancel

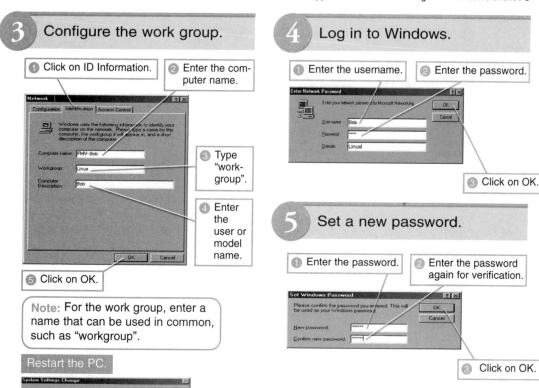

3 Configure the work group.

① Click on ID Information.

② Enter the computer name.

③ Type "workgroup".

④ Enter the user or model name.

⑤ Click on OK.

Note: For the work group, enter a name that can be used in common, such as "workgroup".

Restart the PC.

Click on Yes.

4 Log in to Windows.

① Enter the username.

② Enter the password.

③ Click on OK.

5 Set a new password.

① Enter the password.

② Enter the password again for verification.

③ Click on OK.

Adding TCP/IP Protocol

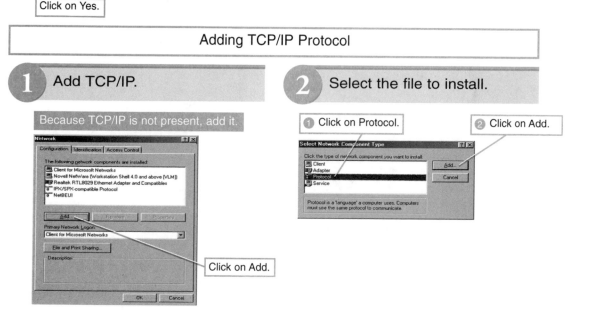

1 Add TCP/IP.

Because TCP/IP is not present, add it.

Click on Add.

2 Select the file to install.

① Click on Protocol.

② Click on Add.

3 Select the protocol to add.

① Click on Microsoft. ② Click on TCP/IP.

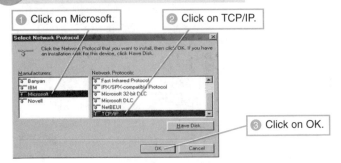

③ Click on OK.

Configuring The Local Area Network Connection

---

1 Set the method for connecting to the Internet.

If the PC had been using a dial-up connection to access the Internet, change the access method.

① Open items in the following order.

> 📁 Start menu
>> 🖥 Settings
>>> 🗔 Control Panel
>>>> 🌐 Internet

② Select the Connections tab bar.

③ Click on LAN Settings.

---

2 Enter the address of the proxy server.

Note: This will run based on the configuration of the proxy server described in Chapter 9.

① Enter your proxy server host name. ② Enter "8080".

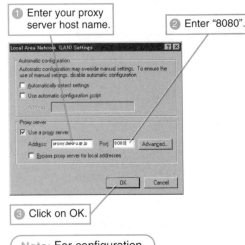

③ Click on OK.

Note: For configuration details, see Section 9.8.

Enabling A Macintosh To Connect To The Internet

1 Insert the network cable.

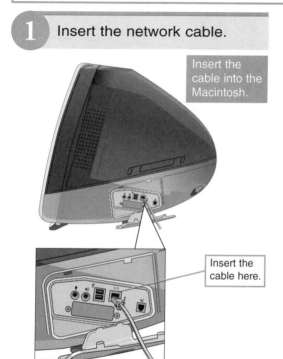

Insert the cable into the Macintosh.

Insert the cable here.

2 Start TCP/IP.

① Open items in the following order.

🍎 Apple menu
  🍎 Control Panel
    TCP/IP

A message asking whether TCP/IP is to be enabled appears.

TCP/IP is currently inactive.
Changes won't take effect until TCP/IP is made active again.

Make TCP/IP active when closing the control panel?

[No] [Yes]

② Click on Yes.

3 Change the TCP/IP setting.

③ Click on Close. ① Select Ethernet. ② Select Reference DHCP server.

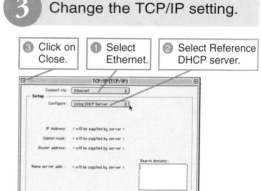

4 Save the settings.

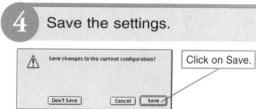

⚠ Save changes to the current configuration?

[Don't Save] [Cancel] [Save]

Click on Save.

TIP!

Proxy Server Configuration

Set the Web browser to use a proxy in accordance with the configuration of the proxy server described in Chapter 9.

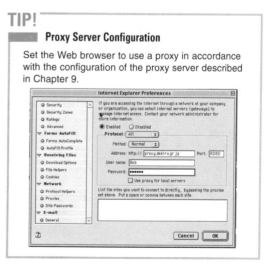

Appendix C | How To Configure The Mail Client

To use mail on a Windows or Macintosh client, configure the mail client software in accordance with your Internet server configurations. Because the mail client uses the Simple Mail Transfer Protocol (SMTP) server for sending mail and the Post Office Protocol (POP) server for retrieving mail, both servers must be configured. Also, to use mail, a user account must have already been created on the Linux machine. The username and password of the created user account are required to configure the mail client.

POP Server Name

Enter the alias for the POP server that you set in the Domain Name Service (DNS) server. If you configured the DNS server as described in this book, this alias will be "pop.*specified_domain_name*". In the example used in this book, it is "pop.dekiru.gr.jp".

SMTP Server Name

Enter the alias for the SMTP server that was set in the DNS server. If the DNS server has been configured as described in this book, this alias will be "smtp.*specified_domain_name*". In the example used in this book, it is "smtp.dekiru.gr.jp".

Mail Address

The mail address is "*Linux_user_name@specified_domain_name*". In the example used in this book, it is "bob@dekiru.gr.jp".

Account Name

The account name is the username that was added on the Linux server.

Password

This is the password corresponding to the username that was added on the Linux server. For APOP, use the password that was set by using the **popauth** command.

Outlook Express (Windows Version) Configuration Example

Enter a combination of the username and domain name as the mail address.

Enter the account name and password.

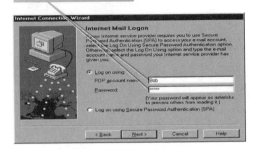

Enter the POP server name and the SMTP server name.

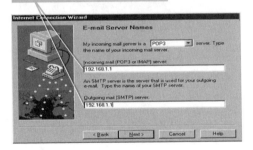

Outlook Express (Macintosh Version) Configuration Example

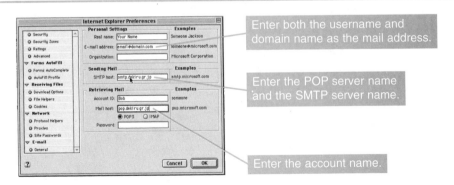

Enter both the username and domain name as the mail address.

Enter the POP server name and the SMTP server name.

Enter the account name.

At Least Two DNS Servers Are Required

At least two DNS servers are required to obtain a domain name. Because the DNS server provides the information needed to access your local domain to the Internet, it should always be running properly (24/7). If you prepare multiple DNS servers on separate computers, you need not worry if one DNS server starts acting strangely. Among the multiple DNS servers, the one that is the master is called the *primary DNS server*, and the slaves are *secondary DNS servers*. You can have more than one secondary DNS server.

The Primary-Secondary Relationship

For each domain, there are two or more DNS servers: one primary DNS server, and one or more secondary DNS servers. Because of the master-slave relationship between primary and secondary DNS servers, multiple DNS settings don't need to be completely rewritten each time a setting is changed. Each secondary DNS server updates its DNS settings by automatically referencing the data of the primary DNS server. Therefore, after the secondary DNS server has been properly configured, you need only modify the configuration file of the primary DNS server. Because the configuration of secondary DNS servers is simple, you can set up two or more secondary DNS servers easily. The transfer of domain data from the primary DNS server to a secondary DNS server is called a *zone transfer*.

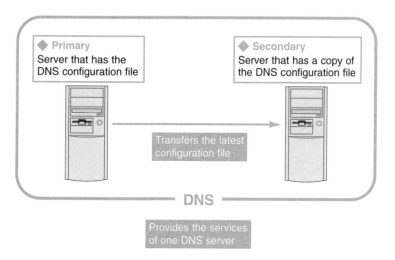

Constructing Two DNS Servers

The DNS server that you constructed according to the procedure described in Chapter 6 is a primary DNS server. Use the Berkeley Internet Name Domain (BIND) software in a similar manner to construct a secondary DNS server. Because a secondary DNS server copies domain data from the primary DNS server, you need to create a domain definition file that differs from that of the primary DNS server configuration. Specify the IP address of the primary DNS server and the file in which the copied definition file is to be saved in the named.conf file.

To create a secondary DNS server, install Linux on another PC. Although you will install Linux according to the procedure described in this book, you must set a hostname and IP address for the secondary DNS server that differ from those of the primary DNS server. In this example, set the hostname of the secondary DNS server to "ns2.dekiru.gr.jp" and the IP address to "210.248.12.99". Also, define the secondary DNS server information for the primary DNS server. Make sure that you replace this example information with your own DNS information.

Primary DNS	server.dekiru.gr.jp	210.248.12.98
Secondary DNS	ns2.dekiru.gr.jp	210.248.12.99

Creating The Primary DNS Server

Install Linux according to the procedure described in this book, and configure the primary DNS server as described in Chapter 6. However, in this configuration, enter the address of your own secondary DNS server, not the address of the secondary DNS server that was provided by your Internet Service Provider (ISP). Also, you must define and add the secondary DNS server host to both the forward lookup and backward lookup configuration files. Add the secondary DNS server definition as follows to both the forward lookup and backward lookup configuration files. When you finish editing the configuration files, use the **ndc** command to reload BIND.

Forward Lookup Information Configuration File (/etc/namedb/dekiru.gr.jp)

```
router      IN   A       210.248.12.97
            IN   MX  10  server
server      IN   A       210.248.12.98
            IN   MX  10  server
ns2         IN   A       210.248.12.99     Define the secondary
            IN   MX  10  server            DNS server.
```

Reverse Lookup Information Configuration File (/etc/namedb/dekiru.gr.jp.rev)

Define the secondary
DNS server.

```
97              IN    PTR     router.dekiru.gr.jp.
98              IN    PTR     server.dekiru.gr.jp.
99              IN    PTR     ns2.dekiru.gr.jp.
```

Creating The Secondary DNS Server

After installing Linux according to the procedure described in this book, configure the secondary DNS server according to the following procedure.

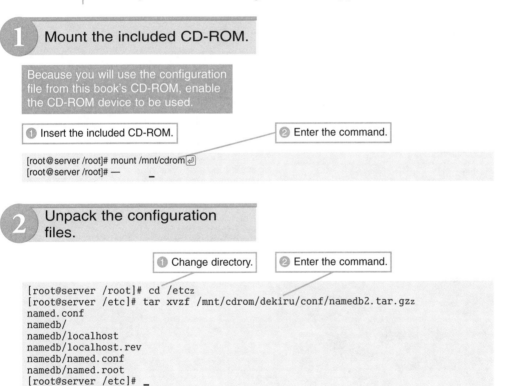

1 Mount the included CD-ROM.

Because you will use the configuration file from this book's CD-ROM, enable the CD-ROM device to be used.

① Insert the included CD-ROM.   ② Enter the command.

```
[root@server /root]# mount /mnt/cdrom⏎
[root@server /root]# —        _
```

2 Unpack the configuration files.

① Change directory.   ② Enter the command.

```
[root@server /root]# cd /etcz
[root@server /etc]# tar xvzf /mnt/cdrom/dekiru/conf/namedb2.tar.gzz
named.conf
namedb/
namedb/localhost
namedb/localhost.rev
namedb/named.conf
namedb/named.root
[root@server /etc]# _
```

The files are unpacked.

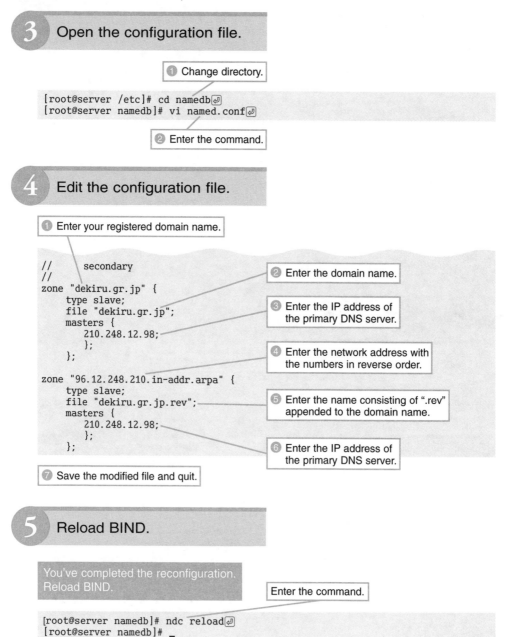

3 Open the configuration file.

① Change directory.

```
[root@server /etc]# cd namedb↵
[root@server namedb]# vi named.conf↵
```

② Enter the command.

4 Edit the configuration file.

① Enter your registered domain name.

```
//        secondary
//
zone "dekiru.gr.jp" {
    type slave;
    file "dekiru.gr.jp";
    masters {
        210.248.12.98;
        };
    };
zone "96.12.248.210.in-addr.arpa" {
    type slave;
    file "dekiru.gr.jp.rev";
    masters {
        210.248.12.98;
        };
    };
```

② Enter the domain name.

③ Enter the IP address of the primary DNS server.

④ Enter the network address with the numbers in reverse order.

⑤ Enter the name consisting of ".rev" appended to the domain name.

⑥ Enter the IP address of the primary DNS server.

⑦ Save the modified file and quit.

5 Reload BIND.

You've completed the reconfiguration. Reload BIND.

Enter the command.

```
[root@server namedb]# ndc reload↵
[root@server namedb]# _
```

The installation process has been made more user-friendly through new features such as:

- **A Graphical User Interface (GUI) Installation Mode**
  The screens are now more intuitive, and mouse navigation throughout the installation is now possible. Help screens are added.

- **Customizable Workstation-Class Installations**
  You can choose between GNOME and KDE desktops.

- **Manual Hard Drive Partitioning**
  You can now set your own hard drive partitions manually instead of using the system's preset partitions.

- **New Scriptable Kickstart Mode**
  Kickstart is extended to allow you to pass it a Python object and to configure your kickstart installation dynamically.

- **User Account Creation**
  You can now set up new user accounts, and determine your root password during installation.

- **Up Front Configuration**
  You can preconfigure your system before committing any of your changes to the hard drive. Changes are not made until after you have completely configured X.

System-Related New Features Include:

- **Automatic Hardware Detection On Boot**
  Upon reboot, the new Kudzu tool detects new hardware and asks if you want to configure it.

- **Support For The 2.2.12 Linux Kernel**

- **Pentium And Pentium III Optimized Kernels**
  These kernels, compiled for chip-specific support, are available.

- **Glibc 2.1.2**
  Support for the newer glibc 2.1.2 library is available.

- **XFree86 3.3.5**
  More driver support is available in this version of XFree86.

- **Support For Lightweight Directory Access Protocol (LDAP) Authentication**
  Now you can set up the LDAP for account information services. It runs over an Internet transport protocol, such as Transmission Control Protocol (TCP), and you can use it to access stand alone directory servers or X.500 directories.

- **Optional Interactive Boot Sequence**
  You can now enter an interactive mode while booting and individually select the services you want to have started. It's a good way to catch error messages and test new configurations.

Other Goodies:

- **Graphical Point-To-Point Protocol (PPP) Configuration Tool**
  You can use a program called RP3 to monitor connections to any configured net work device and to configure a new PPP connection.

- **KDE 1.1.1**
  An alternative GUI desktop environment is provided, including useful window and file managers and many more applications.

- **GNOME 1.0.15**
  This GUI allows end users to more easily use and configure their systems. There are many new applets, control center tools, and a better file manager and login screen.

- **Integrated Services Digital Network (ISDN) support**
  ISDN support is now included.

Linux Resources Online: Web Sites, Mailing Lists, News Groups

The amount of Web-based information on Linux grows by leaps and bounds every day. Here are some of the best:

- **slashdot.org**

This is the main news portal for Linux aficionados and geeks in general. If you only have enough time to check out one Web site to keep up to date on geek news and issues, this is the place.

- **linuxworld.com**

This site has very good and frequent feature articles about Linux, especially about how Linux is actually being used in practical applications. It's a good place to find reviews of recent commercial software that was written for or ported to Linux. The nice thing about the interactive discussion here is that it runs as a standard nntp-based newsgroup that you access through your browser or news reader (i.e., you don't have to sign up, subscribe, or come up with another password, just read and post). The whole online magazine is under the competent and careful editorial direction of Nicholas Petreley, who also writes for *info World* magazine.

- **linuxjournal.com**

This is the home page of the print edition of the *Linux Journal*. It offers the chance to take a look at what's happening in the hard-copy magazine, in addition to providing information that is available strictly online. An example of the online-only content is a column called "The Rockery", which does an excellent job of distilling the latest Linux-related news stories into a few sentences.

- **linuxgazette.com**

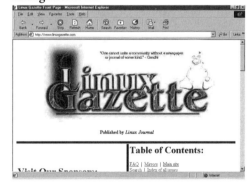

Published by the *Linux Journal*, articles that appear here are also included in the Debian/GNU Linux distribution. A master index to all of the tables of contents for all issues as well as a search engine is available. Make this site a first stop for your research on Linux.

- **linuxtoday.com**

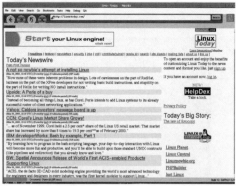

Clean and straightforward, this site has a huge list of Linux news headlines.

- **linux.org**

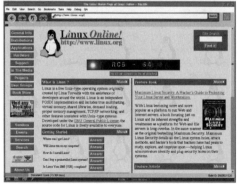

This site provides a wealth of information about where to find things for Linux. A handy world-spanning list of regional Linux user groups is also featured.

- **portalux.com**

Also called "Linux Center", this site provides a wealth of Linux-related links organized by categories such as Applications, Development, Networking, and so on.

- **lwn.net**

This is the home page for the *Linux Weekly News*. The daily update feature is an especially good place to find the latest Linux news stories. Also, links to approximately a dozen other online sources for Linux news are available.

Besides the kernel, there are four other important parts of GNU/Linux. They are the General Public License (GPL) and the thinking behind it, as well as the many applications and utilities that have been produced by GNU Project; the X Window system that provides the basis for nearly all graphics and graphical user interfaces (GUIs) on Linux; mail servers (sendmail, qmail, exim) for the Internet; and the Apache Web server. Here's a brief list of sites to learn more about these parts:

- gnu.org
- xfree86.org
- apache.org
- exim.org
- qmail.org
- sendmail.org

Mailing Lists

Each Linux distribution maintains at least one mailing list. (See the list of major Linux distributions in Appendix G.) Linux user groups also have associated mailing lists. For a list of user groups, see **www.linux.org/users/**. Some of these user groups maintain extensive and informative Web sites. For example, see the Irish Linux User Group (**www.linux.ie**) or the Tokyo Linux User Group (**www.tlug.gr.jp**).

Each free or open-source software project also has at least one mailing list. Some examples taken from the many current projects are as follows:

- AbiWord:

  abisource.org

  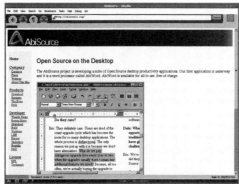

- Emacs:

  www.gnu.org/software/emacs/ or
  www.emacs.org

- GNOME:

  www.gnome.org

  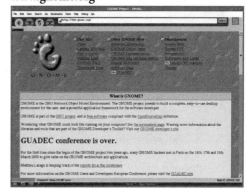

- KDE:

  www.kde.org

- Linux Documentation Project:

  www.linuxdoc.org

- ## Mozilla:
  www.mozilla.org

  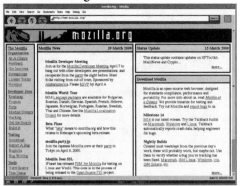

- ## Zope:
  zope.org

- ## Xmlterm:
  xmlterm.org

News Groups

Internet Usenet news groups are a rich source of the latest information about Linux, the Linux distributions, and the multitude of open-source software development projects. The groups listed here are some of the most active. Besides the groups that use English, there are many groups in other languages, especially German, Chinese, Japanese, Korean, French, Russian, and Spanish. A recent search of the news groups retrieved over 350 groups devoted to Linux.

A Selection Of Linux News Groups

- 3dfx.glide.linux
- alt.linux
- alt.os.linux
- alt.os.linux.caldera
- alt.os.linux.corel
- alt.os.linux.mandrake
- alt.os.linux.slackware
- alt.os.linux.suse
- alt.os.linux.turbolinux
- aus.computers.linux
- borland.public.jbuilder.linux
- comp.os.linux.advocacy
- comp.os.linux.announce
- comp.os.linux.development.apps
- comp.os.linux.development.system
- comp.os.linux.hardware
- comp.os.linux.misc
- comp.os.linux.networking
- comp.os.linux.portable
- comp.os.linux.powerpc
- comp.os.linux.security
- comp.os.linux.setup
- comp.os.linux.x
- corelsupport.linux.corellinux
- corelsupport.linux.hardware_compatibility
- corelsupport.linux.install
- corelsupport.linux.networking
- corelsupport.linux.printing
- corelsupport.linux.set_up_config
- corelsupport.linux.wordperfectoffice
- corelsupport.linux.wordperfect_linux
- corelsupport.linux.
- creative.linux
- fa.linux.debian
- fj.os.linux.networking (in Japanese)
- fj.os.linux.setup (in Japanese)
- han.comp.os.linux (in Korean)
- hk.comp.os.linux (in Chinese)
- ibm.software.db2.udb.linux.beta
- ibm.software.java.linux
- interbase.public.linux
- japan.comp.linux (in Japanese)
- linux.debian
- linux.debian.user
- linux.redhat
- linux.redhat.devel
- linux.redhat.digest
- linux.redhat.install
- linux.redhat.misc
- linux.samba
- linux.sources.kernel
- opera.linux
- staroffice.com.support.install.linux
- sybase.public.easerver.linux
- tw.bbs.comp.linux (in Chinese)
- uk.comp.os.linux
- vmware.for-linux.configuration
- vmware.for-linux.misc

All of the distributions try to make installation easy. Whether they succeed largely depends on what hardware each distribution finds or doesn't find on your PC. Check the hardware compatibility lists before installing to make sure that your video card, network interface card (NIC), sound card, and so on are compatible with the Linux distribution you intend to install. (These lists are usually found either in the documentation or on the software firm's Web site.) When there are no hardware conflicts, the easiest distribution to install is probably Corel Linux. Caldera and Mandrake follow closely for ease of use. Thereafter, the line-up would be Turbo, Red Hat, SuSe, Slackware, and Debian, respectively. Experienced users or those who desire a high degree of customization should try the previous order in reverse.

Each distribution offers its own special features. For example, Caldera's customization of XDM is useful. Corel's addition of a network neighborhood extension to the file manager is convenient. Mandrake's capability to switch to an expert mode where you can pick your packages is great, and so on. You will want to examine each distribution.

Home Pages Of Major Linux Distributions

1. Caldera:
www.caldera.com

2. Corel Linux:
linux.corel.com

3. Debian:
www.debian.org

This is the major free (open-source) distribution, the distribution *par excellence* for the true student of Linux. It's easy to update, and it let's the system administrator become very involved in the distribution. You can use the development distribution (unstable) or the latest stable distribution. The biggest problem with Debian is that the stable distributions are very slow to be released. Because the newest unstable distribution is opened up before the final bug fixes on the current frozen distribution are completed, developers tend to lose focus on the frozen distribution before it's released. Debian now has four preconfigured sets of packages to make installation easier.

4. Mandrake:

www.linux-mandrake.com/en/

7. Storm Linux:

www.stormix.com

This is based on Debian.

5. Red Hat:

www.redhat.com

This is the standard for comparison in commercial distributions.

8. TurboLinux:

www.turbolinux.com

This is the most known (internationally, that is) of all of the distributions mentioned here.

6. Slackware:

www.slackware.com

This is one of the first distributions of Linux.

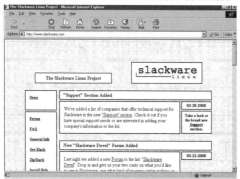

Although you can do most of the work required to get your Internet server/services up and running, the easiest way to go about getting them permanently connected to the Internet is to directly contact your local connection provider. Depending on the size of your budget, bandwidth, and other needs, purchasing a small business or small office home office (SOHO) Internet access package from your local provider may be the best solution. If your connection provider and your ISP are not the same company, you need to coordinate the installation of your connection with your ISP who will provide most of the critical settings for your system.

Whether you will use a telephone company (Telco), cable, or satellite connection,each provider has a plethora of services and product information on their Web site, from which you can begin to evaluate your options. A short list of examples of representative SOHO products and services from a few of the regional big connection providers follows (your area will have different selections):

Telco Companies
Pacific Bell:
www.pacbell.com

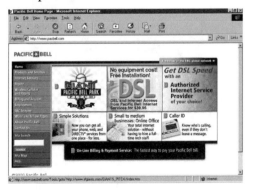

LAN ISDN:
With LAN ISDN, your router automatically places an ISDN call to the PacBell network whenever a user on your LAN needs access to the Internet and a connection is not already up. The

ISDN connection supports speeds up to 128 Kbps (and the Basic Rate Interface provides this speed). When no one is accessing the Internet, the router disconnects the ISDN call. For locations with low to medium usage, your users can enjoy the convenience and speed of a dedicated access service at a fraction of the price.

DSL:
Digital Subscriber Line Internet access is a new technology that runs over standard phone lines. DSL allows you to download files and view graphic-intensive Web pages at speeds up to 10 times faster than ISDN and up to 50 times faster than conventional 28.8Kbps modems. The farther you are from the network switching "node"(the small, inconspicuous cabinets stuffed with electronic components, usually found in neighborhoods on telephone poles or the ground), however, the more questionable the service and or quality of service becomes. The more active people on the node the slower the connection becomes. DSL is not yet available in most rural areas and in some cities. Check with your local Telco.

Frame Relay:
Frame Relay is one of the most cost-effective ways to get dedicated access to the Internet today at speeds up to 1.544Mbps, depending on your location. Frame Relay is a digital service that handles "bursty", high-speed data traffic, making it ideal for Internet access. It's usually less expensive than a leased full-capacity DS1 or T1 line.

Burstable DS1:
This 1.544 Mbps digital service is well-suited for large organizations requiring high capacity Internet connections. Depending upon your organization's location, you may also want to consider a 1.536 Mbps Frame Relay service, which— unlike DS1 — does not include a mileage charge. For further information, please see the Web site.

Burstable DS3:

If you want high-speed private line service but don't want to pay for a set bandwidth level, you may want to subscribe to the Burstable DS3 service. With Burstable DS3 service you can burst up to 45 Mbps, as your needs dictate.

ATM (Asynchronous transfer mode):

ATM is an attractive Internet access option because it provides cost-effective access for companies requiring higher speeds than DS1 leased lines (1.544 Mbps), but not needing the full speed of DS3 leased lines (45 Mbps).

Other similar and regional Telcos are:

US WEST:

www.uswest.com

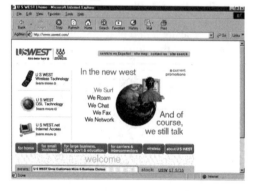

Bell Atlantic:

www.bell-atl.com/about/business.htm

Sprint:

www.sprint.com

Internet On Cable Provider Companies:

Companies such as Roadrunner offer a suite of dedicated connections to the Internet with bandwidths necessary for company LANs and other SOHOs.

Roadrunner:

www.roadrunner.com

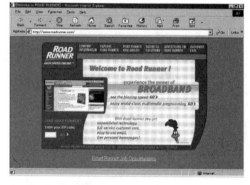

Again the more active people there are on a "node", the slower the connection becomes. This service is also not fully available nationwide, please check with your local cable provider for service.

Other Internet On Cable Provider Companies

AT&T:

www.att.com

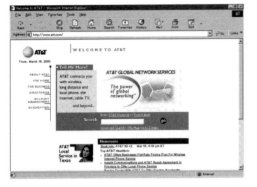

Excite @work:

www.work.home.net/dedicated.html

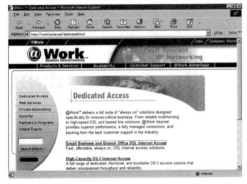

Internet on terrestrial and non-terrestrial wireless Satellite:

Uses a combination of terrestrial and non-terrestrial connections to upload and download Internet content. Simply having one side of the link is useless to an Internet server. You must be able to both upload to and download from the Satellite. The new upload capability is only recently beginning to become available. Advantages are deployment, scalability of bandwidth, logistical availability.

GE Americom:

www.geamericom.com

Microwave:

A comparatively cost effective, logistical solution. See Microwave provider.

CowboyZ.com at www.cowboyz.com

Disadvantages are transport environmental interference.

* Brackets [ ] around a command argument in the syntax sections indicate that the argument is optional and can be omitted.

cd

Changes the current directory.
- Syntax
  cd [*directory name*]
- Commonly used option
  - (hyphen) Change to previous directory.
- Related commands: **ls, pwd**
- Examples
  cd /etc   Change to /etc.
  cd   Change to home directory.

chgrp

Changes the group owner of a file.
- Syntax
  chgrp *group name file/directory name*
- Commonly used option
  -R   Changes all files and directories in the specified directory.
- Related commands: **chown, chmod, ls**

chmod

Changes file permissions.
- Syntax
  chmod *permission setting file/directory name* ...
- Commonly used option
  -R   Recursively changes all files and directories in the specified directory.
- Related commands: **chown, chgrp, ls**

chown

Changes the owner of a file.
- Syntax
  chown *username[.group name] file/directory name* ...
- Commonly used option
  -R   Recursively changes all files and directories in the specified directory.
- Related commands: **chgrp, chmod, ls**

cp

Copies files.
- Commonly used options
  -a   Maintains original file permissions as much as possible.
  -i   Asks for confirmation to copy each file.
  -f   If the file already exists at the destination, the copied file overwrites the existing file.
- Related commands: **mv, rm, ls, ln**

date

Displays and sets the current time and date.
- Syntax
  date [*string representing date*]
- Related command: **rdate**
- Note
  Only root can set the date. If no argument is specified, the current time and date displays. If an argument is specified, the time and date is set.

df

Displays the disk capacity used by a file system.
- Syntax
  df [*directory name*]
- Commonly used options
  -k   Displays amounts in kilobytes.
  -h   Displays in an easy-to-understand format.
- Related commands: **du, mount, umount, fdisk**
- Note
  Executing the **df** command without specifying a directory displays the disk capacity used by all mounted file systems.

diff

Displays differences in files.
- Syntax
  diff *file1 file2*
- Commonly used options
  -c   Displays the results in a *context output format.*
  -u   Displays the results in a *unified output format.*
  -d   Makes the set of changes as minimal as possible.
  -b   Ignores differences in the number of blank spaces.
  -B   Ignores differences in the number of blank lines.
  -r   If a directory is specified with this option, all files in that directory are compared.
- Note
  The results of **diff** can be used as a batch file.

dmesg

Displays the kernel log.
- Syntax
  dmesg

du

Displays the disk capacity used by each directory.

- Syntax
  du *[directory name]*
- Commonly used options
  - -k   Displays amounts in kilobytes.
  - -x   Stays in one file system.
  - -s   Displays totals only.
  - -S   Displays only the disk capacity used within each directory.
  - -h   Displays in an easy-to-understand format.
  - -a   Displays all files as well.
- Related command: **df**

find

Searches files.

- Syntax
  find *starting directory conditions*
- Commonly used options
  - -name - *file name*   Searches for the file name.
  - -size - *number*   Searches for files this size.
  - -type - *character*   Searches for or finds matches only with files of this type.
- Note
  When specifying a number (n), [+n] indicates a value greater than n, [n] indicates a value equal to n, and [-n] indicates a value less than n. For the size, appending [c] after the character displays the result in bytes, [k] in kilobytes, and [b] (or nothing at all) will display the result in blocks of 512 bytes. After -type, appending [d] displays directories, [f] displays normal files, and [l] displays symbolic links.

fsck

Checks and repairs file systems.

- Syntax
  fsck *[device name]*
- Commonly used option
  - -y   Answers yes to all questions.
- Related commands: **mount, umount, df**
- Note
  When Linux boots, the **fsck** command executes automatically if the drive has been mounted more than 20 times since the last check. Additionally, **fsck** executes automatically if the shutdown command did not execute properly or if a file system error occurs.

fuser

Displays the processes that are using files and file systems and sends a signal.

- Syntax
  fuser *file/directory name*

- Commonly used options
  - -l   Displays a list of signals that can be sent.
  - -v   Displays details.
  - -m   Displays the processes that are using file systems containing specified files and directories.
  - -HUP   Sends hang-up signal. Often used when re-reading settings in a daemon.
  - -kill   Sends a signal to forcibly quit. Use sparingly, such as when a program refuses to quit.
- Related commands: **mount, umount, kill**
- Note
  If processes are using files within a file system, you cannot unmount the file system. Using the **fuser** command allows you to search for these types of processes and quit them.

grep

Searches within files and displays the results in line units.

- Syntax
  grep *character string filename* ...
- Commonly used options
  - -n   Outputs line numbers.
  - -i   Does not distinguish case.
  - -v   Displays non-matching lines.
  - -w   Searches words.
  - -number   Displays the specified number of lines both before and after a match.
- Related command: **less**

gzip

Compresses files.

- Syntax
  gzip *file*
  gunzip *file*
- Commonly used option
  - -d   Extracts compressed files.
- Note
  The **gzip** command compresses files and then saves them with the extension .gz appended. A function to collect files is not included in **gzip** itself. In Linux, use the **tar** command to collect files. Generally, **tar** will call on **gzip** to compress files.

id

Displays user ID and group ID information.

- Syntax
  id *[username]*
- Related commands: **su, useradd, userdel**
- Note
  If a username is not specified, the user who executes the **id** command will be specified.

kill

Sends a signal to a process.

- Syntax
  kill *process ID*

- Commonly used options
  - -l   Displays a list of signals that can be sent.
  - -HUP   Sends hang-up signal. Often used when re-reading settings in a daemon.
  - -KILL   Sends a signal to forcibly quit. Use sparingly, such as when a program refuses to quit.
  - -TERM   Sends a signal to quit (default).
- Related commands: **top, ps, pstree, killall**

killall

Sends a signal to a process.

- Syntax
  killall *command name*
- Commonly used options
  - -l   Displays a list of signals that can be sent.
  - -HUP   Sends hang-up signal. Often used when re-reading settings in a daemon.
  - -KILL   Sends a signal to forcibly quit. Use sparingly, such as when a program refuses to quit.
  - -TERM   Sends a signal to quit (default).
- Related Commands: **top, ps, pstree, kill**
- Note
  The difference between the **killall** command and the **kill** command is that **killall** specifies processes using the command name, while **kill** specifies processes using the process ID (number to specify the process). Each process has a unique ID number, but multiple processes can have the same command name. **killall** sends a signal to all processes having the same command name.

last/lastlog

Displays user login sessions.

- Syntax
  last *[username]*
  lastlog
- Related command: **w**
- Note
  If a username is not specified, the **last** command displays the entire log. If a username is specified, the **last** command displays only the login records for that user. The **lastlog** command displays the time and date of the last login for each user.

less

Displays the contents of a file.

- Syntax
  less *filename* ...
- Key Operations
  - f, b   Moves up/down one screen.
  - d, u   Moves up/down half screen.
  - · /, ?   Searches forward/backward.
  - -i   Search is/is not case-sensitive (toggle).
  - n, N   Search forward/backward again.
  - F   Read from the end of the file. (If appended to a file, the file will quickly display.)
  - v   Starts the vi editor and edits a file.
- Related command: **more**

ln

Creates a link.

- Syntax
  ln *file/directory file/directory*
  ln *file/directory _c. directory*
- Commonly used option
  - -s   Creates a symbolic link.
- Related commands: **cp, mv, rm, ls**
- Note
  If the -s option is not specified, a hard link is created. Hard links, however, are seldom used.

locate

Searches for files.

- Syntax
  locate *filename*
- Related commands: **find, updatedb**
- Note
  In contrast to the **find** command, which searches all directories, the **locate** command first makes a database of file names, and then searches for file names in the database. Consequently, the **locate** command can search significantly faster than the **find** command.

ls

Displays file names.

- Syntax
  ls *file/directory*
- Commonly used options
  - -l   Displays in long format.
  - -F   Displays with the file type appended to the end of the file name.
  - -a   Displays all files including those starting with a dot (.).
  - -R   Displays all files and directories in the specified directory.
- Related command: **find**

man

Displays a manual.

- Syntax
  man *[section] name*
- Commonly used option
  - -k   Searches titles of manuals.

mount/umount

Mounts and unmounts file systems.
- Syntax
  mount *device name mount point*
  umount *device name or mount point*
- Commonly used option
  -o   Mount option.
  -t   File system type.
- Related commands: **df, fuser, fstab**
- Note
  If you execute the **mount** command without specifying a device name or mount point, the file system currently mounted displays.

mv

Moves files and directories.
- Syntax
  mv *file file/directory*
  mv *file _c directory*
- Commonly used options
  -f   If the file already exists at the destination, the moved file overwrites the existing file.
  -i   Requests user confirmation for each move.
- Note
  The **mv** command can also be used to change file names.

newaliases

Implements changes in /etc/aliases for Sendmail when used to maintain a mailing list.
- Syntax
  newaliases

ndc

Starts or restarts the Berkeley Internet Name Domain (BIND) to reload configuration settings.
- Syntax
  ndc *[command]*
- Note
  Specify **start**, **restart**, or **reload** for *[command]*. If **ndc** is executed with no option being specified, it starts in conversational mode.

nslookup

Used to look up any type of DNS resource record or to query any name server. For example, it finds the hostname from the IP address or the IP address from the hostname.
- Syntax
  nslookup *[host_name/IP_address]*
- Commonly Used Options
  -type=MX   Searches MX records
- Note
  If **nslookup** is executed without an option being specified, it starts in conversational mode. You can specify any of the individual record codes that are used in the BIND configuration settings for the -type option.

passwd

Changes passwords.
- Syntax
  passwd *[user name]*
- Related commands: **chfn, chsh**
- Note
  Only root can specify usernames. Ordinary users can only change their own passwords.

ping

Verifies whether a network is connected.
- Syntax
  ping *host name/IP number*
- Note
  When ping is executed, data is sent to the host with a request to return that data as is. The ping display is related to the returned data.

popauth

Sets the APOP password.
- Syntax
  popauth *[username]*
- Commonly Used Options
  -init   Initializes the APOP password database
  -list   Displays a list of registered usernames
  -delete username   Deletes the APOP password of the specified user
- Note
  Only root can specify a username. Ordinaly users can change only their own password.

ps

Displays processes.
- Syntax
  ps *[process ID]*
- Commonly used options
  a   Displays processes of all users.
  x   Displays processes not controlled by a terminal.
  u   Displays in username format.
  w   Expands the display width for each line.
  c   Displays only executable file names in the command name column.
- Related commands: **top, pstree, kill, killall**
- Note
  If you execute the **ps** command without specifying a process ID, only the processes of the user who executed the command will display. If a process ID is specified, only the process of the specified process ID will display. You must enter an option after the process ID.

pwd

Displays the current directory.
- Syntax
  pwd
- Related commands: **cd, ls**

reset/resize

Carries out terminal settings.
- Syntax
  eval 'resize'
  reset
- Related commands: stty
- Note
  The **resize** command is used to change the size of a window. The **reset** command is used when unintelligible characters are encountered, as when a binary file displays on screen.

rm

Deletes files.
- Commonly used options
  -r   Deletes all files in the current directory.
  -f   Deletes read-only files as well without confirmation.
  -i   Requests user confirmation to delete each file (Red Hat default).
- Related commands: cp, mv, ln
- Note
  Deleted files cannot be recovered, so exercise caution when using this command.

shutdown

Quits the system.
- Syntax
  shutdown *[-h:-r] time [message]*
- Commonly used options
  -h   Quit.
  -r   Reboot.
  -c   Cancels a scheduled shutdown.
- Related command: sync
- Note
  If you specify "now" in the time option, the shutdown operation begins immediately. A shutdown that has already begun cannot be canceled. If -h or -r are not specified, the system switches to single-user mode. In single-user mode, all services are stopped. Use this command when necessary during administrative tasks.

sort

Sorts files by line.
- Commonly used options
  -n   Sorts arithmetically. (The default is alphabetically.)
  -r   Sorts in reverse order.
  -u   Lines having identical content display only once.
  -b   Ignores leading blank characters.

su

Changes the user ID.
- Syntax
  su *[username]*

- Commonly used options
  -l   Matches environment settings to the user being changed to.
  -m   Matches environment settings to the current user.
  -c *command*   Executes a command.
- Related command: id

sync

Writes the cache to the disk.
- Syntax
  sync
- Related commands: shutdown, df
- Note
  The **sync** command executes automatically when you remove a mount or shut down the system. Use the **sync** command as often as you want: this can help avoid situations where data remaining in the cache cannot be written to a file.

tar

Collects files (archive).
- Syntax
  tar *option directory*
- Commonly used options
  c   Creates an archive.
  t   Displays a list of files in the archive.
  x   Opens an archive.
  v   Displays the progress of the command.
  f file   Specifies a file.
  z   Uses compression.
- Examples
  tar cvfz bakup-home.tar.gz /home
  tar tvfz aaa.tar.gz
  tar xvfz aaa.tar.gz
- Note
  The **tar** command was originally a tape archive. Consequently, if you do not specify a file name by using the f option, Linux will attempt to send the data to a tape archive.

tcpdchk

Tests the tcp_wrappers configuration file. Along with **tcpmatch**, it can be used to verify the settings in the hosts.allow and hosts.deny files.
- Syntax
  tcpdchk
- Commonly Used Options
  -v   Displays the contents of the access restrictions
- Related Commands: **tcpdmatch**

tcpdmatch

Checks the access restrictions in the tcp_wrappers file. Predicts how the tcp wrapper will handle a specific request for service.
- Syntax
  tcpdchk
  tcpdmatch *server_name client_IP_address*
- Related Commands: tcpdchk

top

Monitors the status of processes.

- Primary Key Operations

Space bar   Rewrites the new status.

u   Displays only specific users
(enter *username*).

k   Sends signals
(enter the process ID and type of signal).

?   Displays Help.

- Related commands: ps, pstree, kill, killall

- Note

This command is like repeating the ps acux command over and over again with the results displayed continuously on screen. With ps, only the current status is displayed. With top, however, you can use key operations to send a signal.

touch

Changes the time stamp of a file. If the file does not exist, this command creates a file with a size of 0.

- Syntax

touch *file*

umask

Specifies the permissions given to a new file or directory when it is created.

- Syntax

umask *[umask value]*

- Commonly used umask values

022   Other users are read-only.

077   Other users cannot read or write.

- Related commands: ls, chmod

- Note

A umask value sets the initial permissions of a file or directory when it is created. All permissions are open before umask values are set. If a umask value is not specified, the current umask value will display.

useradd/userdel

Creates/deletes users.

- Syntax

useradd *username*
useradd -D
userdel *username*

- Commonly used options

-g *group*   (useradd) Sets the primary group.

-p *password*   (useradd) Sets the password.

-r   (userdel) Deletes the home directory as well.

- Related command: id

- Note

useradd -D sets the default values.

vi

Edits text files.

- Syntax

vi *file*

w

Displays users who are logged in.

- Syntax

w

watch

Executes and displays commands at fixed intervals.

- Syntax

watch *command*

- Commonly used option

-n *number*   Sets the interval in seconds.
(The default is two seconds.)

- Related command: top

- Note

Quit by pressing c + C.

wc

Displays the number of lines, words, and characters in a file.

- Syntax

wc *file*

- Commonly Used Options

-l   Displays the number of lines.

-w   Displays the number of words.

-c   Displays the number of characters.

- Note

The default display is: lines, words, characters, and file name.

which

Displays which file will be executed when a command is entered.

- Syntax

which *command*

- Related commands: whereis, find, locate

- Note

In Linux, if a command does not contain a slash (/) to specify a directory, the default directory path is searched for the executable file. The which command displays the location of the file to be executed.

Finding Out Which Commands Are Available

When you want to know which commands are available, enter the first characters of the command and then press t t to display the command names that begin with those characters. Pressing only t t displays all the commands.

To learn how to use a command, use the man command to view the command's manual. Enter "man *command name*" to display the manual for the command.

Appendix J GNU General Public License

We have included the GNU General Public License (GPL) for your reference as it applies to the software this book is about. However, the GPL does not apply to the text of this book.

Version 2, June 1991

Copyright © 1989, 1991 Free Software Foundation, Inc.

59 Temple Place, Suite 330, Boston, MA 02111-1307 USA

Everyone is permitted to copy and distribute verbatim copies of this license document, but changing it is not allowed.

Preamble

The licenses for most software are designed to take away your freedom to share and change it. By contrast, the GNU General Public License is intended to guarantee your freedom to share and change free software—to make sure the software is free for all its users. This General Public License applies to most of the Free Software Foundation's software and to any other program whose authors commit to using it. (Some other Free Software Foundation software is covered by the GNU Library General Public License instead.) You can apply it to your programs, too.

When we speak of free software, we are referring to freedom, not price. Our General Public Licenses are designed to make sure that you have the freedom to distribute copies of free software (and charge for this service if you wish), that you receive source code or can get it if you want it, that you can change the software or use pieces of it in new free programs; and that you know you can do these things.

To protect your rights, we need to make restrictions that forbid anyone to deny you these rights or to ask you to surrender these rights. These restrictions translate to certain responsibilities for you if you distribute copies of the software, or if you modify it.

For example, if you distribute copies of such a program, whether gratis or for a fee, you must give the recipients all the rights that you have. You must make sure that they, too, receive or can get the source code. And you must show them these terms so they know their rights.

We protect your rights with two steps: (1) copyright the software, and (2) offer you this license which gives you legal permission to copy, distribute, and/or modify the software.

Also, for each author's protection and ours, we want to make certain that everyone understands that there is no warranty for this free software. If the software is modified by someone else and passed on, we want its recipients to know that what they have is not the original, so that any problems introduced by others will not reflect on the original authors' reputations.

Finally, any free program is threatened constantly by software patents. We wish to avoid the danger that redistributors of a free program will individually obtain patent licenses, in effect making the program proprietary. To prevent this, we have made it clear that any patent must be licensed for everyone's free use or not licensed at all.

The precise terms and conditions for copying, distribution, and modification follow.

Terms And Conditions For Copying, Distribution, And Modification

This License applies to any program or other work which contains a notice placed by the copyright holder saying it may be distributed under the terms of this General Public License. The "Program", below, refers to any such program or work, and a "work based on the Program" means either the Program or any derivative work under copyright law: that is to say, a work containing the Program or a portion of it, either verbatim or with modifications and/or translated into another language. (Hereinafter, translation is included without limitation in the term "modification.") Each licensee is addressed as "you."

Activities other than copying, distribution, and modification are not covered by this License; they are outside its scope. The act of running the Program is not restricted, and the output from the Program is covered only if its contents constitute a work based on the Program (independent of having been made by running the Program). Whether that is true depends on what the Program does.

1. You may copy and distribute verbatim copies of the Program's source code as you receive it, in any medium, provided that you conspicuously and appropriately publish on each copy an appropriate copyright notice and disclaimer of warranty; keep intact all the notices that refer to this License and to the absence of any warranty; and give any other recipients of the Program a copy of this License along with the Program.
   You may charge a fee for the physical act of transferring a copy, and you may at your option offer warranty protection in exchange for a fee.

2. You may modify your copy or copies of the Program or any portion of it, thus forming a work based on the Program, and copy and distribute such modifications or work under the terms of Section 1 above, provided that you also meet all of these conditions:

a) You must cause the modified files to carry prominent notices stating that you changed the files and the date of any change.

b) You must cause any work that you distribute or publish, that in whole or in part contains or is derived from the Program or any part thereof, to be licensed as a whole at no charge to all third parties under the terms of this License.

c) If the modified program normally reads commands interactively when run, you must cause it, when started running for such interactive use in the most ordinary way, to print or display an announcement including an appropriate copyright notice and a notice that there is no warranty (or else, saying that you provide a warranty) and that users may redistribute the program under these conditions, and telling the user how to view a copy of this License. (Exception: If the Program itself is interactive, but does not normally print such an announcement, your work based on the Program is not required to print an announcement.)

These requirements apply to the modified work as a whole. If identifiable sections of that work are not derived from the Program, and can be reasonably considered independent and separate works in themselves, then this License, and its terms, do not apply to those sections when you distribute them as separate works. But when you distribute the same sections as part of a whole which is a work based on the Program, the distribution of the whole must be on the terms of this License, whose permissions for other licensees extend to the entire whole, and thus to each and every part regardless of who wrote it.

Thus, it is not the intent of this section to claim rights or contest your rights to work written entirely by you; rather, the intent is to exercise the right to control the distribution of derivative or collective works based on the Program.

In addition, mere aggregation of another work not based on the Program with the Program (or with a work based on the Program) on a volume of a storage or distribution medium does not bring the other work under the scope of this License.

3. You may copy and distribute the Program (or a work based on it, under Section 2) in object code or executable form under the terms of Sections 1 and 2 above provided that you also do one of the following:

a) Accompany it with the complete corresponding machine-readable source code, which must be distributed under the terms of Sections 1 and 2 above on a medium customarily used for software interchange; or,

b) Accompany it with a written offer, valid for at least three years, to give any third party, for a charge no more than your cost of physically performing source distribution, a complete machine-readable copy of the corresponding source code, to be distributed under the terms of Sections 1 and 2 above on a medium customarily used for software interchange; or,

c) Accompany it with the information you received as to the offer to distribute corresponding source code. (This alternative is allowed only for noncommercial distribution and only if you received the program in object code or executable form with such an offer, in accord with Subsection b above.)

The source code for a work means the preferred form of the work for making modifications to it. For an executable work, complete source code means all the source code for all modules it contains, plus any associated interface definition files, plus the scripts used to control compilation and installation of the executable.

However, as a special exception, the source code distributed need not include anything that is normally distributed (in either source or binary form) with the major components (compiler, kernel, and so on) of the operating system on which the executable runs, unless that component itself accompanies the executable.

If distribution of executable or object code is made by offering access to copy from a designated place, then offering equivalent access to copy the source code from the same place counts as distribution of the source code, even though third parties are not compelled to copy the source along with the object code.

4. You may not copy, modify, sublicense, or distribute the Program except as expressly provided under this License. Any attempt otherwise to copy, modify, sublicense or distribute the Program is void, and will automatically terminate your rights under this License. However, parties who have received copies, or rights, from you under this License will not have their licenses terminated so long as such parties remain in full compliance.

5. You are not required to accept this License, since you have not signed it. However, nothing else grants you permission to modify or distribute the Program or its derivative works. These actions are prohibited by law if you do not accept this License. Therefore, by modifying or distributing the Program (or any work based on the Program), you indicate your acceptance of this License to do so, and all its terms and conditions for copying, distributing, or modifying the Program or works based on it.

6. Each time you redistribute the Program (or any work based on the Program), the recipient automatically receives a license from the original licensor to copy, distribute, or modify the Program subject to these terms and conditions. You may not impose any further restrictions on the recipients' exercise of the rights granted herein. You are not responsible for enforcing compliance by third parties to this License.

7. If, as a consequence of a court judgment or allegation of patent infringement or for any other reason (not limited to patent issues), conditions are imposed on you (whether by court order, agreement, or otherwise) that contradict the conditions of this License, they do not excuse you from the conditions of this License. If you cannot distribute so as to satisfy simultaneously your obligations under this License and any other pertinent obligations, then as a consequence you may not distribute the Program at all. For example, if a patent license would not permit royalty-free redistribution of the Program by all those who receive copies directly or indirectly through you, then the only way you could satisfy both it and this License would be to refrain entirely from distribution of the Program.

    If any portion of this section is held invalid or unenforceable under any particular circumstance, the balance of the section is intended to apply and the section as a whole is intended to apply in other circumstances.
    It is not the purpose of this section to induce you to infringe any patents or other property right claims or to contest validity of any such claims; this section has the sole purpose of protecting the integrity of the free software distribution system, which is implemented by public license practices. Many people have made generous contributions to the wide range of software distributed through that system in reliance on consistent application of that system; it is up to the author/donor to decide if he or she is willing to distribute software through any other system and a licensee cannot impose that choice.

    This section is intended to make thoroughly clear what is believed to be a consequence of the rest of this License.

8. If the distribution and/or use of the Program is restricted in certain countries either by patents or by copyrighted interfaces, the original copyright holder who places the Program under this License may add an explicit geographical distribution limitation excluding those countries, so that distribution is permitted only in or among countries not thus excluded. In such case, this License incorporates the limitation as if written in the body of this License.

9. The Free Software Foundation may publish revised and/or new versions of the General Public License from time to time. Such new versions will be similar in spirit to the present version, but may differ in detail to address new problems or concerns.

Each version is given a distinguishing version number. If the Program specifies a version number of this License which applies to it and "any later version", you have the option of following the terms and conditions either of that version or of any later version published by the Free Software Foundation. If the Program does not specify a version number of this License, you may choose any version ever published by the Free Software Foundation.

10. If you wish to incorporate parts of the Program into other free programs whose distribution conditions are different, write to the author to ask for permission. For software which is copyrighted by the Free Software Foundation, write to the Free Software Foundation; we sometimes make exceptions for this. Our decision will be guided by the two goals of preserving the free status of all derivatives of our free software and of promoting the sharing and reuse of software generally.

No Warranty

11. BECAUSE THE PROGRAM IS LICENSED FREE OF CHARGE, THERE IS NO WARRANTY FOR THE PROGRAM, TO THE EXTENT PERMITTED BY APPLICABLE LAW. EXCEPT WHEN OTHERWISE STATED IN WRITING, THE COPYRIGHT HOLDERS AND/OR OTHER PARTIES PROVIDE THE PROGRAM "AS IS" WITHOUT WARRANTY OF ANY KIND, EITHER EXPRESSED OR IMPLIED, INCLUDING, BUT NOT LIMITED TO, THE IMPLIED WARRANTIES OF MERCHANTABILITY AND FITNESS FOR A PARTICULAR PURPOSE. THE ENTIRE RISK AS TO THE QUALITY AND PERFORMANCE OF THE PROGRAM IS WITH YOU. SHOULD THE PROGRAM PROVE DEFECTIVE, YOU ASSUME THE COST OF ALL NECESSARY SERVICING, REPAIR OR CORRECTION.

12. IN NO EVENT, UNLESS REQUIRED BY APPLICABLE LAW OR AGREED TO IN WRITING, WILL ANY COPYRIGHT HOLDER, OR ANY OTHER PARTY WHO MAY MODIFY AND/OR REDISTRIBUTE THE PROGRAM AS PERMITTED ABOVE, BE LIABLE TO YOU FOR DAMAGES, INCLUDING ANY GENERAL, SPECIAL, INCIDENTAL, OR CONSEQUENTIAL DAMAGES ARISING OUT OF THE USE OR INABILITY TO USE THE PROGRAM (INCLUDING BUT NOT LIMITED TO LOSS OF DATA OR DATA BEING RENDERED INACCURATE OR LOSSES SUSTAINED BY YOU OR THIRD PARTIES OR A FAILURE OF THE PROGRAM TO OPERATE WITH ANY OTHER PROGRAMS), EVEN IF SUCH HOLDER OR OTHER PARTY HAS BEEN ADVISED OF THE POSSIBILITY OF SUCH DAMAGES.

How To Apply These Terms To Your New Programs

If you develop a new program, and you want it to be of the greatest possible use to the public, the best way to achieve this is to make it free software which everyone can redistribute and change under these terms.

To do so, attach the following notices to the program. It is safest to attach them to the start of each source file to most effectively convey the exclusion of warranty; and each file should have at least the "copyright" line and a pointer to where the full notice is found.

```
<one line to give the program's name and a brief idea of what it does.>
Copyright C 20yy  <name of author>
```

This program is free software; you can redistribute it and/or modify it under the terms of the GNU General Public License as published by the Free Software Foundation; either version 2 of the License, or (at your option) any later version.

This program is distributed in the hope that it will be useful, but WITHOUT ANY WARRANTY; without even the implied warranty of MERCHANTABILITY or FITNESS FOR A PARTICULAR PURPOSE. See the GNU General Public License for more details.

You should have received a copy of the GNU General Public License along with this program; if not, write to the Free Software Foundation, Inc., 59 Temple Place, Suite 330, Boston, MA 02111-1307 USA

Also add information on how to contact you by electronic and paper mail.
If the program is interactive, make it output a short notice like this when it starts in an interactive mode:

Gnomovision version 69, Copyright C 20yy name of author Gnomovision comes with ABSOLUTELY NO WARRANTY; for details type 'show w'. This is free software, and you are welcome to redistribute it under certain conditions; type `show c' for details.

The hypothetical commands 'show w' and 'show c' should show the appropriate parts of the General Public License. Of course, the commands you use may be called something other than 'show w' and 'show c'; they could even be mouse-clicks or menu items—whatever suits your program.

You should also get your employer (if you work as a programmer) or your school, if any, to sign a "copyright disclaimer" for the program, if necessary. Here is a sample; alter the names:

Yoyodyne, Inc., hereby disclaims all copyright interest in the program 'Gnomovision' (which makes passes at compilers) written by James Hacker.

<signature of Ty Coon>, 1 April 1989
Ty Coon, President of Vice

This General Public License does not permit incorporating your program into proprietary programs. If your program is a subroutine library, you may consider it more useful to permit linking proprietary applications with the library. If this is what you want to do, use the GNU Library General Public License instead of this License.

Glossary

Number

10Base-T
100Base-TX
See Ethernet.

A

Absolute path
See path.

Address
Number or name for specifying another device location. On the Internet, an address is a number called an IP address used to specify a computer or device. An email address is a character string that specifies a destination for email.
See also email and IP address.

Administrator, admin
See root and user.

Alias
Refers to defining another name for a command in Linux.

Apache
Name of the most widely used Web server in the world.
URL: **www.apache.org**
See also Web.

APOP
A more secure alternative to POP that send encrypted passwords to the POP server.

Archiver / archive
An archiver refers to a program that collects numerous files and places them in one file and a file created by an archiver is called an archive. The archiver most often used in Linux is tar. Archivers often used in Windows are WinZip and lha, and Stuffit in Macintosh. All these programs have a compression utility. In Linux the archiver and compression software are considered to be separate programs and in many cases an archive file is compressed separately.
See also compress.

Argument
See command.

Attribute type domain name
A domain name that uses two letters to represent the type of organization in the second level of the domain is called an attribute type domain name. For example, in dekiru.gr.jp, the .gr stands for the type of organization, in this case, a 'group'.

B

Back up
Saving and storage of data at a separate location to prevent catastrophic data loss due to software and/or hardware failure.

BIND
The Berkeley Internet name domain software that is used to implement, manage and maintain the Internet DNS specifications.

Binary number
A numeric value represented by zeroes and ones.

Bit
The smallest unit manipulated by a computer, represented as binary number, i.e., either zero or one.

Boot disk
A floppy disk used when loading a PC OS.

Boot manager
A program that allows you to select a bootable OS during a system boot.

Broadcast address
The address to which devices send packets that are intended to be received by all hosts in the given network.
See also IP address, and network address.

Bug
An error in a program.

Byte
A unit of data or memory represented by a computer, generally assumed to represent one ASCII character. Normally, one byte is composed of eight binary bits.

C

Cascade
See hub.

CF

Program to create a settings file (sendmail.cf) for sendmail.
See also sendmail.

Clear text

Human readable, plain text files that may be encoded in any of many, publicly available encodings, such as ASCII or UTF-8, but do not contain any proprietary encoding or markup.

Client

The client side of the client-server model for the distributed database known as DNS. These are often just library routines that make queries and send them over a network to a name server. As such, they are called resolvers.
See also Server.

Command

Called a command line in Linux, the command line forms the core interface where character strings (commands) are input and results returned. Using spaces after commands on the command line allows character strings called arguments to be passed to commands. From among the arguments, an option is the device that influences the way a command operates. When using many options for a Linux command, specify the options by continuing one character after a hyphen (-) or continuing the character string after a double hyphen (--). However, an exception is the ps command (a (-) is not prepended) and the tar command (a (-) need not be prepended).

Compile / compiler

Compiling is the operation to convert source code into an executable file. A compiler is a program that translates source code into an executable file. In Linux the compiler command is make.
See also source, make, GNU.

Compress

Refers to reducing the size of data. Returning the data to its original state is called *extraction*. In Linux, the compression program mainly used is gzip.

Cross-over cable

See Cross cable and Straight cable.

Current directory

Refers to the present location within the file hierarchy. The current directory is indicated by a period and a slash (./). The directory just after logging in is the home directory. The home directory is the directory from which user operations initially start.
See also directory and path.

D

Dedicated line

A line leased from your telco that is not shared with other customers. Sometimes called a leased line.

Default

A fixed value that is assumed if nothing is specified. The default value can also be changed.

Development environment

A set of files and programs needed to create programs. Even if you don't create programs, it will be necessary to compile programs from source in order to install software. The main development environment used in Linux is GNU.
See also compiler, source, make, and GNU.

Device

A piece of peripheral equipment. Hard drives, keyboards and mice are peripheral equipment devices. Device names are attached to each device. In Linux, files exist that correspond to devices, and access to the devices is made through these files. The file name of the file that corresponds to a device is the device name, and these files are always placed in the /dev directory.

Device name

See device.

DHCP (Dynamic Host Configuration Protocol)

Method to automatically handle the network settings of an operating PC (such as IP address or netmask).
See also IP address and netmask.

Dial up connection

A line connection to your ISP's network made by dialing a phone number each time you want to establish a connection with the Internet.
See also Permanent connection and Dedicated line.

Directory

A location where files are placed, equivalent to a folder in Macintosh and Windows systems. In Linux, there is one large directory structure and the root of that structure is called the root directory and is represented by a slash (/). Files and other directories are placed within a directory. To represent that directory B is contained within directory A, directory B is called a subdirectory of A or, in contrast, A is called the parent directory of B. A parent directory is represented by two periods and a slash (../).
See also user, current directory, and path.

Distribution

See kernel and Linux.

Domain name

The top level of the FQDN is called the domain name. A domain name is a character string that represents the system to which the address belongs. Alphanumeric characters and hyphens are used for domain names and separated by dots (.). Even larger names can be made by appending characters to the end of a string. These larger names are called the top and second level domain. You can also express domain and hostnames by appending a dot.
See also hostname.

Domain name system (DNS)

Domain name system or domain name service, is a distributed database, that uses a client-server model. The server side is represented by name servers that contain information about their own respective segment of the database and make it available to clients, called resolvers.

Dot files

Files that have a dot (period) as the first character of their file name. They are usually used as configuration or resource files for programs running under Linux.

Driver

A driver is a piece of software necessary to use hardware (device driver).

Dual speed hub

See hub.

E

Email

A method to transfer messages across a network.
See also sendmail, SMTP, qpopper, and POP.

Ethernet

Communications protocol and hardware that enable two or more computers to share information. Divided into two types: 10Base with a maximum data transfer speed of 10Mbits/sec and 100Base with a maximum data transfer speed of 10Mbits/sec. There are many cables and connection methods but 10Base-T and 100Base-TX are mainly used, which utilize a modular type telephone jack for the connections.
See also LAN.

Extended partition

See partition.

F

fdisk

Name of a program to set disk partitions.
See also partition.

File system

A structure that defines access to files. Linux uses many different file systems. ext2 is mainly used for Linux, iso9660 is used for CD-ROMs, and vfat is used for Windows. When mounting a disk using the mount command, append a -t option to specify a file system or specify a file system by using the fstab command.
See also mount.

Folder

See directory.

Forward lookup

Used in DNS, to obtain the IP number of a host by means of the hostname.

FQDN (Fully Qualified Domain Name)

The complete form of a hostname in which the domain portion has not been truncated. For example, plumtree is the single-word hostname of the machine whose FQDN is plumtree.kanji.com.

FSF (Free Software Foundation)

See GNU.

fstab

Settings file in which information is written about file systems to be loaded automatically during the boot procedure.
See also mount and file system.

FTP (File Transfer Protocol)

Communication conventions used when transferring files in a TCP/IP network.
See also HTTP.

G

Global IP address

In contrast to a private IP address that identifies a machine internally, only on your LAN, a global IP address is an IP address that is used to identify a host publicly, on the Internet at large.

GNU

A freely distributed and changeable software development project. GNU (short for GNU's Not Unix) software is distributed by the FSF (Free Software Foundation). All distributions of Linux make use of many GNU software packages such as compilers, basic commands and editors. A GPL (General Public License) is a software license that defines the GNU software, which protects the freedom to re-distribute and change the code. The Linux kernel is also distributed based on GPL.
URL: **www.gnu.org**

GPL (General Public License)
See GNU and source.

H

Home directory
See current directory.

Hostname
A character string that represents the name of a computer. The hostname can represent the FQDN or just the host portion of the FQDN.

HTTP (Hypertext Transfer Protocol)
Communication conventions used when transferring Web pages in a TCP/IP network.
See also FTP and Web.

Hub
A device for connecting PCs by Ethernet. There are different types of hubs, including: hubs that transmit only a given speed in a network, dual speed hubs that correspond to both 10BaseT / 100BaseTX, and switching hubs that regulate the transmission of information to increase network efficiency. A special port is sometimes attached to a hub, allowing the network to be expanded by connecting this port to another hub. This is known as cascading.
See also Ethernet.

I

IDE (Integrated Drive Electronics)
A standard for connecting peripheral devices such as hard disks and CD-ROMs to PCs.
See also SCSI.

IMAP (Internet Message Access Protocol)
An Internet mail protocol used for storing and accessing mail. Creates a mail file on the mail server side to store mail which can then be repeatedly accessed by the same recipient regardless of which machine the recipient uses.

Index file
The default file that is displayed when a URL references the top page of a Web site. It is usually called 'index.html', 'index.htm', or 'default.htm', but your Web server can be configured to use any name here.
See also Apache and Web.

Internet
A worldwide network of networks. A network connects computers and devices, and the Internet connects networks. The communication protocol used on the Internet is TCP/IP.
See also intranet.

InterNIC
Provides public information on Internet domain name registration services. For example, it lists those ICANN-accredited registrars that are currently taking registrations in the .com, .net and .org domains.
URL: **www.internic.net**

IP address
An address for detecting computers in a network. Uses numbers from 0 to 255 organized in four groups, separated by a period (.), which is called dotted quad notation. In this book, for example, the IP address 192.168.1.1 was set to the Linux server.
See also netmask and broadcast address.

IP Masquerade
The name of software that is used to apply NAT under Linux.

ISA (Industry Standard Architecture)
A standard for connecting peripheral devices such as network cards and SCSI cards to a PC.
See also PCI and PCMCIA.

iso9660
See file system.

ISP (Internet Service Provider)
The establishment that connects your computer or LAN to the Internet via its LAN.

J

JPNIC (Japan Network Information Center)
Organization that manages and assigns domain names and IP addresses for the jp domain.
URL: **www.nic.ad.jp/jp/**

K

Kernel
The portion of code that forms the core of an OS. As introduced in this book, Linux is the name of a kernel. Additionally, it is also used with systems that utilize a Linux kernel. When installing Linux, you install what is known as distribution. Here, "distribution" is a system comprising a set of a kernel, basic commands, and applications. In this book, a method is introduced to set up a server using a distribution called Red Hat Linux.
See also Linux.

L

LAN (Local Area Network)
Two or more computers in relatively close proximity to each other (same building), connected in such a way that they can share information.
See also Ethernet.

Library
A file consisting of various collected program parts.

LILO (Linux Loader)
See boot manager.

Link
See symbolic link.

Linux
A Unix-based OS. This book describes how to set up a server by using Linux. Linux is actually the name of the kernel that forms the core of the OS. Note that in many cases, Linux is used to refer to systems that use the Linux kernel.
See also kernel.

Location type domain name
A domain name that shows the name of a geographic location in the second level label is called a location type domain name. For example, in chiyoda.tokyo.jp, the chiyoda stands for the 'chiyoda' ward, and 'tokyo' on the second level, is the city name.

Log
The log is a record of daemon and kernel operations.
See also daemon and kernel.

Log in
Refers to a situation when the user begins work. In Windows, logging in is called logging on.
See also log out.

Log out
Refers to a situation when the user completes work. In Windows, logging out is called logging off.
See also log in.

Logical partition
See partition.

M

Mail address
A character string that represents the sender and recipient of mail. If a mail address is broken down, the right side of the at symbol (@) represents the address of the system to which the address belongs and the left side of the (@) represents the address within the system (name of user that corresponds to the mail address).
See also address.

make
The make command executes a procedure to write to a file named "Makefile". The make command is often used to compile programs so many people say "make" when referring to the compiling of a program.
See also compile and development environment.

Mode
The word "mode" has many meanings. For example, the "mode of a file" indicates permissions. A "vi mode" indicates the state of the vi editor (input mode / edit mode).
See also vi and permissions.

Mount
Linking a file system to a specified directory. In Linux, one large directory structure is used. When a hard drive or CD-ROM is initially used, it will link to one portion of this large structure.
See also file system.

N

NAT (Network Address Translation)
The translation between a private network address on a LAN and a public IP address that can be used on the Internet.

NE2000 compatible
An NE2000 compatible card is a network card that can be used by Linux. NE2000 compatibility is defined as having functions compatible with the standards of a network card named NE2000.
See also Ethernet and network card.

Netmask
A figure for dividing addresses of an entire network and addresses within a network.
See also network address, broadcast address, and IP address.

Network
A network connects computers and allows communication.

Network address
An address that indicates the entire network.
See also network address, broadcast address, and IP address.

Network card
An expansion card for connecting a network. Also called an Ethernet card, LAN card and a NIC (network interface card).
See also Ethernet and LAN.

O

Open source
URL: **www.opensource.org**
See source.

Option
See command.

OS (Operating System)
Fundamental software program for using a computer. An OS allocates resources of the computer to users and processes.

Owner
A user that corresponds to a file used to manage permissions of files and directories. Usually, the user who created the file becomes the owner of the file. The owner of a file can be changed by using the "chown" command.
See also user and permissions.

P

Package
In Linux, a package is a format that allows software to be quickly and easily installed.

Parent directory
See directory.

Partition
A region on a hard drive. On PC/AT compatible machines the following restrictions exist when creating partitions due to limitations of MS-DOS. There can be a maximum of four primary partitions. When setting more than four primary partitions, from among the primary partitions, one partition will be set to an extended partition, and the extended partition will be divided into a several logical partitions.

Password
A key to access a computer. During log in on Linux, the user name and password typed verify the user.
See also user and log in.

Path
A route followed to a file. Directories in a path are separated by (/). The path that starts from the root directory (/) is called an absolute path, and paths that start from current directories other than the root directory are called relative paths.
See also directory.

PCI (Peripheral Component Interconnect)
A standard for connecting peripheral devices such as network cards and SCSI cards to a PC.
See also ISA and PCMCIA.

PCMCIA
A standard for connecting peripheral devices such as network cards and SCSI cards, to a PC. Used mainly for notebook PCs. Originally, the name of an organization (Personal Computer Memory Card International Association) that managed standards but now, it mostly concerns the use of slots or cards.
See also ISA and PCI.

Permanent connection
Unlike a dialup connection, which is temporarily connected, a permanent connection is always connected to your ISP's network and through that to the rest of the Internet. Typical permanent connections are leased lines and DSL lines.

Permissions
Access rights to files and directories. In Linux, you can set whether or not to allow reading, writing, and executing for three types of users; owners, groups, and other users. Also called file attributes and file modes.
See also user and group.

POP (Post Office Protocol)
Communication method for sending your email located on a mail server to another address in a TCP/IP network.
See also qpopper and SMTP.

Port
A port of a hub is an inlet for connecting cable connectors. Moreover, in TCP/IP, another location is specified by an IP address, and a service is specified by a port number.
See also hub, IP address, and server/service.

Primary partition
See partition.

Private address

An IP address that cannot be used on the Internet. It is recommended to use private addresses on an intranet. The range of private addresses can be: 10.0.0.0 – 10.255.255.255 (a network that has 16,277,216 addresses X 1), 172.16.0.0 – 172.31.255.255 (65,536 X 16), and 192.168.0.0 – 192.168.255.255 (256 X 256). The instructions introduced in this book on how to set up a network used addresses of 192.168.1.0 – 192.168.1.255. *See also* IP address, Internet, and intranet.

Process

An executed program running on an OS. Each process is managed by an integer value called a process ID. When a program is executed, a process is created and a process ID assigned. At this time, processes that have identical process IDs cannot exist simultaneously. When the execution completes, the process is deleted. *See also* program.

Program

Computer code that can be executed (run) on a computer. Almost all programs are saved in files. *See also* process.

Prompt

A character string displayed on screen, such as a command line for eliciting input. In addition to the command line prompt displayed by the shell, there is also a login prompt and a LILO prompt during the boot sequence. *See also* command.

Protocol

Rules and formats by which computers communicate with each other.

Proxy

A server that stands in for one or more other machines for Internet access. The IP addresses of the other machines are not made public.

Pseudo tty (virtual terminal)

A virtual terminal allows identical operations from another networked PC as if you were using a PC with Linux directly installed on it. A Linux screen emulated by an application such as telnet is called a virtual terminal (pseudo tty).

Q

qpopper

Name of a POP server introduced in this book. URL: **www.eudora.com/freeware** *See* POP.

R

Red Hat

Company that produces a Linux distribution and is also the name of the distribution. Red Hat Linux CD-ROM is available for purchase. URL: **www.redhat.com** *See also* Linux and distribution.

Relative path

See path.

Relay

To pass along mail that has been handed over to a mail server but that is destined for another server.

Reverse lookup

Used in DNS, to obtain the hostname of a host by means of its IP number.

root

User who administers a Linux system. Also called a super user. Root is a user who is not restricted by Linux security. For example, permissions attached to files and directories are not valid for root. The root user can read and write all files and directories. *See also* user.

Root directory

See directory.

Router

A device at an Internet node used for forwarding TCP/IP packets.

Routing

The process of passing packets from router to router before they finally arrive at the host corresponding to their destination address.

rpm (Red Hat Package Manager)

Name and file format of a Red Hat Linux package (a software format that allows quick installations). Also the name command for operating rpm files. *See also* Red Hat.

S

SCSI

Small Computer System Interface. A standard for connecting peripheral devices such as hard drives and CD-ROMs to a PC. Pronounced "scuzzy." *See also* IDE.

Second level domain label

Countries outside the U.S. use a two-letter code to indicate the type of organization. For example, .co (companies), .ac (academic institutions), .ne (network service), .gr (volunteer group) and so on.

sendmail

Name of an e-mail delivery server introduced in this book.
URL: **www.sendmail.org**
See also SMTP and server / service.

Server / service

A service provides some type of useful service or utility to other computers, and a server is a program that provides these services. In this book a dhcpd server that provides DHCP services and a Samba server that provides sharing services with Windows were introduced.
See also daemon and network.

shutdown

Stopping the system. When exiting Linux, rebooting or turning OFF the power, a correct shutdown procedure must be executed. This happens because there is a chance that data may be lost before being written to the disk if the power is suddenly turned OFF.

SMTP

Simple Mail Transfer Protocol. Set of communication rules for delivering email under TCP/IP.
See also email and sendmail.

Source

A text file written by a person when creating a program. The execution procedure of a program is written in source. Compiling a source file produces an executable file. It was often the case that source was the property of developers only. Due to the success of Linux and (to a greater degree) GNU/FSF, however, great interest developed in the idea of making source publicly available and allowing all interested people to develop programs (open source).
See also Linux and Apache.

Source file

See source.

Source list

See source.

Spool

A location where data is temporarily stored when sending data to another device or program. In Linux, the data is often placed in the /var/spool and /usr/spool directories. The spool is used to store mail not yet received and data sent to a printer.

Squid

A proxy server discussed in this book.
URL:**www.squid.cache.org/**

Straight cable

A cable for connecting a PC and a hub by Ethernet.
See also cross cable and Ethernet.

su (substitute user / switch user)

Command to change user IDs. The default reverts to root.
See also user and root.

Subdirectory

See directory.

Super user

See root and user.

Symbolic link

A file that indicates a file located at another separate location. When a symbolic link is accessed, the file indicated by the symbolic link will be accessed. In Macintosh and Windows these same types of links are called an "alias" and a "shortcut," respectively.

Swap

A file or disk partition used by the operationg system to give the impression of having more memory than is physically present. A hard drive partition is often used as swap space.
See also partition.

Switching hub

See hub.

T

TCP/IP (Transmission Control Protocol / Internet Protocol)

A communication method widely used on the Internet.
See also Internet and intranet.

Text file

The simplest document file format in which only character information is written. Text files do not depend on specific applications and have many uses, such as settings files and program source. Text files in Linux are handled in the same manner as Windows and Macintosh, although the Return/Enter key codes are different.
See also source.

Top level domain label

This is usually omitted in the US; else-where, it repre-sents the name of the country by means of a two-letter country code. For example, .ca (for Canada), .jp (for Japan), .uk (for England), and so on.

In the US the top level domain label represents the type of organization.

U

Unauthorized entry

To gain access to a networked computer at will without the computer owner's permission.

Uncompress (extract)

See compress.

Unix family OS

Unix was initially developed in the Bell laboratories of AT&T in 1971. Since then, it has developed into various forms and presently many varieties of Unix-based systems are being developed. These systems are part of the Unix family OS. The Linux program was written from scratch, but was modeled after the Unix family OS.

See also Linux and OS.

Unmount

See mount. Linux uses the umount command to detach the specified file system from the file hierarchy.

Up-link

The port on a Ethernet hub that is used to connect to another hub rather than directly to a computer or device on the LAN.

See also Hub.

User

An individual registered to use Linux. A user is the basic unit in Linux when managing permissions.

See also root, permissions, and group.

V

vfat

See file system.

vi

Name of a screen editor. Used to edit text files.

See also text file.

Virtual host

To the outside it appears as a separate host machine, but it is actually operating on the same machine as one or more other hosts.

W

Web

Refers to the World Wide Web, also called WWW. It is called a Web because pages located in the Internet are joined by links like a spider web. Presently, the Web is the name used to refer to the Internet as a whole and cur-rently an approximate 70% of the data flowing through the Internet is said to be related to the Web.

WWW (World Wide Web)

See Web.

See also IP address and network address.

Z

Zone

A part of the domain space that is under the authority of a particular name server. It is like a domain, but contains only the domain names and domain information that is not delegated elsewhere.

Index

What's On The CD-ROM

The Setting Up A **Linux Internet Server Visual Black Book**'s companion CD-ROM contains elements specifically selected to enhance the usefulness of this book, including:

- Red Hat Linux 6.0—A special package of the Linux installation and core files needed to run and manage the Internet servers described in this book.
- Apache—A robust, commercial-grade, full-featured, and freely available source code implementation of a Web server.
- QPopper 3.0—A Post Office Protocol (POP3) server, enhanced by QualCom to include extensions such as UIDL and bulletin support to the normal pop3 daemon.
- Sendmail 8.51—A unified "post office" sofware package, to which all mail can be submitted.
- CF3.7Wp12—An archive file containing CF, a sendmail configuration-file editing tool, that enables you to create sendmail configuration files with relative ease.
- All the configuration files needed for projects in this book.

System Requirements

Software
- Your original operating system must be Windows 95, 98, or NT4 before you can install Red Hat 6.

Hardware
- An Intel (or equivalent) 80486 processor is the absolute minimum platform required; an Intel or equivalent Pentium 120MHz (or faster) microprocessor is recommended.
- 16MB of RAM is the minimum requirement. 64MB or more of RAM is recommended.
- The basic Red Hat Linux 6.0 installation requires (at an absolute minimum) approximately 500MB of disk storage space. Hard disk space of 2GB or more is strongly recommended.